Leviathan 2.0
Inventing Modern Statehood

Charles S. Maier

The Belknap Press of Harvard University Press
CAMBRIDGE, MASSACHUSETTS
LONDON, ENGLAND

Originally published as Chapter 1 of *A World Connecting: 1870–1945*, ed. Emily
S. Rosenberg (Cambridge, MA: Belknap Press of Harvard University Press, 2012), a
joint publication of Harvard University Press and C. H. Beck Verlag.
German language edition © 2012 by C. H. Beck Verlag.

Maps by Isabelle Lewis
Book design by Dean Bornstein

Library of Congress Cataloging-in-Publication Data

Maier, Charles S.
    Leviathan 2.0 : inventing modern statehood / Charles S. Maier.
        pages   cm
    Includes bibliographical references and index.
    ISBN 978-0-674-28132-5 (alk. paper)
    1. State, The—History—19th century. 2. State, The—History—20th century.
3. World politics—19th century. 4. World politics—20th century. I. Title.
    JC201.M34   2014
    320.1—dc23   2013031958

For Pauline, not yet just memory:
A companion departed, a conversation interrupted

Contents

Leviathan 2.0

Introduction: Last Stands

Start perhaps in the foothills of southern Montana on a summer day almost a century and a half ago—not a long time really, indeed in the very year that my grandfather was born in a densely settled neighborhood of Central Europe five thousand miles to the East. The United States Army has deployed about seven hundred cavalry against an alliance of Lakota, Arapaho, and Cheyenne communities concluded the year before under the leadership of Chief Sitting Bull, after white miners, beckoned by reports of gold discoveries in the Black Hills of South Dakota, had streamed into lands allocated to the Indians by treaty in 1868. There have been clashes through the spring of 1876, and Washington has sent three columns of troops into the Montana territory to engage the Indian warriors and press them back westward. On this day, June 25, the soldiers of the southern column, comprising the 7th Cavalry, are attacking an Indian settlement in the valley of the Little Bighorn River and realize belatedly that they face more enemies than they had anticipated.

Were these endangered soldiers really confident that these hills and river valleys were their country's own? What might such an assertion signify? What status did it portend for the Lakota people, whose own grandparents had welcomed the explorers Lewis and Clark three-quarters of a century earlier but now faced a continuous incursion of miners, ranchers, and homesteaders? The Native Americans have their own economic relationship to these lands that includes hunting and seasonal migration as well as cultivation, confirmed by custom, but apparently unrecognized by the new settlers who keep arriving to mine, farm, and graze. Perhaps neither side really comprehends why the other must claim such a vast landscape. Under pressure the Indians have signed many agreements they believed would preserve diminished but guaranteed territory; but they have watched as these pacts have been unilaterally amended and their lands reduced. On this day, at least, they will give pause to their pursuers. Finally aware that he has imperiled his forces, General George A. Custer will divide his men in the river valley into three detachments. Two of them will hold off their attackers after costly retreat, but the 210 men under his command, forced against the crest of the bordering hills, will be overwhelmed within an hour. By the end of the day they will all be dead, their equipment stripped, most of them with heads scraped of flesh and hair.[1]

In the long run, however, the victors of that day will be the losers. Their reservation will be diminished again. More cavalry will come, the railroads will bring new settlers, and the tribes will be continuously pressed into the inhospitable highlands over the years to come, until one of their leaders makes a final capitulation a generation later. The victorious chief of the summer of 1876 will be killed on the allotment his people were granted, an old man, in 1913. Still, let us start with them, with those who across the world resisted the encroachments of the modern state, with its aspirations for territorial expansion, its exploitation of steam and steel, and its highly developed organization of government. Let us give the communities who faced these instruments of domination (for so they encountered them) a last chance to preserve their homelands under their own control. The tableau they offer is a familiar one captured in nineteenth-century novels, paintings, and the engravings commissioned for weekly newsmagazines, and later, after the administration of final defeat, by the haunting melancholy of silver halide photographs of "noble" warriors or disconsolate families confronting the unrelenting pressure of settlers and explorers and soldiers.

Communities we used to label casually as nomadic or tribal—whether (to cite only a few generic cases) of desert Bedouins on the fringes of the Ottoman Empire, the villagers of the Caucasus or the highlands of Central Asia facing the tsar's administrators, the Indians of the North American arid lands, and the peoples of the African savannas—were slowly but inexorably subjugated. Their long and difficult retreat, of course, had started well before the late nineteenth century: when Europeans reached the Americas, the Portuguese and Dutch pressed inland from the coasts of southern Africa, the French and British sought to control the North American Great Lakes, or the Qing and Romanov dynasties established adjacent imperial control over Xinjiang and Mongolia. By the twentieth century they survived as depleted units, allowed legalized or de facto tribal habitations, sometimes even subsidiary states within the empires, but their earlier confederations and international roles were just a memory—often neglected by the later anthropologists who studied their local customs and family structures but not their politics, or ignored by the historians who were encouraged by all the resources of the victorious states to focus on their nations' success stories.

But just occasionally, the indigenous defenders of these sprawling regions gave pause to the steamroller of "civilization." This is what happened on June 25, 1876, at the Little Bighorn. So, too, three years later, when Zulu soldiers destroyed an encroaching British encampment at the Battle of Isandlwana. Between 1881 and 1898, the extensive Mahdist uprising in the Sudan, waged in the name of a purified Islam, inflicted costly defeats on the Turco-Egyptian governors in Cairo and the British commanders who led their makeshift armies. In 1893 the Rif tribesmen, in theory subjects of the king of Morocco, besieged and defeated Spanish troops at Melilla. Ethiopian soldiers wiped out Italian detachments at Dogali in 1891 and even more catastrophically at Adwa in 1896. Ethiopia, of course, was no mere tribal region, but one of the globe's oldest kingdoms. The Europeans, set back for a decade or two—until 1935–1936 in the case of Italy's assault on Ethiopia—hardly took account of the complex political and religious polities that managed to slow their conquest. They beheld a series of savage last stands on the part of nomads and tribes.

In fact, the common word *tribes* does not adequately summarize any of these regional peoples' political existence, for they too had states or quasi states.[2] Tribes refers to communities who believe themselves organized by descent from early founders or chiefs, which, after all, was also the theoretical claim of the Ottoman Turks and of the Qing Dynasty, which had ruled China since 1644. But tribes were also political units, sometimes taking decisions of war and peace in confederal assemblies, although usually without the population density and the differentiated offices that marked the European states. The Spanish had conquered two elaborately organized tribal empires in central Mexico and Peru in the sixteenth century. The early United States repeatedly signed (and then unilaterally revised) treaties with the Indian nations of North America that recognized aspects of tribal statehood, including control of territory, as well as degrees of incorporation within the international boundaries of the North American republic. The Creek and Seminole, and Cherokee, Iroquois, Comanche, Sioux, and Apache, occupied extensive territories, sometimes exclusively, sometimes in symbiotic exploitation of rival peoples. Under their charismatic and ruthless leader Shaka, the Zulu had created a robust nineteenth-century polity that dealt with neighboring Boer republics and British intruders. Some tribes might find it advantageous to move their abodes in a yearly or periodic pattern, whether to take advantage of animal hunts, as on the Great Plains, or of different elevations and their seasonal climates for animal husbandry. But many others had become sedentary and agricultural. Along the steppe lands of Russia, dozens of tribal confederations and hundreds of subunits recognized only the wispy remote claims of a Russian power thousands of miles away, as did the communities on the southern sides of the Himalayas and

Afghan frontiers who dealt with Queen Victoria's local agents. As in the American West or Zulu South Africa, the Islamic khanates of the Turkestan region were subjugated as political units only in the 1870s and 1880s, as were the Kurdish tribes of southeastern Anatolia and northern Iraq at the hand of Ottoman military forces throughout the 1880s and 1890s.[3]

These decades signaled the last stand for indigenous political autonomy, for many reasons that will be explored below. Despite the lethal capacity of spears and bows and tomahawks, tribes recognized the advantage of firepower and had acquired rifles. But they depended on the horse (or camel), and had not developed the more recent railroad, which limited the size of their military mobilizations. They might claim large areas of terrain as their own but imposed no fixed boundaries and moved about without efforts at permanent settlement throughout. Although their statesmen might negotiate compacts and alliances, tribes also fought each other over decades, often in ritualized and savage warfare. And, fatal for their own collective survival, they had often solicited the European peoples encroaching on their lands to help tilt the balance in their own intertribal warfare. Still, for all its momentum the state did not penetrate everywhere. Large regions of upland or deep forest remained refuges for smaller peoples stubbornly seeking not to be governed, in the phrase of James C. Scott, who has celebrated their refractory evasiveness, which in part can be attributed to the inaccessible terrains they inhabited.[4]

The winners were the well-organized representatives of Europeans and their American or African or Asian descendants organized into the most efficient engine of expansion and governance that the world had seen for centuries: the modern nation-state. This was a large-scale unit organized to permeate and master territory, to pursue sedentary agriculture and industrial technology, possessing complex legal systems that allowed the preservation and transmission of family and individual property, the salaried employment of large-scale private and public workforces, the rapid communication of commercial and policy decisions by electrical telegraph, the ministerial archives and records that ensured institutional memory, and ideologies of rivalry and group purpose that generated intense loyalties.

Looking at the forces that drove the historical development of the modern state over two centuries, I would emphasize three. Critical thinking was crucial in undermining the old regimes; formal ideas but also the dramaturgies of discontent and protest played a major role in the constant questioning of existing institutions and the imagining of new ones that operated so powerfully after 1750. Technological inventiveness—that is, a different range of ideas, thinking applied to the material world—was crucial to the transformations of the mid-nineteenth century. The inventions that overcame the constraints of distance and time allowed the global restructuring of territory that transformed the states of the mid-nineteenth century. At the same time they introduced new forms of social stratification that renewed intellectual discontent, no longer just with a timeworn status quo but impatience with the new results of economic and political transformation. For the eighteenth and nineteenth century these impulses tended to originate in Europe and its New World offshoots and radiated outward, compelling the massive societies of Asia to take up the same processes by the twentieth century. The third major force was more a condition of global territorial organization and less an active agent. It was the fact that states have always existed in the plural—in continuing competition, if not open warfare. Any history of the state, like it or not, must follow an institution whose organization and social divisions have been premised on insecurity. The fact that this circumstance has continually contributed to the maintenance of internal hierarchies, even in modern societies, does not make it less real.

⌢

State is a heavy word, not so easy to define. It refers to the institution to which human communities have entrusted the coercive power they find necessary for the legal regulation of collective life.[5] How much power, with what limits, for what ends remain issues contested in the West since at least the ancient Greeks. Much of the history of the world's peoples has been told in terms of the rise and fall of their states. States, of course, are ancient structures, hierarchies of political and administrative decision-making designed to ensure ongoing control for elites and continuing security for those who accept their claims to rule. States are abstractions. While they have often been represented in the person of their rulers, they usually generate an ideology of existence as communities in their own right. States claim to operate according to general laws or norms (although they may legislate different levels of privilege and entitlement for different groups within their jurisdiction), and these rules are the basis for their claims to legitimacy—that is, to their meriting loyalty from citizens and recognition from foreigners on grounds that go beyond the mere exercise of coercive power.

The fact that states have remained stubbornly plural throughout history means they each have claimed a degree of supreme authority (usually defined in terms of geographical reach or territory), which theoretically excludes the writ of other states—a condition called sovereignty. Although political theorists have often insisted that sovereignty is absolute, in practice it has often been partial or nested within imperial or associative structures. States have sometimes accepted some overarching claims against their freedom of action, whether as protectorates or tributary units, and often even large states have had to grant privileged legal enclaves or functions to other powers. Increasingly states have agreed to cede functions and authority, whether over their economies or their military or even their frontiers, to common authorities such as today's European Union. Sovereignty has never excluded the prerogative of making self-limiting treaties.

Because states are always interacting, sometimes peacefully through trade, migration, or diplomacy, sometimes through warfare, it is natural enough that they often reform themselves as a group and not just one by one. Renovation therefore has come in waves. From time to time states are reorganized, reconstituted on new principles, endowed with new goals, and claim new capacities. This does not mean that all states successfully renovated themselves. Some, especially the old imperial structures such as China or the Ottoman Empire, made important efforts but could not sustain their territorial integrity or capacity to ensure internal "order." Still, a global perspective suggests that a "long century of modern statehood," proposed here as a meaningful description for political modernity, extended from about 1850 to the 1970s. What follows is a history of how it arose, what innovations it brought, and why it seems to have ended.

The modern Western language of statehood and sovereignty emerged in the sixteenth and seventeenth centuries to assert the superiority of political rulers over contending secular or religious claims. By the end of the sixteenth century, so Quentin Skinner explains, the concept of the state had become "the most important object of analysis in European political thought" as the "form of public power separate from both the ruler and the ruled, and constituting the supreme political authority within a certain defined territory."[6] This European-wide discourse reflected the vast transnational splintering of post-Reformation Christian authority, the intensive communication of ideas in an era of print culture, and the painful search for alternative nonreligious principles of legitimacy. Late sixteenth- and seventeenth-century writers (such as Jean Bodin in the 1570s and Thomas Hobbes in the 1640s and 1650s) focused on the absolute authority that such sovereignty required. Without a powerful ruler, so Hobbes argued in *Leviathan* (1651), individuals within territories must live in the same insecure and violence-prone "state of nature" as nations did in the international realm.

The international properties of statehood and sovereignty are usually deemed to have been defined most decisively with the end of the Thirty Years War and the Treaties of Westphalia (Münster and

Osnabrück) in 1648 that finally closed that long and complex struggle in Central Europe. The idea of sovereignty thus emerged with a dual thrust. Looking "inward," sovereignty was defined as the prince's governmental supremacy within the territorial unit—supremacy especially above any rival claims of religious authority. Looking "outward" to the collection of states as a whole, sovereignty was defined as the international independence sanctioned by the Treaties of Westphalia or recognition by other states more generally. Precisely because these properties of statehood—a supreme legal power within a home territory and full rights vis-à-vis other states—continued to be highly theorized after 1648, we tend to refer today to the "Westphalian" order.[7]

We should not overgeneralize. Such a vision of state sovereignty, absolute and integral, was foreign to large areas of the world with respect to both external relations and internal authority. Within South Asia, for example, the Mughal Empire and its successor, the British Raj, recognized partial sovereignty for hundreds of princes or rajas or sultans, and claimed only what medieval European law often defined as suzerainty. In East Asia, where the massive and venerable Chinese Empire dominated the mainland, the Westphalian paradigm of state equality would have seemed unnatural. The communities around the rim of that megastate recognized its primacy but expected no real interference in their domestic affairs.[8]

Just as fundamental, the inner coherence of the Chinese state seemed to rest on a particular relationship with the realm of the sacred. Whereas in Christian realms, religion was invoked to support the state and its leaders, the religious sphere still remained distinguishable from what the state had come to be about. At least since the Investiture Conflict of the eleventh century, popes and emperors alike insisted on distinguishable, if sometimes overlapping, missions. That dualism was reaffirmed implicitly even as the seventeenth-century construction of Leviathan 1.0 subordinated the political claims of religious officials to secular rulers. To be sure, wherever an anointed monarch reigned, the separation was hardly absolute. Religious officials still often claimed the authority of an autonomous normative order, and it was the task of the monarch to protect their claims. Roman Catholic Church officials served as the political rulers of various territories within the Holy Roman Empire until 1803 and in Italy until 1870. In Islamic regions, the relationship was fully as complex. Although Islam originally envisaged a political domain coterminous with the community of believers, a succession of rival imperial units had come to contest the vast territories where Muslim affiliations prevailed. Ottomans, Persians, and Mughal rulers in India usually made allowance for alternative worship but in so doing often conceded the preeminent role of Islamic religious authorities and law. The Ottomans, moreover, sought to claim the earlier extensive idea of Islamic political rule and the function of the caliphate until the Turks abolished the empire in 1922 and their claim to the office in 1924. In East Asia the claims were different still. The Japanese emperor, no matter how weak over the centuries, retained an aura of divine origin that was celebrated through special rites; and until 1945 modern nationalists sought to strengthen his divine status. The Confucian legacy perhaps overcame to the greatest degree the dualism of sacred and political authority that persisted elsewhere at least until recent decades. Somewhat as in the earlier Mesoamerican polities destroyed by the Spanish, the Chinese emperor, deep into the nineteenth century, was to ensure the good order of a society by ritual practice in a cosmos that extended from the family to the heavens. Any tourist who follows his and his servants' processions to ensure the year's crops through the precincts of the Temple of Heaven in Beijing can sense that the world's largest state had an aura of its own.[9]

Not that Chinese imperial functions and structure cannot be compared with Western institutions—they certainly can—but the language developed in the West, and taken for reasons of familiarity as a discursive base for this history, does not capture the vibrations that filled other realms. The Westphalian concepts were thus restricted in scope, but as European influence spread through trade, diplomacy, and conquest, the more absolute categories of state and nation also diffused. By the late nineteenth century, states possessed a degree of dedication to governance, of bureaucratic functionality, of at-oneness with fixed territorial space, of belief in their own competitive mission, that was unprecedented.

Nonetheless, that climax was also a renewal and partial transformation. New technologies of communication and transportation allowed a decisive intensification of state ambition and governmental power in the second half of the nineteenth and first half of the twentieth century, sufficient to justify the numerical suffix used for computer software: Leviathan 2.0. The fundamental properties of the state—the supremacy of its legal norms at home and its reliance on a territorial base—remained the same. But territorial ambitions became vastly greater in an age of renewed imperialism, no longer content with trading rights and enclaves, but pursuing enclosure of vast tracts of land abroad.

Moreover, the older ideals of an autonomous and supreme legal order, of government by law, whether bureaucratic and monarchical or based on popular sovereignty, also changed. Leviathan 2.0 seemed to accept that its own supposedly transcendent legal norms become entangled with economic interest groups and political caucuses. To be sure, the Anglo-Scottish (and later North American) interpretation of a legal order never separated the law so formally from the world of commerce and association as did continental legal theory. With the struggle against supposed Stuart absolutism behind them by the eighteenth century, British Whig, if not Tory, publicists measured human progress less by the unsullied transcendence of law than by economic progress and the development of civility. Continental liberal thinkers, struggling until the mid-nineteenth century to limit monarchical authority, still retained a more transcendent concept of law as "above" interests, just as it was above personal rule. Still, by the early twentieth century the ideal of a pristine state was difficult to maintain. It was hard to disentangle from the web of corporate interests, labor unions, and political parties that claimed the right to govern, whether in a competitive system or exclusively and without tolerating rivals. Only a century or so after the idea of a government of laws had slowly disengaged itself as the ideology of Enlightenment politics, the state seemed about to be reabsorbed as just a regime of party or of interests.[10]

How far any of those trends might be pursued without undermining the state as such remained a question for political actors and—in retrospect—for scholars. Looking ahead to the late twentieth century, we can grasp that the abuses of single-party and military regimes became so terrifying that political activists wanted to revive the theory and the practices of liberal government. But the old idea of a transcendent state and legal order no longer promised a realistic liberal refuge. Instead theorists and practitioners accepted, and sometimes celebrated, the entanglement of the public legal order in the welter of associative interests, churches, unions, economic enterprises, and the media. These entanglements might seem menacing or beneficial. When economic difficulties threatened, as in the 1970s, many analysts envisaged a recourse to private–public bargaining they labeled neo-corporatism. When authoritarian rule crumbled, as in the later 1980s and 1990s, they celebrated the benevolent forces of civil society that had resisted dictatorship. In either case state and society seemed hard to disengage. Not, however, that those forms seem inscribed for permanence. By the late twentieth century many commentators were theorizing the state as a regime of discursive expertise, hopefully protected from untutored populist pressures—perhaps to be designated by some future historian as Leviathan 3.0.

⌒

To return to the 1870s, arrayed against the encroaching machinelike national communities, the momentary tribal victors of the Little Bighorn or southern Africa did not really have a chance. The states had superior weaponry, particularly the rapid-firing guns, railroads, and river gunboats decisively improved in the late nineteenth century. The states had the agencies to persist in policy and to replace those boastful military leaders who so often courted defeat. States came back—they wore down the tribes, reduced them by disease and, from time to time if resistance persisted, by genocidal repression and driving them into the deserts, where they could be left to die of thirst, hunger, and exposure. Still, many of these tribal communities survived to bear witness. Some clung to highland areas whose arduous climate did not encourage dense settlement. Some continued on the steppe, driving their animals in yearly patterns from summer pasturages to more sheltered winter terrain. Some emerged as the components of the states created in the wake of decolonization after 1945. The desert Bedouins benefited from the inhospitable margins of a weak empire. The American Indians were settled in hardscrabble reservations, continually diminished in size, where the price they often paid for the continuity of their tribal life was economic stagnation and alcoholism, or chose assimilation and intermarriage, retaining only the memory of their collective past and perhaps nurturing revivalist myths and folklore.

"Bury my heart at Wounded Knee," or at Kokand in Turkestan, or Melilla in Morocco, or Omdurman in the Sudan—battles occasionally won by those resisting, usually lost, in any case episodes in the global triumph of the modern state and the marginalization of a nomadic alternative. In some locations, as in Central Asia, the tribes might continue traditional modes of life, wandering across new and weakly established frontiers. In the Americas they gave up their collective property rights, and access to land, and the rights to mineral wealth they might have developed. Where the Europeans came from afar, as in Africa, the tribes faced harsh regimentation, reinforced by doctrines of racial hierarchy. The states won, expanded, and then turned with murderous single-mindedness on each other and sometimes on their own citizens.

The rest of this book examines the ascent and transformations of the modern state. From the 1860s to the 1970s these units of territorial organization prevailed without any real alternative institutions to contest their triumph. Then they entered a period we still live in, one that seems to have imposed some important limitations on their freedom of action and even perhaps on the loyalties they compel. In the course of their trajectory, the violence they inflicted on each other dwarfed in scale the casualties they took at their tribal margins.

CHAPTER ONE

The World Is Weary of the Past

The line is from Shelley, the twenty-nine-year-old British poet living in Italy and intoxicated by the opening of the Greek rebellion against the Turks:

> The world's great age begins anew,
> The golden years return,
> The earth doth like a snake renew
> Her wintry weeds outworn . . .
> The world is weary of the past,
> Oh might it die or rest at last!

When did the past die at last? Sadly, the impatient Shelley went first, drowning a year after he wrote his ode "Hellas" in 1821. This history proposes that insofar as statehood and public institutions were concerned, the past died in the mid-nineteenth century. As the poet suggested, the end of an old order and the birth (or rebirth) of a new are part of the same process. Still, rather than presenting the revolutionary era of 1776 to 1830 or even to 1848 as the seedtime of a global future, I argue that we better understand the entire century from 1750 to 1850 as one of institutional meltdown. Assuming that the ideas and practices of the early modern state—call it, after Thomas Hobbes's tough-minded treatise of 1651, "Leviathan 1.0"—arose in the seventeenth century, then fell into difficulty in the later eighteenth century, they were reconstituted after 1850 as "Leviathan 2.0." That process of reconstruction lasted, I will suggest, through the 1960s and 1970s, since which time the edifices of modern statehood have begun to decompose in their turn.

To propose the importance of two roughly hundred-year epochs divided at 1850 raises a labeling problem, as they straddle the more familiar divisions of the eighteenth, nineteenth, and twentieth centuries.[1] Neither do they coincide with such conventionally inscribed periods as the Enlightenment, "the age of revolution," or "the era of world wars." In particular, most historians have seen the decades around the French Revolution as so fundamental a rupture (at least for Europe) that they have tended to divide the prerevolutionary era from that which followed. For modern Middle Eastern history, they pivoted "before" and "after" around 1798, the year of Napoleon's invasion of Egypt. For China, until recently historians regarded the Opium War of 1840–1842 as a crucial rupture. Similarly, many have accepted the notion of a short twentieth century, an epoch of ideological and military conflict beginning with the outbreak of World War I and ending with the fall of the communist system in Russia and Eastern Europe between 1989 and 1991. Without denying that such dramatic moments structure what I have called our moral narratives, I am urging that we need to keep a different tempo and follow long-term processes.[2]

Still, the argument here is not simply that institutions fell apart from 1750 to 1850, whereas in the subsequent long century strong leaders reasserted the capacity to rule. Revolutionary crises in the first epoch simultaneously reshaped institutions. New principles of political recruitment, new concepts of rights, a redefined sphere for religious authority, administrative rationalization, geographical reconstruction, and legal codification mark the history of the American territories and of French-dominated Europe from the 1760s on. Conversely, widespread and protracted upheavals in Asia and Latin America as well as political violence in Europe punctuated the long century of state formation after 1850. Within that second extended century we have also lived through an extensive era of crisis, which brought a world war, widespread revolution, massive unemployment, and a second global conflict and the replacement of colonial empires with the Soviet and American spheres of influence. Both century-long spans were periods of transformation; both constituted long episodes in the creation of what historians think of as modernity. This chapter examines the era from 1750 to about 1850; those that follow discuss subsequent developments. The conclusion attempts to take stock of what trends have intervened since 1970—that is, the world in formation. Older readers of this book have been imprinted with experiences and mentalities shaped by the long century of modern statehood that began in 1850. Younger readers have come of age since 1970 in the flux of newer currents and rapidly evolving institutions. Hopefully what follows makes sense of both.

Contagious Ideas

Return for now to the years after 1850 and generalize extravagantly, as must any history on a global scale. In the decades receding into the past as of the mid-nineteenth century—remain for the moment in the domain of Western culture and sensibility—youthful, enthusiastic, sometimes utopian and even violent yearnings marked advocates of change. Conservative opponents summoned up visions of allegedly organic communities that would be arbitrarily destroyed. In the decades ahead, harsher and more realistic calculations will govern group behavior. There will be no less a recourse to violence, but it will be governed more by the alleged requirements of ethnic and national necessity, and less frequently by utopian hopes. Already dissipating as of 1850 is a fervor for revolution, although such exiles in Paris as Richard Wagner or Alexander Herzen echo accents of a generation earlier (again we choose that Romantic radical, Shelley):

To defy Power, which seems omnipotent . . .
Neither to change, nor falter, nor repent:
This, like thy glory, Titan, is to be . . . free;
This is alone Life, Joy, Empire, and Victory.[3]

By midcentury such a sentiment seems more bombast than enthusiasm. Dated, too, is the fervor for "young" national societies (Young Italy, Young America), for utopian communities, for socialist equality among radicals, or for enchanted estatist hierarchies for conservatives. Instead, for those who followed after 1850, a different spirit will dominate: a utilitarian commitment to "order and progress," the Comtean motto that foreswore revolutionary juvenilia and came to terms with power—the power of soldiers, of machines, of artillery and repeating rifles, of finance, of electricity. Summoned to serious work, the post-1850s generation will grow the heavy white beards of mature citizens. They will take precautions against the rebellious potential of the threatening street, become attuned to the "survival of the fittest" (misinterpreting Darwin's work to mean survival of the strongest) and the apparently inexorable laws of social development. In fact, the generation that straddled that mid-1800s line will make the conversion in their own lifetime, passing from romantic fervor to convinced sobriety—as over a century later, the protesting youth of the 1960s will buckle down as middle-aged adults to programs of realistic reform or even repentant reaction.

The currents of ideas—first romantic, then realistic—coursed through Europe and the societies settled by Europeans in North and South America or dominated by their colonial administrators in Bengal, Batavia, and elsewhere. In the first half of the nineteenth century they were already exerting a powerful and unsettling impact in the Ottoman Empire, whose administrators and intellectuals had confronted Europeans across their borders and in the Mediterranean for centuries. The Ottomans had fallen under increasing pressure in military encounters—having had to cede territory on the north shore of the Black Sea to Russia and in 1798 having experienced a disastrous French invasion of Egypt, which only the British fleet and not their own soldiers had compelled to withdraw, and then in the first decades of the nineteenth century facing open rebellion in Greece and then Serbia.

Traditional Islam, represented by a conservative establishment of judges and scholars, collectively known throughout the Middle East as the 'ulama', and ethnic Turkish loyalty to the house of Osman no longer seemed to provide the legitimacy for this large domain to stand up to more universal concepts of citizenship that had come with the French armies and books. Its organizational principles—based on the management of religious and ethnic diversity by drafting talented Albanians, Greeks, and others to high office, allowing non-Muslims their own communal authorities (the *millets*), and relying on extensive clientelist networks with regional notables—had served a vigorous expansionist empire well. But in an era of unrelenting pressure and the fashionable emerging European notions of homogeneous nationhood, they appeared creaky and backward.[4] East and south of the Ottoman Empire, throughout the great arc of South Asia, a great ferment of Islamic revivalist ideas challenged rulers in Persia, in the Central Asian khanates, and in the decrepit Mughal Empire. Emerging in religious schools and focusing on nonpolitical moral renewal, Islamic revivalism tended to undermine the regimes in which their doctrines took hold, whereas the Western currents were increasingly oriented toward enhancing political structures.

European missionaries had arrived in China and Japan by the sixteenth century. Once the Tokugawa leaders secured decisive control of their realm, they moved to reverse Christian inroads and extirpate the converts by the 1620s. Jesuits and Franciscans would vie for influence at the Ming court, but the Chinese seemed interested primarily in assimilating the Westerners' ideas to their own Confucian principles. Insofar as Chinese policy intellectuals later tuned into the ferment in the West, they latched on to practical writings of the Victorians, such as Samuel Smiles's tract on self-help. The Japanese listened more closely, and a few of the quasi-autonomous feudal domains into which the Tokugawa rulers had divided the islands sought Western learning, but the age of intellectual infatuation and importation would come after the mid-1800s. Still, contemplating the diverse global currents of intellectual ferment, any observer from outside the planet would have had to admit that the clash of ideas in the West was claiming increasing attention. Emanating from the West were notions of citizenship, that is, the idea that ordinary male adults, at least those with some property of their own, could claim a voice in constituting a nation and judging its policies; concepts of inherent rights; appeals to a literate and propertied middle class as a key political actor; and the appropriateness of becoming wealthy.

We shall have to examine more closely the physical milieu and built environments in which this remarkable moral trajectory took place. The technological transformation was leaving obvious tracks across on the landscape. The Industrial Revolution is usually dated from the accumulation of mid-eighteenth-century innovations in British textile production and the breakthroughs in harnessing steam power. Its effects increased exponentially after the Napoleonic wars. Textile factories brought new urbanization: the metropolises of 1800 had been administrative and court centers or commercial ports: London, Paris, Madrid, Dublin, Naples, St. Petersburg, Constantinople, Edo/Tokyo, Guangzhou (Canton), Calcutta (Kolkata). Alongside these cities after midcentury would emerge the industrial suburbs and conurbations of the Midlands, the Ruhr, eventually New York, Chicago, and so on. Steam power, and the capacity to smelt iron and then steel, meant the feasibility of railroads and new migration and production for distant markets. The telegraph meant that empires and large nations could be run in real time. Midcentury wars—the large, brutal combats that severed the first half of the century from the second: Crimea, the

American Civil War, the German wars of unification—accelerated the technology and the movement of individuals.

Everyone could see the impact of these changes and write, as did William Cobbett early in the century, about their effect on the landscape or their creation of an impoverished urban laboring mass— sometimes in factories, often in small workshops or performing casual physical labor—that nineteenth-century social commentators a generation later, following the German historian of French social movements, Lorenz von Stein, would now define as a proletariat. Nonetheless, the gradual transformation of life on the land acted as profoundly on world populations even if unattended by such obvious visible signs. These were the changes, after all, that affected the overwhelming mass of global population, involving the transition from agriculture as a communal, subsistence-oriented activity, with prescribed routines set in village structures, to a market-oriented enterprise, where land could be bought and sold and peasants could depart for the city or across oceans to new continents, or, if less fortunate, lose their inherited protected status and become wage laborers or bound to their plots as indebted tenants. Market relationships, long established in Britain, and to a degree wherever peasants had to supply cities, were intruding into all the settled ways of rural life.

What was new was the growing liberalization of markets for land and labor. Until the nineteenth century, land and labor had been mutually shielded from market relations in a web of status restrictions and customs. Now in the most fundamental transformation of those under way, they lost their fixity.[5] Peasant emancipation, the vendibility of land, and market insecurities came as a piece, and provided the underlying seismic shifts that helped generate rural uprisings in the seventy-five years before 1850 and then again new revolutions at the threshold of the twentieth century.

These cumulative interacting transformations—in the constitution of the countryside, the application of an energy technology with radical consequences for moving goods and peoples, the altered mentalities—divided the conventionally demarcated nineteenth century into two epochs. Between them lay the mid-1800s watershed: a generation-long set of shocks that inaugurated the era of the modern. Not that what went into that transition was all of a piece culturally, religiously, or in terms of politics and economics. Nor that what emerged would be all of a piece, although the diverse cultures of the second half of the nineteenth century would be far more interconnected than they had been before 1850. But across the world each great geographical or cultural region would be recast and reshaped across that long caesura. And the states and nations that organized political life on the global surface would likewise reemerge transformed.

Interactive Geographies

States are authorities generally based on the control of territory and its inhabitants. Most states have claimed to control the behavior, the loyalty, and often the beliefs of those who resided within their boundaries. Land and sea gave states their most fundamental opportunities and set them basic challenges. High-density settlement required a settled and productive agriculture, whether based on rice, wheat grains, maize (corn), or root crops, such as manioc and potatoes. It usually entailed an ecology in which some of these grains supported animal husbandry, whether for meat, milk, or textiles. Animals in turn provided fertilizer that helped in grain production. High population densities existed in much of Europe, the Valley of Mexico (before devastating European diseases depopulated many of their settlements in the sixteenth century), South Asia, and East Asia. Societies that allocated large expanses of land for animals or left areas forested usually supported a lower density. Sparsely settled areas where hunter-gatherer populations still existed had the lowest density of all, excluding the great deserts and the arctic zones.

Historical transformation often involved an imperial dynamic between "crowded" and "empty" lands, sometimes within already existing empires, sometimes newly joined in imperial units. Earlier epochs had seen nomadic inhabitants of low-density areas (who probably felt the spurs of shortages more immediately than those in regions of settled agriculture and food distribution) conquering contiguous high-density regions. Peoples from the Asian highlands contested Han state expansion (the dynasty ended in 220 CE) and perhaps impelled confederations in western Eurasia against the Roman Empire (third to fifth centuries CE). Islamic Arabs surged across the Byzantine and Persian Middle East, North Africa, and Spain in the seventh century; again when the Mongols of Central Asia conquered the same territories and China itself in the eleventh century; the Turkic Timurids (the term derived from the name of their feared ruler, Timur or Tamerlane) subjugated Asia to the borders of China in the sixteenth while the Ottomans took Anatolia, the Balkans, Syria, Egypt, and Mesopotamia. These conquests were facilitated by the fact that the areas were all part of one land mass with grasslands enough to support horses.

By the end of the fifteenth century, high-density European populations were sending first soldier-adventurers and then settlers into remote territories. Sometimes these might appear as relatively empty lands. Muscovy reversed the Tatar invasions and expanded into the steppe lands of the Urals and farther east. In the New World the population dynamics changed as the Europeans arrived. The Spanish conquerors of Mesoamerica and the Andes quickly subjugated populations themselves precariously organized as recent imperial federations and soon depleted by European-borne diseases. The "discovery" and conquest of the Americas ultimately provided the Spanish, French, and British with vast territories of low population density. For the next two centuries, European conquerors sent enough soldier-adventurers, church organizers, and eventually settlers to exploit their acquisitions for their home states. But high-density populations did not simply flow out in some hydraulic surge to low-density areas. As Alfred Crosby famously described the Columbian exchange, the Europeans exported lethal pathogens that decimated native populations and imported New World crops—corn and later the potato—that allowed population growth at home. Kenneth Pomeranz has relatedly attributed the dynamism of the late eighteenth-century British economy vis-à-vis Chinese stagnation to the "shadow acreage" that British settlers overseas could occupy. North America became a British plantation, producing over time its great cash crop, sugar, then the cotton that was the basis of industrial development, and the grain that allowed it to shift its own growing labor force into commercial and later industrial activities.[6]

The dynamics of population growth changed the land itself. China's population had doubled from two hundred million to over four hundred million, and had pushed toward the north and west, although the Qing expansion into Mongolia or Xinjiang expanded the territory even beyond the newly settled regions. Western Europe's population surged ahead from the mid-eighteenth century on. In part this reflected the fluctuation in climate that ended the relatively cold interval sometimes called the little ice age of the seventeenth century and brought milder temperatures. There were fewer crop failures, fewer famines, more children reaching the age when they could themselves have children, whether in households solemnized by marriage or not. In China yams, maize, and soybeans, intensively cultivated in the North, provided the expanded carbohydrate base for population growth, with the destabilizing ramifications discussed below. The innovations we associate with the agricultural revolution—new crops, legume rotations that restored the nitrogen content of the soil, ditching, fencing, enclosure—meant higher yields in Europe. Advocates of potato culture helped the crop's spread in Ireland, northern France, and the Low Countries, such that the caloric yield per acre soared. The advent of cotton and more textiles meant the spread of proto-industrialization—multiple households taking on spinning or weaving under the organization of district entrepreneurs—conducive again to families raising more children who in turn founded their own families at an earlier age, and favorable, too, to higher consumption of tea and sugar and thus a surge in colonial settlement and wealth.

These trends, however, meant a pressure on world forest reserves. Britain could live with depleted woodland as it turned toward coal for fuel and got its naval timber from New England and Scandinavia. Japan, which did not pursue the coal option, worked to reverse deforestation. China suffered vast depletion—as a consequence not of industrialization but of the population growth of the eighteenth and nineteenth centuries. The forests were "largely gone by 1820, almost wholly by 1860, but mainly as a result of peasant subsistence cutting, clearing for agriculture and for local sale as both wood and charcoal."[7] Mark Elvin, historian of Chinese ecology, suggests three waves of deforestation: the impact on northern woodlands in the five centuries BCE, a second transition of a millennium ago in the lower Yangzi and the west, and the severe deforestation since about 1700 with commercial timber operations and widespread theft of wood. Deforestation meant not only a shortage of timber but erosion of vast areas and silting of the rivers, including the Yellow River, whose course shifted drastically in the 1850s. The silting had already produced a major crisis in the early 1820s, for where the Yellow River crossed the Grand Canal, the erosion blocked the Canal and with it the provision of rice from the south for the capital. Woodland penury continued in many locations. "We have reached a moment in time when the mountains have been ruined. . . . Our locality is in a state of decomposition and decline," announced a stele of 1851 in the south of Hunan, ordaining that no more cutting could take place.[8] The Brazilian Atlantic rain forest was stripped by different dynamics. It fell prey first to the rapid expansion of coffee cultivation for export and later to the pressure of the immigrant population brought to man the industry. "There is no tool readier to hand than the matchbox for establishing a coffee plantation," has written the historian of the long assault on Brazil's ecology.[9]

The zones of contact where those pushing outward from crowded land met the sparser residents of "empty" land, the Anglo-Americans called the frontier. This frontier was different from what in Europe was called frontier, the borders between settled states. The frontier bred a characteristic "type"—the independent, sometimes quarrelsome and violent leader, who felt that the state on whose borders he settled should protect his acquisitive impulses but otherwise not interfere with his ambitions. This populist roughneck became a character type basic to national self-images: the gaucho or the cowboy or the self-made soldier-politician. Andrew Jackson, the truculent soldier of the southern frontier, anti-elitist American president, domineering over the American Indians, suspicious of the northeastern banking cliques, was one personification. The Argentine dictator Juan Manuel de Rosas, depicted by the Argentine statesman and writer Domingo Faustino Sarmiento, was another. For Sarmiento, the contest between the cultivated elite of the great port of Buenos Aires and the gauchos of the neighboring pampas was that between civilization and barbarism.[10] The cultivated residents of the Roman Rhine frontier and the court poets of Isfahan who had to deal with Mongols in the eleventh century and with Turkic Timurids two hundred years later must have felt the same way. The cinematic depiction of the frontier type continued through the twentieth century in countless Westerns, one of the major genres of popular narrative.

In the crowded lands, population increase and the division of labor that overseas commerce stimulated meant wealth and sometimes development. They were not the same. No traveler to Iberia or to the former Spanish and Portuguese colonies today can fail to note the incredible architecture that colonial wealth and commerce could bestow even on societies that did not generate self-sustained economic growth.

Travel out of Oaxaca to the Mixtecan highlands north of the city and marvel at the monasteries and churches—alas, some now damaged by repeated earthquakes—built by the combined effort of Indian and Spanish artisans, that rise from the sparsely populated arid lands; or admire the richly adorned cathedral fronts, whether in the metropole or in the former colonies. Take note of the size and scale of public buildings and grand houses that crowded lands could indulge in. But recall, too, the immense social distance between the masses of population that toiled near subsistence and the grandees or corporations that enjoyed these possessions. Much of that wealth—whether in Europe, or Mughal India, or China—rested on accumulation at home, and the steady improvements of cultivation and willingness to reinvest that constituted what has been termed the "industrious revolution."[11] The surpluses that created modern armies, monuments, music, and art did not require colonies. Nonetheless, the juxtaposition of empty and crowded land created new opportunities for subjugation, on the one hand, and enrichment, on the other.

Imperial Tandems

Major geopolitical patterns were emerging from the juxtaposition of crowded and empty land and would dominate international politics and rivalry throughout the whole era of modern statehood. Empires constituted the state structures that optimally united the flows of commodities, labor, and cultural values between crowded and sparsely settled regions. Economists would say that these assemblages lowered the transaction costs of territorial governance that separate sovereign units would have entailed. This is not to claim that empires were founded for such a sophisticated motive—although Western mercantilist theory by the seventeenth and eighteenth century implicitly posited this premise—only that its logic made imperial expansion "rational," within limits. If we judge by outcomes, the logic of imperial power worked itself out best not by single empires in constant contention but by imperial combinations or tandems. Certainly it remains instructive to compare the particular institutions created by national empires for their own internal organization, such as the colonial assemblies encouraged by the British in North America versus the *audiencias* or royal investigative commissions that reviewed the administration of New Spain and Mexico.[12] But from the viewpoint of global rivalry, what proved decisive were ambitious coalitions for empire negotiated by a cosmopolitan elite across state lines on the basis of dynastic and cultural affinities and common adversaries. Such partnerships constituted in effect three or four imperial enterprises at any time. As of 1800 some had a past, others a future.

After the War of the Spanish Succession and the advent of the Bourbon dynastic line in Spain, French and Spanish interests tended to converge in opposition to British ambitions. In effect a Bourbon colonial realm and agenda emerged involving defense of French and Spanish overseas possessions against British sea power. But between the Treaty of Utrecht in 1713 and the revolts in Latin America a century later, the Bourbon New World empire collapsed in fits and starts. The so-called Bourbon family pact, based on the shared royal-family cousinage and the renewal of conflict in 1739, as the British Whig leader Robert Walpole lost his influence, led to a series of major contests in and for the far-flung peripheries outside Europe—Canada, Hispanic America and the Caribbean, and Bengal. In the mid-eighteenth century, the Franco-Spanish colonial coalition had lost the Canadian coast and Saint Lawrence Valley, but it still played a major role dominating the Great Lakes and the length of the Mississippi Valley, thence west to the California coast and south to Mexico, Central and South America, and half the Caribbean. This was a vast juxtaposition of imperial and European interests, potentially as formidable as the Anglo-American association. Later in the nineteenth century, Southern US slaveholders would from time to time be attracted as possible co-participants, but their bid for secession from the American union came fifty years too late, for by then the French had sacrificed their assets in the Mississippi Valley (as they had earlier in India and Canada), and the Spanish had lost their possessions to the Creoles of Latin America and did not have the means to recover them. Even Napoleon's effort to reconquer the half island of Haiti on behalf of French slave owners was defeated by yellow fever and inspired, if brutal, resistance by the communities of African descent. Bonaparte calculated, probably correctly, that in the long run the French could not retain the Mississippi and New Orleans against the United States' westward expansion, and by 1803 he sold the vast French colonial domain on the lower Mississippi to the American republic. What is more, his very effort to integrate Spain into his continental blockade of British trade by putting his own family candidates on the Spanish throne severed the remaining loyalties that the Spanish Creole elites (the colonists of European family descent but born in the New World) felt toward either the Bonapartist regime in Spain or the restored Bourbons after 1815. French and Spanish dreams of regaining their lost colonies after 1815 were preempted by implicit American and British agreement to prohibit any such moves—what Washington termed the Monroe Doctrine. A later French effort at Mexican conquest, taken while the United States was involved in civil war, also collapsed.[13]

Whereas the Franco-Spanish condominium of the New World was doomed, the Anglo-American co-imperial sphere was soon ascendant. Essentially a large English-speaking Anglo-American association of cotton and wheat growers on the trans-Appalachian as well as coastal lands of the former colonies was increasingly interlocked with the banking, investment, and industrial communities of the British islands. From the beginning of the American republic, both North American ruling groups shared a common language and a Protestant commitment (which more than matched the Bourbons' loyalty to the Roman Catholic Church). Both cooperated in prohibiting any Bourbon reconquest of Hispanic America. After American forces failed to conquer Canada, first in the American Revolution and then later in the War of 1812, Britain and the United States would reach a de facto compromise over Canada. The British would grant it autonomy, the United States would renounce annexation, and the Canadians would finally (by the 1850s) resolve to thrust toward the west and not link up with the country to their south. Such an implicit settlement meant that Anglo-American elites might overcome disputes to claim shared leadership in global politics—an emerging trend confirmed at several junctures before 1850 and then in the century after. By the 1890s the bonding of Anglo-American elites was being cemented in social as well as policy spheres, and this despite the mass of US immigrants who remained outside its charmed circle. Both powers would resist any German efforts to wrest economic influence in Latin America. Finally, from the early twentieth century on, both would effectively cooperate across the Pacific in trying to defend a faltering Chinese state against Japanese efforts to dominate East Asia. The Americans desisted on making any claims in the Indian Ocean area until 1945, while the British refrained from hindering the US claims in Oceania and accepted the US Open Door doctrine with respect to China's future. The Japanese, in fact, remained the most isolated of the imperial contenders in the Pacific, colliding as they did with Russians, Chinese, and eventually British and Americans. Despite the energy of their efforts to develop the extensive colonies they did acquire—Taiwan and Korea and a growing presence in Manchuria even before its formal takeover in 1932—they never kept a tandem partner. Their later effort in the 1940s to lead an Asian movement against European colonizers recruited some collaborators but ultimately could not prevail against Anglo-American and Anglo-American-Russian resistance.

Anglo-American imperial cooperation rested on maritime strategy. There were potential alternative combinations based on landed domination—above all a possible German-Russian condominium resting on gradually winding down Austrian and Turkish possessions while precluding the reemergence of a Polish nation. German-Russian imperial association promised domination of Eurasia, as the professors of geopolitics during the second half of the nineteenth century would recognize. Dynastic interconnections, the large number of German bureaucrats that the Russian monarchs employed, the common interest in suppressing the independence of Eastern European Slavs, and the growing economic exchanges of the late nineteenth century would all bode well for this coalition between 1850 and 1890. But German politics was too fitful (and in fact too liberal, for all its military trappings) to follow this strategy consistently. Efforts at cooperation could not overcome the tendencies toward mutual suspicion, which would culminate in the two world wars of the twentieth century. The alternative for Germany of keeping the Austrian Empire viable while working with the Ottomans to dominate the Middle East would have rested on partners inherently too weakened by their nationalities problem. The Portuguese, the Dutch by the nineteenth century, and later the Belgians exploited their rich colonial holdings but claimed no larger role of global order, as had the Bourbons earlier and as did the Anglo-Americans or Germans.

No stable combination of Russo-German, Russo-Japanese, or German-Japanese imperium in Asia was easily envisaged. Even when Germans and Japanese shared much common ambition in the Second World War, they could not make their association, the so-called Axis, function in any more than a nominal sense. Between them lay Russia and China, empires too extensive to conquer despite the huge efforts that would be made between 1937 and 1945. There was, however, the potential for a Russo-Chinese combination of interests, which did in fact emerge to dominate inner Asia in the eighteenth century. By the mid-nineteenth century, China, like the Ottoman realms, would be simultaneously the protagonist of an old empire and the object of other empires' piece-by-piece (and function-by-function) colonization. But this had not been the case for the great Qing imperial structure of the late seventeenth and early eighteenth centuries—itself an imperial assemblage of diverse peoples run by a non-Chinese dynasty. From the close of the seventeenth century the Qing negotiated with Russia a frontier settlement that allowed them in effect to constitute an imperial tandem to finally suppress the Zunghar nomadic state in Mongolia and decimate its population by the late 1750s. The subsequent expansionist campaign west to secure the "new dominion" of Xinjiang added a huge territory, but one that remained beset by continuing ethnic and religious resistance to Beijing. The Russians would suppress their "nomads" a century later but face continuing resistance in the Caucasus territories that abutted the weaker Persian and Ottoman states.[14] Empires the world over proved most successful when they could operate as dyads.

Commodification of the Countryside

The immense turbulence of the first half of the nineteenth century did not require the impact of the Industrial Revolution. That development played a large role in some societies. But concentrations of factory labor were still rare outside zones of Western Europe and the northern United States before 1850. The larger reservoirs of unrest lay on the land. Perhaps 75 percent of the world's active population worked the land or rendered services that supported those who farmed directly. The share went from about a third of the population in the England of 1800 to perhaps 70 percent in eastern and southern Europe and probably higher in Asia and Africa.[15] It is customary to think of agricultural communities as traditionalist and quiescent. But the burden of taxes and rents and labor services had ignited frequent protests, most confined to one village or another, but sometimes sweeping up large areas in frightening rebellions. The century or so after 1750 or 1760 was to add a further cause for unrest as market relationships invaded the countryside. Land and labor, fundamental factors of world production, hitherto locked into customary or legally stipulated relations, would become far freer to be bought and sold as ordinary commodities. Peasants who had been bound to a village or a landlord could depart for other villages or towns. Rural estates, controlled for generations by a given family or religious foundation, might be seized by state authorities and auctioned off to a new owner. They were to be swept into the flux of the market, and in the process would shake up state and society.

Market relationships were not, of course, the only transformative agent in play. But they were the newest (and for the moment, at least, perhaps the strongest) among three basic forces that together undermined the structures of the premodern world and prepared for the new regime of modern statehood. Warfare and its inexorable appetite for higher taxes and military modernization continued to exert the pressure it had since the seventeenth century, when Jean Bodin had called money the sinews of war. And as a countervailing pressure, religious revivalism sometimes emerged as a manifestation of communal resistance to change, what E. P. Thompson called the "chiliasm of despair."[16] Perhaps it is more accurate to say that new religious movements represented an alternative impulse to change—one that radically denied fulfillment through the market, although in some cases, such as the American Latter-day Saints, market skills were annexed to communal and not individualist ends. Commodification of the countryside, the state's search for greater penetration of society to meet the demands of modern war, and religious evangelization would interact in the transition to modern state politics.

Such processes played themselves out within a triangular framework constituted by laboring families on one side, by landlords and their agents on another, and by representatives of the state on the third. The state varied in its role. Peasants might encounter its agents as oppressive tax collectors or dreaded army recruiters. But the state also had an interest in defending hard-pressed peasants against rapacious landlords. The rights of the landlords themselves emanated from different principles, and the revenues they collected were based on different sorts of claims. As "owners" or as stable leaseholders, landlords could collect rents from peasants to whom they let out the land, whether on an individual basis or as residents of a village community. As members of a privileged, legally defined "estate" *(état, Stand)*—that is, a legally defined social stratum with defined tax privileges and conveying in some cases an aristocratic title, and the right to representation in local or national assemblies consulted by the monarch—landholders could claim payments and services by virtue of their inscribed legal status as well as rents from the tenants on their land: an arrangement that Western lawyers often termed feudal. Sometimes these landlords—or recognized local headmen, even if not proprietors—were given the right to collect payments on behalf of the state as well. They became local tax collectors (*zamindars* in Indian agriculture), or even regional tax "farmers" for large areas, being assigned a quota they had to pass on to the state but allowed to collect whatever the market or custom might bear. In some societies, including Britain and Prussia, landlords retained the right to act as local judges in civil and minor criminal cases until the 1870s. In some cases they had the duty of conscripting peasants for military levees, as the Prussian state imposed until 1806. With each layer of duty came new honorific status and "offices" and claims for financial compensation. Over the centuries, "deference" of tenants toward landlords, expressed by gestures of submission, had also become integral to the texture of rural life. In times of hardship or under the influence of charismatic concepts of equality, agrarian subjects might abandon deference for direct efforts to destroy hierarchies they had earlier lived with. Such rebellions, elemental and violent, meant frightening times, and when they were finally suppressed, those in charge usually administered the dismemberment, torture, and executions needed to "teach a lesson."

Mass rebellion seemed infrequent enough and the privileges of aristocratic office sufficiently desirable to attract the wealthy and ambitious. A major attraction was that they often brought the right to be transmitted by inheritance to one or more children. Crucial to the system was the long-term embeddedness of many public functions in the land, specifically in the role of landlords. Thus the laboring peasantry, the class or estate of landowners—who had pretensions to grander living in imposing houses with servants—and the agents of the state, which needed taxes for military expenses, interest payments, display, and public projects, all vied for a share of the earth's yield in a triangular contest. But there were often religious functionaries who also had the right, as officers of great or small churches or monastic communities, to claim a share of rents as landed proprietors along with state-sanctioned taxes (tithes). Monastic organizations were numerous and strong in Roman Catholic countries, in the Orthodox Church of Russia, and among Buddhist communities in Southeast Asia, Japan, and China. In the Islamic lands of the Ottoman Empire, there were some rural monastic communities, but also urban religious communities supported by generations of pious gifts as foundations or *waqfs*.

There were innumerable variants and complications even in small areas. No automatic correlation made village communities or those benefiting from commercial and market relations in the countryside into revolutionaries. Explanations that serve for one episode sometimes fail for others. Many studies have sought to account for the divergent political choices of adjacent regions in France. William Taylor has found that in the Mexican war of independence Oaxacan Indians engaged in numerous village protests and uprisings but generated no overall revolutionary movement until the southwestern peasant war of the early 1840s—a protest against commercial agriculture exploited by rival elite leaders. To the north, however, Jalisco peasants, whose village bonds were more frayed and their clergy new arrivals, joined in the early war for independence.[17]

Still, we can attempt to sort out the major patterns of agricultural life and labor. Especially in upland communities or frontier zones where population was sparser, or among tribal confederations, the supervisory community remained weak or perhaps nonexistent and freehold farmers produced for their own subsistence and/or brought their goods directly to market and retained the proceeds. This situation pertained in parts of western and northern Europe and North America. The families involved retained legal independence although they might live in grinding poverty and sometimes indebtedness. At the opposite end of the legal structure, usually in areas of dense lowland population, landlords dealt with peasant labor, sometimes as tenants but also as hired labor (or even legally coerced labor) who lived in cottages grouped apart from fields (though they might retain small garden and livestock plots). These sorts of agrarian enterprises were often described as *latifundia* (a term inherited from Roman antiquity), and in North America tended to become known as plantations. Plantations specialized in crops that benefited from "gang" labor—whether the arduous cultivation of sugar cane in Brazil and the Caribbean or cotton and tobacco in the mainland of the American South. Mediterranean agriculture retained such factory-like agricultural enterprises, which would become more important in the late nineteenth century as land reclamation projects and commercial agriculture increased in significance. The Dutch and the French organized such enterprises for the cultivation of Javanese sugar and Vietnamese rubber.

Such plantation laborers were usually deemed the lowest in status, especially when they were racially segregated, as in the case of black slavery. For about two centuries slaves had been captured in the interior of Africa, herded to the coasts, then forcibly transported in overcrowded, sweltering ships from Africa to the Americas. By the mid-nineteenth century, perhaps ten to twelve million Africans had been transported and reproduced and formed an absolutely basic constituent of the economic interchange between Europe, the Americas, and

Africa. The transoceanic slave trade was suppressed in 1808 in the United States by the terms of a compromise at the time of the Constitutional Convention. The French Jacobins abolished slavery in French colonies in 1794, although Napoleon reinstated it. The British abolished the trade throughout their domains in 1807, and the condition of slavery itself in 1832–1833. Still, for slaves "bred" in captivity, the status continued until 1863–1865 in the United States, 1887 in Cuba, and 1889 in Brazil. The Mexican government sold some captured Mayan rebels into Cuban slavery as late as the 1860s; slavelike labor conditions persisted in the mines of the Belgian Congo and elsewhere in Africa, and in the nitrate and copper mines of the Andes, long after formal abolition. Slaves had no legal rights against their owners in court (although a slave supposedly could not be put to death if he did not take up arms or commit ordinary crimes). Slaves could be beaten (as could Eastern European serfs), often at will, their marriages were not given legal status, and, most disabling, the status was deemed hereditary, to be removed only by legal manumission. The fact that the slaves of the New World were defined as distinct according to racial features rendered them particularly tainted, and the racial disabilities were legally enshrined in the United States and South Africa (as were de facto systems for preserving subjection) long after inherited legal bondage formally ended.

Most agrarian laboring families occupied an intermediate status between freehold independence and outright slavery. In areas where slavery had not been sanctioned (as in most of colonial Mexico, where the Spanish had granted *encomiendas* or tracts of land together with their Indian population) or later abolished (as in the United States), peasants could slip into such total dependence on landlords for their seeds and housing that they became bound de facto by their recycled debts. In Europe east of the Elbe River and in Russia, peasants had been reduced to serfdom in the sixteenth and seventeenth centuries; this condition of legal inherited bondage was not alleviated or dissolved until varying points between the 1770s and 1860s. Serfs needed land-lords' permission to leave their villages or to marry, and often had to work a varying number of days per week on the lands that their lords farmed directly. Serfs in some locations in Slavic Europe, in particular, could be transferred from one owner to another, whether for purchase or to settle debts, although in the German areas they were usually seen as an appurtenance of the estate to be transferred along with the land. In contrast to slaves, serfs retained higher legal status, including recognition of marriage; their families could not be broken up by landlords. Through the course of the first half of the nineteenth century (and in some areas after 1850), both slavery and serfdom would be eliminated. Traditionalist landlords fought bitterly against the waves of emancipation, but in fact would find that market pressures and control of credit provided most of the enforcement mechanisms they required to retain a compliant labor force.[18]

Crucial to this "old regime" was not just the superiority of the land-lords, but the village structure and the claims on the land itself. Emancipation did not usually bring a transfer of ownership to the former slaves or serfs. The idea of endowing each ex-slave family head in the American South with "forty acres and a mule" was never enacted; in Prussia emancipated peasants could claim land only if their assets fell above a certain threshold, and within a generation or two many had fallen into the status of hired hands. In Russia, former serfs would be taxed to redeem the bonds given to landlords for compensation, while the village communes retained control of the land. For better or worse, the village provided a corporate existence: its elders could periodically redivide the farmland among different families, and it retained control of a common pasturage or woodland. We have learned that like a modern trade union, the village could confront a landlord with enough collective strength to keep rents and services tolerable.[19] Elsewhere, including Japan and China, it provided a structure that was often more disciplinary than protective. It stood as an enforcement mechanism in a hierarchy of duties and expectations. Villages could control land, allocate labor, enforce obedience—but they did not own land.

Outright ownership, as envisaged under ancient Roman law or British "freehold" or today's American home ownership, thus remained an alien idea across much of the globe. Land went with people—whether organized in families or villages—and people with land. In Russia estates were graded by the number of attached peasants or "souls." In some societies, especially where a conquering or formally invested sovereign claimed supreme power, ownership was theoretically retained by the conquering sovereign, as in the Ottoman Empire, and rights of "use" (usufruct or the old feudal notion of *dominium utile*) alone were ceded. In fact, after a generation or two it would become almost impossible to reclaim effective control, although programs of national "restoration" might try to reinstitute this claim.

Land ceded by sovereigns or pious donors to monasteries passed to an institution from which it could not easily be reclaimed—until the governments of the sixteenth century in Britain, or the eighteenth and nineteenth centuries in Roman Catholic states. Governments, it was understood, could confiscate, or at least compel sale to the state. Possession of land by charter conferred status rights, but also restricted sale, often to owners who possessed the same "noble" qualifications. This made it hard to hypothecate, or use as collateral for a mortgage loan, and was thus seen as a disadvantage. Such restrictions on marketability or hypothecation were termed entail, and they became less a protection for magnates than a burden. Still, the privileges over control of land that were inherited from feudalism determined the horizontal layering of estatist society and what in Europe was termed the Old Regime.

In some tribal societies, the concept of ownership as Europeans conceived it did not really exist. Land was plentiful, its cultivators—who used it for pasturage and hunting as well as agriculture—scarce, and the idea of exclusive possession (with its rights to sell or bequeath) played no role because use seemed guaranteed. One must be cautious about ascribing such a pastoral or collective mentality: many traditional societies constructed institutional equivalents to family ownership and certainly to tribal custody. White colonizers moved to purchase these residual rights for insignificant sums and sometimes, as in Australia, to claim that the land was *terra nullius* (unclaimed) and theirs for the taking or by right of conquest—modes of expropriation that would exert a devastating impact in the American, Australian, African, and Indonesian settlements. Those who spoke for taking possession pointed to the poverty of collectivist societies. "Several nations of the Americas," John Locke had written, "are rich in Land, and poor in all the Comforts of Life . . . for want of improving [the materials of Plenty] by labour, have not one hundredth part of the Conveniences we enjoy: And a King of a large fruitful Territory there feeds, lodges, and is clad worse than a day Labourer in England."[20] Thus possession, vendibility, tax burdens, and labor claims were all woven together in a complex tapestry of honorific, economic, and political claims. Untwisting the fabric was the work of modernization—the great process of legal and economic change from traditional societies across the globe to their modern successors. Even in China, where family claims on land remained strong, the eighteenth century strengthened the idea of definitive sales and contracts retained importance.[21]

This process added immensely to the unrest that already was inherent in the countryside's economy of scarcity. Peasants and magnates, and indirectly rulers and city dwellers, all depended on the physical extraction of food from the countryside. It was natural enough that the pressures of population increase, the vicissitudes of weather and harvest, and the ravages of disease would produce conflict. Villages living on the margins of subsistence could be provoked by rigorous tax collection and bad harvests, and their discontents could be rendered ideological by popular millenarian religious doctrines. Prosperous peasants might be angered by efforts to tighten up rules that had grown softer over time. Rising prices worked to the advantage of the party that marketed the harvest. If the peasant paid relatively fixed money rents but could bring grain or rice to market on his own, then the landlord and the state would be squeezed in an era of inflation. If the landlord collected his rents in kind, then he benefited from inflationary trends. Peasant revolts, usually localized but occasionally coalescing into broad protest movements, were a frequent seasoning of rural life.

But add to these latent tensions in the years from 1750 to 1860 a new transnational impulse: the penetration of rural land and labor relations by market forces, that is, the commodification of the countryside. Much of the globe's arable land had been farmed in one or another fabric of collective relationships or at least under arrangements that guaranteed tenure and fixed terms of labor and deference. Public authorities had a role: they protected landlords against major protest, raked off shares of harvest proceeds, might call on manpower for military uses. But states needed money. Eighteenth-century war was expensive and endemic. Current ideas among reformist European philosophers and statesmen—above all those who deemed themselves Physiocrats—envisaged that dissolving all the restrictions on the market for land and its crops could significantly increase national wealth. The fruitfulness of land, claimed the Physiocrats, was the ultimate source of society's wealth or surplus. One of their major theoreticians, François Quesnay, had devised a table that showed the cycle of production. Agriculture brought to market yielded more than was spent by the peasants and middlemen who dealt with it. On the basis of that surplus landlords received their rents and the urban sector its payments for its goods and services. From these continuing dividends created by agriculture would be built the roads, harbors, palaces, all the nonagricultural products that a society consumed. Agriculture paid for government and the military and private incomes.

The key to the process was encouraging those who owned land and sowed it to expand their production. That meant creating a broader class of owner-entrepreneurs who would respond to market incentives. It also suggested, in contrast to centuries of efforts to keep grain prices down for fear of public unrest, that the traditional price controls be suspended so that higher prices would entice producers into producing more. Of course, in the eighteenth century, where crops could fail and the harvest might be precarious, higher prices could mean shortages, inflation, urban riots, and unrest. This had been the result of the freeing of grain prices in France and Spain in 1764–1765, and the monarchs retreated. Still the basic insight was amazingly influential.

Americans think of Physiocracy as a curious adulation of the soil held by intellectuals who had visions of agrarian republics. But in fact the underlying insights were broadly influential. The British governor of Bengal, the monarchs of the Iberian states and their Latin American colonies, the reform-minded ministers of the Italian states, whether Austrian-governed Lombardy in the north or prosperous Tuscany or Bourbon Naples and Sicily, all agreed on the major outlines of reform. Transform peasants from downtrodden ignorant workers in thrall to landlords, priests, and religious foundations into an agricultural middle class. Remove the personal restrictions that bound peasants to their village and their owners: let them marry and migrate and contract at will; remove the inherited stigmata of serfdom and slavery, and they would become a class of sturdy yeomen producers. Increase the output of grain, of olives, of wine, of forests, or rice and silk in Japan, tea in India. Invest in agrarian infrastructure— canals, roads, harbors—and in improved techniques of cultivation. Consolidate the patchwork of taxes and spread the burden to the landlords or nobility, who were often exempt, so that it might be lowered overall. Free grain prices to encourage higher production. Remove the impediments to free purchase, sale, and mortgaging of land, and wrest land from churches and abbeys and village communes.

But the concept did not work out so easily. In the late 1760s, following decades of criticism of Roman Catholic institutions, the monarchs of Spain and Portugal decided that they could expropriate the extensive lands of the Jesuit order held in Iberia and in Latin America. As in most such auction procedures, the beneficiaries were not poor peasants but substantial proprietors who could participate in the market. The French revolutionary peasants who freed their holdings from the remaining rents, *corvées,* and occasional labor exactions that still persisted (what French lawyers called feudalism) perhaps fared the best. In most places—whether Central Europe, Ireland, Iberia, and Italy, eventually the American South—the new peasant proprietors fell into the snare of growing indebtedness. The British may have dreamed of awakening the torpid villages of Bengal and making the agrarian middle classes into gentry-like farmers and agents of indirect rule. Their governors thus proposed a "permanent settlement," or freezing of the taxes on agriculture that would supposedly benefit farmers who could turn toward commercial agriculture without fearing tax hikes. They ended up, however, tending to reinforce the power of the tax farmers *(zamindars)* and the reduction of the peasants *(ryots)* from whom they collected rents and taxes into further dependency and poverty.

Physiocracy was only the most formalized version of the underlying trend, which saw the growing commodification of land and the labor that worked it. All the traditional restraints on a pervasive market mentality, whether religious teachings, feudal privileges, the inscribed status of nobles or churches, or the customary village control of common lands, were under pressure. Population growth, the cost of military and colonial competition, and the burdens of alleviating poverty ratcheted up the demands for extracting resources and money from the countryside. Economic development, not yet labeled as such, became a major preoccupation in China, the reform-minded semiautonomous feudal domains or *han* of Japan (such as Tosa), the lands of the East India Company (EIC), the Ottoman Empire, as well as the reformist monarchies of Maria Theresa's Austria and Archduke Leopold's Tuscany, Frederick the Great's Prussia, the Spain of Charles III,

Turgot's France, and throughout the global state system. But the result was agrarian unrest, and there was a cluster of major rural revolts in the 1770s and 1780s: the great Pugachev rebellion in Russia in 1773–1775, the Bohemian revolts in the same period, the French upheaval of 1789 once it spread to the countryside—and outside Europe, the 1780 Inca uprising led by Túpac Amaru II in the viceroyalty of Spanish Peru, and from 1796 the White Lotus rebellion in China.[22]

These diverse upheavals cannot be ascribed solely to commodification or inflationary pressures, although population and markets increased. A great deal depended upon the state of harvests from year to year and the state's pressure to collect taxes and ultimately the tactics it used to assuage grievances or to repress disorder. It would certainly be too simple to ascribe the two great Western political transformations of the late eighteenth century—the American independence movement and formation of a constitutional republic (1775–1787), and the French Revolutions of 1789–1799—to rural turbulence. For even as the idea of a liberal market percolated in the countryside, the accompanying concepts of human rights and participation in government undermined aristocratic and monarchical political claims. Despite such voices for conciliation of the North American colonies as Edmund Burke, George III and his ministers insisted on preserving the decisive rights to raise money and limit colonial voices in government, and the resulting demonstrations and efforts at repression escalated into forcible resistance, thereby provoking claims for the colonies' assumption of independent statehood. As a struggle for independent statehood in a society of middling incomes, class division was not a major theme. Modest family farmers in the interior of the respective colonies often felt resentments at wealthier coastal planters or urban merchants, and in the inland South might align with British forces. Urban concentrations, however, were relatively small, and local opinion leaders, including slaveholders, seized the leadership of the movement and inscribed its claims in traditional terms of English constitutionalism. British efforts to raise slave uprisings limited American slavery opponents from acting more decisively.

French-speaking societies were not so immunized. The sequence of late eighteenth-century fiscal crises and constitutional conflicts led in the late 1780s and 1790s to the astonishing collapse of the French monarchy, and as the European states became involved in this great upheaval, the *gens de couleur* in Haiti and the Creole elites of Mexico and Spanish America decided to follow the same path. Given the great social inequalities in French society, the tax immunities enjoyed by its class of hereditary nobility, and the claims of the French church in the countryside, a political upheaval in that populous country (twenty-five million versus the Americans' four million) was bound to target the privileges accruing to land in the estatist structure of the Old Regime.

Great revolutions and sometimes minor ones as well become vortices that suck in outside rival powers even as they radiate principles of upheaval abroad; and this was true of the American and the French. The French armies (Republican after 1792) who sought to establish an international coalition of like-minded revolutionaries abroad in the Austrian Netherlands (Belgium), the Rhineland territories of the Holy Roman Empire, Switzerland, and the Italian kingdoms, ended up playing on all the tensions that were built into the estatist societies of the late eighteenth century. The French armies took advantage of these tensions, and forced victories that brought their ideological allies to power in the late 1790s. But in some of the societies the new revolutionaries faced opposition not only from the old rulers allied with the anti-French coalition (British, Austrian, Prussian, and fitfully the Russians), but peasant masses who were the uneasy victims of the Physiocratic transformations described above. They helped sweep away the early collaborationist republics in Italy and, during the Bonapartist phase of French expansion a decade later, often joined the indigenous forces opposing the French occupation of Spain. The reimplantation of the revolution abroad step by step after 1801—no longer under the hodgepodge of local Jacobin radicals, but by middle-class or aristocratic reformers working under Napoleon's rationalization of fragmented German and Italian territories—had more enduring effects. The recruits to this cause were often reformers, who wanted to rationalize fiscal burdens, mobilize clerical wealth, modernize law codes, and use French patronage to reorganize their own territories by absorbing all the manifold subordinate jurisdictions—a program that the emperor of the French pushed through from 1803 to 1806, largely at the cost of the Habsburg traditionalist claims. When Prussia resisted and was disastrously defeated in 1806, its aristocratic bureaucrats decided to emulate similar reforms such as formal abolition of serfdom and thereafter to introduce military conscription.

~

Thus by 1810, the historian can discern throughout Europe and the Americas the outlines of the next generation's transnational alignment of social forces and political programs. They included, first, a conservative cohort of dispossessed or threatened aristocrats aligned with landed church officials—still dominant in Britain, Austria, and among the French exiles—who would recover partial and temporary power after 1815; and, second, a reformist phalanx of leaders who sympathized with the French reforms and were willing to administer Napoleon's European satellites and would establish themselves after 1815 as a more liberal alternative to the Restoration governments. Many of these benefited from the sale of church properties that the French secularized and auctioned off—more to commercially minded bourgeois who formed corporations to buy them than to aspiring peasants.[23] Similar acquisitions, which purchasers could finance by government loans, became available to the Mexican men of property as the revolutionary and then successive governments sold off monastic and Holy Office properties.[24] On the far left the small groups of republican revolutionaries who had supported the Jacobin republic remained in the political wilderness. They comprised preeminently literary intellectuals and political amateurs throughout Western Europe (including some in Britain) and the Americas.

Finally, there were masses of peasants who felt threatened by rural capitalism and resented the attacks on the Catholic Church in the countryside. The Church, after all, at least as represented in the parishes and monastic settlements, was the institution par excellence that resisted the market, baptized their children, knit together their families in marriage, and offered hope as they buried their parents and, alas too often, children. Those peasants who remained religiously loyal (many did not, of course) sustained the anti-French guerrilla forces in occupied Spain and southern Italy and remained pro-Bourbon and pro-clerical and hostile to any whiffs of French-inspired elite reform. After the restoration of the Spanish Bourbons, the aging painter Goya would depict them as superstitious, brooding, ignorant Catholic masses. The proponents of agrarian reforms and the emancipation of landed society from its traditional hierarchies ignored this rural populism at their peril. The Church remained a major strand of peasant protest and revolution deep into the twentieth century, sustaining Catholic guerrillas in Spain and Mexico and peasant mobilization in Russia, China, and Japan.[25]

How these groups might combine or quarrel, and which might prevail, often depended upon the military outcomes—although these in turn reflected the forces that revolutionary principles awakened. Where the French armies conquered, political reorganization usually followed. Russia and Britain remained outside the reach of French armies and thus under traditional rule, which in the latter country meant the government of an oligarchical parliament—a regime that the British sought to strengthen in Sicily, which they occupied while Napoleonic forces held mainland Italy. As of 1815, when the twenty-five-year-long warfare and economic turmoil provoked by revolutionary France and its contagious principles were finally extinguished, revolutionary claims appeared defeated, but like some dormant volcano they still rumbled under the surface of the Restoration. Certainly they did not triumph. The Bourbon monarchs returned to France (to be succeeded by their Orleanist cousins from 1830 to 1848), but in both cases under regimes that gave a role to an elite drawn from finance, industry, engineering, and the educational establishment. These new forces counted for more than they ever had before, as technological change began visibly to transform the economies and mentalities of the literate classes in France, Belgium, the German states, and Lombardy by the 1830s and 1840s. The political question in the West was whether the traditions of the countryside and its rural hierarchies could keep these new forces in check.

The upshot was more complex, in that rural hierarchies were themselves not just barriers to change but its very agents. As a recent revisionist study of Prussian rural life suggests, "over the centuries the two parties, manor and village, approached one another as combatants, probing for weaknesses and opportunities for gain, now accepting truces, now breaking them to pursue strategic advantages with the court bailiff's lash, at the strike front, or on the judicial battlefield." Nonetheless, in all their contention they acted together as agents of change. "Estate owners and landed villagers need rethinking as market producers open to the nineteenth and early twentieth centuries' technological, material, and political opportunities."[26] However, they also were undermining the old rural order. The stability that had rested on legal estates and patterns of deference and the teachings of religion would have to be reestablished, if at all, by the ligaments of rural capitalism— the pressure of rents and debts and credits. It helped that aristocrats would be flanked by new ambitious peasant proprietors with a stake in rural order.

Historians recognize the Congress of Vienna, which concluded peace after the Napoleonic wars, as a fundamental settlement among nations. The statesmen at Vienna, however, also believed that an enduring peace required a settlement *within* each country that precluded a rekindling of revolutionary energy. Just as Woodrow Wilson would later insist that peace rested on liberal democratic regimes, the Vienna leaders took for granted that it required a conservative social base. They were willing to accept monarchs whom Napoleon had put in place in Sweden and initially in Naples but wanted to reinforce the rural hierarchies of the old regime and guarantee the stability of the countryside. They left behind a structure of periodic consultations that could coordinate transnational counterrevolutionary intervention as well as curb threats to peace, the so-called Congress System. For the restored French Bourbons the Vienna settlement meant accepting a constitution and recognizing that the distribution of land by the intervening revolutionary regime would not be reversed. However, even the moderate Vienna program was soon in shambles. The domestic restoration was breaking down by the 1830s and 1840s. International arrangements collapsed in the 1850s and 1860s. Rick burning in Britain; peasant organization in Ireland; agricultural protest on the continent; that harbinger of discontent, anti-Semitic agitation in Germany; and, outside Europe, creole revolutions throughout Latin America, peasant protests in Japan, and a huge insurrection in China, would characterize the stormy decades from the 1820s into the 1850s. The rhetoric of change could be that of liberal rights and equality; it also could be millenarian, the expression of religious protest. Each society played out these conflicts with different ideological traditions and hierarchical structures, but giving impetus to all of them was the great tension produced by the advent of market transactions for land and of the labor on the land.

The implications were contradictory: yes, expand the market energies of the countryside, mobilize the capacity for wealth; but stifle the unrest that was likely to occur. This is why the early nineteenth century was so punctuated by agricultural unrest. On the one hand, the encroaching market principles undermined the old claims of aristocratic supremacy and the sacramental legitimacy of church and religion. On the other, the actual economic results seemed to bring hard times to the countryside as well as the emerging industrial cities. In the long run the Physiocratic mechanisms might encourage surplus and wealth, but a painful transition of several decades lay in between. Faced with the turmoil, the elite faced a stark alternative. Either they might rule by repression and force (this was the stance that English Tories, frightened by the French Revolution, sought to impose from the trials of alleged "Jacobins" in the 1790s through the "Peterloo massacre" of 1819, when soldiers fired on a crowd of demonstrators in Manchester); or, alternatively, they might seek to hasten the triumph of the market and commodification. This latter course constituted the Liberal program that prevailed after the elections of 1830 and 1832, after the narrow British political class absorbed the lesson of the 1830 revolution across the English Channel and passed the Reform Act of 1832, which expanded the suffrage to the substantial middle classes and redistricted Parliament to accommodate new industrial cities.

Markets, Reforms, Resistance

The rise of British liberalism meant far more than a political transition in an island of twelve million. Perhaps to an even greater degree than the principles and armies of revolutionary France, its ramifications were to be felt worldwide. No friends of revolution, the Tory ministries of the 1820s were still resolved to block any Franco-Spanish reconquest of their rebellious colonies in the Caribbean. In 1807 Britain abolished the transport of slaves on its own ships and after the end of the Napoleonic Wars patrolled West African waters to intercept slave traders. Abolition of slavery itself in British colonies followed in 1833, although the voracious demand of English cotton mills kept the institution continuously profitable in the southern United States. British intervention required a global naval presence, although its financial capacity for underwriting foreign loans would also serve as a continuing asset. Britain's long-serving Whig foreign secretary and later prime minister Lord Palmerston (Henry John Temple), vigorous spokesman for his nation's liberalism, helped midwife a peaceful secession of Belgium from Holland, and indirectly encouraged the Turkish reforms of the mid-nineteenth century. The British adherence to market principles—that is, on the right of the East India Company to sell opium in China and to protect the legal rights of brawling sailors—undermined the Confucian order, as China's resistance resulted in a clamorous military defeat in 1842.

By 1846 the political mobilization that led to abolition of the protective tariff on grain confirmed the country's commitment to industry, international finance, and free trade. This so-called repeal of the Corn Laws was among the most decisive legal affirmations of early nineteenth-century social change. It confirmed Britain's industrial vocation—the calculation of the Whigs that by letting wheat prices sink for a hungry working class (and indirectly the wages that workers needed to pay their food budgets), they would do better than putting tariffs on textile competitors and keeping the prices of industry high. Simply put, there were no major competitors for British or third-country markets. The industrial cities grew; paradoxically the sentimental affection for a rural Britain of pastoral villages also increased.

British loans would support the first generation of independent state leaders in Latin America after the Napoleonic wars and the wars for independence from 1810 to 1825 threw the finances of New Spain, including Mexico, into disarray. The breakdown of Bourbon fiscal systems (which remained efficient in the late eighteenth century far longer than often maintained) and the recourse to local finances advanced the federalist options supported by Latin American liberals but sparked endemic conflicts as well. The new republics and the empire of Brazil depended on British loans and investments. Until the 1850s the relative weakness of the international economy weakened the new states and aggravated the conflicts within them and between them. New loans, taxes, discounted state salaries, and the tendency to localize fiscal systems characterized the threshold of independence.[27] We can construe the financial and market connections between Europe and the Americas and Asia as an early form of what 1970s commentators would call interdependence—what today's analysts call globalization. Perhaps most important, if indirect, was the impact of these early financial and commercial currents on the Ottoman Empire, India, and China. These huge, conglomerate societies already faced deep internal crises, which the interventions of foreign powers only magnified. Whereas French concepts of citizenship backed by military interventions from 1792 to 1815 had forced the harsh choice of resistance or subservience, the British connections after 1815 were weaving a fabric of markets and credits that compelled local elites either to develop liberal reform or to resist at the price of disabling backwardness.

In the Middle East the Ottoman Empire descended into intensified crisis. Ottoman state and society had certain traits that emerged both from its multinational imperial legacy—its responsibility for the European Balkans in the north and west, Arab communities in the southeast, Anatolian Turkish populations threatened by Russian expansion, and religious and ethnic minorities organized into partially self-governing communities in the major cities and the coastal regions—and from its ambitions as an encompassing Muslim state. In the outlying regions of the empire the strength of local notables and their clienteles generated long-term feuds that were impossible to discipline. The practice of administration amounted to divide and rule (and protect) the multifarious identities within the realm. The state had no secure monopoly of violence, often resorting to irregular troops and private forces to keep order.[28] The eighteenth century had brought almost continual warfare and net renunciation of territories, against Habsburgs and Venetians in the west, Persians to the east, Russians to the north.

Selim III, who ruled from 1789 until he was deposed and executed in 1807/1808, understood the need for reforms as he confronted Russian military threats and watched Europe plunged into new, seemingly total warfare. In theory the army with its two branches—the cavalry of the frontier whose officers were supported by landed fiefs and the garrisoned army of the capital, the Janissaries, who were the sultan's personal force—was totally at odds with the idea of a citizen army that the French Revolution had made so central. What united army and society were the tax obligations of the subjects, which in turn rested upon their well-being within a framework of justice and Islamic law (shari'a) that the sultan had also to guarantee. Over the centuries the societal framework had calcified into a collection of privileged groups defending their privileges, whether urban guilds, local notables, or waqfs. Selim planned a "New Order" based on a new army, including Western uniforms, and a more efficient tax system, but the reforms threatened, on the one hand, the quasi-feudal notables *(ayan)* who during the previous centuries had entrenched themselves as de facto rulers of the countryside and, on the other hand, the privileged Janissaries of the capital, who originally, centuries earlier, had been recruited from conscripting dragnets among the Balkan Christian populations.[29]

Supported by the conservative Muslim judiciary and fomenting rioting in Constantinople, the Janissaries deposed and executed the sultan and those identified with the New Order. In turn they provoked the Balkan *ayan* to march on the capital, kill about a thousand of the opposition, and install a new sultan, Mahmud II, who was compelled to sign a covenant of union that limited his power and that of the viziers. The compromise did not last long. The sultan turned to limit *ayan* ascendancy, then finally moved against the obstreperous Janissaries in 1826, murdering them en masse and burning their barracks. But his regime faced a Greek revolt supported by Western public opinion, then the Russian destruction of the sultan's Black Sea fleet in 1827 and a confrontation with the ambitious reform pasha of Egypt, Muhammad Ali, in the next decade.

Born in what is today Greek territory as the son of an Albanian in the service of the Ottomans, Muhammad Ali would attempt to bring Egypt into the nineteenth century, destroying the Mamluk military caste, expanding irrigation canals, establishing it as a major cotton-growing territory, and reforming its fiscal system and military. He was commissioned by the sultan to quell the advance of the Arabian Ibn Saud dynasty, adherents of the austere Islamic movement, Wahhabism, that had taken hold in the Arabian hinterland. After the Saudis had taken the Holy Cities and interrupted the Hajj or annual pilgrimage routes from Damascus in 1803, Constantinople enlisted its dynamic Egyptian governor to push them back. Although Muhammad Ali retained too great a sense of Ottoman loyalty to challenge the empire or even seize the throne, Constantinople was naturally leery of his power and freedom of action even as they called on him to help suppress the Greek rebellion and added Crete to his territory. Muhammad Ali and his son conquered Syria and Mt. Lebanon (the Beirut region with a significant Christian population) and defeated the sultan's army on the Anatolian frontier, until the British routed them from these territories. For London, a fragile Ottoman state was a useful, if vulnerable, barrier to Russian expansion.[30]

But propping up the Ottoman imperial structure hardly restored its vitality or overcame the multiple challenges that afflicted it. European support for the Greek revolution in the Balkans, continuing Russian pressure in the Black Sea, French efforts to protect Christians in Lebanon, Islamic religious radicalism in the Arab interior, and an ambitious Egyptian modernization effort meant that Constantinople faced crises on almost every front. The question was whether a vast and creaky empire that for the last few centuries had been governed increasingly through pervasive clientelism and had continually to contend with powerful veto groups—if no longer a corporatized army dominating the capital city, certainly a conservative Muslim establishment claiming to legitimize the monarchy—could change the basis of government.

Emerging from the violence and setbacks of the 1820s, a group of reform-minded bureaucrat-diplomats with particular sensitivity to the dangers from abroad embarked on a modernization of the state in the 1830s and a series of reforms from 1839 into the mid-1870s that would be known as the Tanzimat. They established government departments, a prime minister, public taxation to replace tax farming, and a reform council whose proposals the sultan pledged to institute. The reforms were originally justified as aiming at the regeneration of the role of Islam, and the adherents of civic and political reform could be allies of a vast intercontinental movement for Islamic reform that was culminating in the 1830s.[31] Part of the motive was to appeal to the British Whigs, who would have to provide the backup for the empire against the Egyptian and Russian dangers. All very well, but the more that the Ottoman state moved toward importing principles of citizenship and general law, the more it undermined its traditional cultivation of privileged groups. Could the six-centuries-old empire make the transition from subjects to citizens without disintegrating?

Chinese state and society were also under increasing pressure—even before the Anglo-Chinese Opium War of 1839–1842, which an earlier generation of historians, at least, took as the opening of a national crisis that only deepened in the course of the nineteenth century. Contemporary interpretation has tended to examine the strains arising within the Qing order from its very dynamic growth in the eighteenth century. Population was increasing dramatically—from 300 million in 1700 to perhaps 450 million by 1850—as New World crops, sweet potatoes, maize, and peanuts allowed the relaxation of Malthusian constraints.[32] This brought with it population pressure in the south and the expansion of Han Chinese into the northern provinces that were supposedly the homeland of the Manchu people and its Qing Dynasty that had displaced the Ming in 1644. It put pressure on the earlier Manchu effort to preserve domination of public office as Han officials played an increasingly larger role. The Chinese elite differed from that in Europe: it comprised the provincial and national "gentry," a class that had to pass continuing examinations based on Confucian classics, but then enjoyed office holding and exemptions from state service and corporal punishment. Meritocracy, however, is hard to divorce from class privilege. As population increased, the spread of clientelism, bribes, and the resort to exam schools to gain access to the gentry revealed the strains on the ancient system.

Over the course of the eighteenth century, the Manchu state, under the leadership of two remarkable long-lived monarchs, the Kangxi emperor and his grandson, the Qianlong emperor, had devoted major military efforts to expand into the Mongolian west and had vastly increased the effective territory of the state. But the dense habitations of the southern and central provinces and the two great southern river systems (the Pearl estuaries with Guangzhou, and the Yangzi winding eastward from Sichuan to Shanghai and the coastal cities) proved as major a challenge to effective government. The commercially active populations despised immigrants from other provinces, and the networks of bandits, smugglers, and mafia-like "triads" who exploited the wealth and the conflicts among the "immigrants" challenged the precepts of a Confucian moral order. Outside the channels of social mobility and well-ordered commerce and farming, messianic religious doctrines known as White Lotus Buddhism flourished. Government efforts to suppress the congregations led to massive rebellion in 1796 in the provinces of Taiwan, Sichuan, Guangxi, Hunan, and Guizhou, which would require almost a decade to overpower.[33]

Still, as late as 1800 China could be counted as a wealthy society. The question of how it compared with the West has produced a cottage industry of recent scholarship. In his 1776 *Wealth of Nations,* Adam Smith explained that to account for the prosperity of labor, the critical issue was less the degree of wealth than the comparative rate of growth: a stagnant rich nation was in greater trouble than a poorer but dynamic one: "The poverty of the lower ranks of people in China far surpasses that of the most beggarly nations in Europe."[34] There was trade in land; feudal tenures had been eliminated, although debt relationships kept many in dependency; great estates rarely exceeded 250 acres. Probably a third of agricultural production went into trade, some of it over great distances. Proto-industrial organization produced a great deal of cotton cloth and silk, some of which was processed by owners of several hundred looms. Letters of credit issued by emerging banking houses were replacing shipment of silver bullion. Luxury items such as porcelain and furniture were prized in the West.

Difficulties recurred and increased in the early 1800s. If outright rebellion was stanched, the inner bleeding of the state continued. The grain tribute administration, which had charge of ferrying the major taxes in rice eight hundred miles northward along the Grand Canal from Hangzhou on the Yangzi to Beijing, was undermined by corruption, overhiring, a tripling of boat fees, and growing commercialization of the grain tribute as local officials had to purchase rice from private traders to meet their quotas. If bureaucratic friction, corruption, and monopolistic labor practices were not enough, Yellow River silting blocked the major crossing of the Grand Canal in 1824–1825, even as the vested interests of the river merchants vetoed the alternative of shipment along the coast. The canal route would be restored by borrowing water from the Yellow River to augment the canal, but the sea route had to be adopted by 1845, and by 1853 the advance of the Taiping rebels and the Yellow River's change of course (itself attended by catastrophic flooding and environmental challenges) ended the canal route. The price inflation of the eighteenth century brought a trebling of grain prices. Because taxes on commodities were fixed in quantities of silver, peasants could initially keep up their income as the tax rates increased, but by the 1830s the rapidly expanding opium imports began to drain silver from the country and increased the tax burden in real terms. "Not a year has passed without fears of Yellow River floods, not a year without having to raise funds for river control," lamented the leading intellectual of the era, Wei Yuan, before the Opium War. "This is something unknown in previous ages. Foreign opium has spread throughout the country, and silver flows overseas. Because of this the grain tribute tax and salt monopoly develop ever more evils, the officials and people are ever deeper in trouble.... Standing in the present and surveying the past, the difference is as between black and white."[35] Within the constraints that continuing interpretation of ancient Confucian texts mandated for the elite, he reinterpreted the almost twenty-five-hundred-year-old Book of Odes as a summons for a renewal of literati activism in the public interest and for the court to use the lettered elite to break the bureaucratic blockages the country faced. In a British context one might label such an approach Tory reform, certainly better than no reform but rarely sufficient to master the tides of nineteenth-century economic and demographic change. In the United States its functional equivalent perhaps was the belief, expressed by the Virginian Democratic Republicans of the 1790s, that a "natural aristocracy" could pursue the disinterested public interest—a vision soon submerged under the pressures of commercial development and electoral democracy.

The Daoguang emperor from 1840 did allow a reinvigoration of intellectual life and the cautious application of traditional learning to practical problems such as defense and management of the coasts and frontiers.[36] Pressure from the avid world of commerce abroad, however, came too soon and too rapidly for any gradualist or traditionalist coping. The opium boom, of course, involved China in a disastrous military defeat. Opium had been prohibited by the Chinese in 1821, but traded nonetheless. Addiction grew above all for the smoked leaf. It was an Indian product and the EIC had charge of the trade with China. Growers in Indian territories outside EIC control sought to break into the trade, and rather than cede control, the EIC decided to buy and export greater quantities, although it consigned these exports to Chinese merchants. Because the British sold no other products to

China, opium sales also promised a way to balance growing their imports of silk and tea. Moreover, as the EIC also explained at home, even the purchases from the independent Indian producers would let the Indian population buy more British cottons and manufactures.

Chinese merchants and smugglers and even foreign trade officials might connive in the imports, but concern grew that London was insisting on the principled defense of free trade to profit from the addiction of the Chinese population. By the mid-1830s the EIC no longer had a legal trading status, but British representatives spoke for the English merchants based in the official entrepôt of Guangzhou. Chinese officials also believed the trade was responsible for the rise in silver prices and thus the tightening of monetary conditions, although three-quarters of British proceeds flowed back into the country for purchases of tea and silk. The British expected the Chinese to legalize imports, but after a vigorous debate Beijing reaffirmed the ban in 1836. The Beijing court entrusted its policy response to an official, Commissioner Lin Zexu, whose war against drugs led him to confine the British merchants at Guangzhou to their factories until supplies of opium were surrendered. The conflict escalated over the rights of merchants and British citizens, in particular the immunities of British sailors from Chinese law. Still, British authorities and the Chinese court debated policies of concession and resistance, and full-scale warfare followed only after a series of British attacks and withdrawals. At that point British progress upriver toward Nanjing with successive Chinese defeats finally led to Beijing's military humiliation, which compelled the state to cede Hong Kong and extraterritorial rights.[37]

On the face of it Japan was as vulnerable as China. But the unrest provoked by the rise of commercial pressures mobilized not rebels against a nominally unified empire but the ambitious leaders of autonomous feudal domains. Attendance of these *daimyō* at the emperor's court involved a large percentage of their public expenses. Although public order seemed under far better control than in China, the pressures of market forces had an effect in Japan as well. The early Tokugawa after 1600 had thought to escape from decades of anarchic civil strife and to fix a stable order on Japan, to freeze it into a pyramid of isolated and hierarchical Confucian peace and order. The Christianity that had begun to make inroads was violently suppressed between 1600 and 1620; foreign contacts were prohibited by 1630. But over the next two centuries, population rose, a money economy made inroads with all the inflation and debt that entailed; some peasants went into market farming for the cities or specialized in crops such as rapeseed oil or silk worms; merchants and artisans proliferated; new self-made men bought office and title, the samurai lost their military virtues, and the administrative offices within the *han* and at the center proliferated. Peasants began to produce for the markets and became more disputatious as they entered market relations. Retainers, lords, and the shogunate itself fell further into debt—some of the domains owed up to a couple of years of expected revenues—the currency was periodically debased, samurai debts had to be periodically canceled, while after 1800 occasional crop failures, tax gouging, and corruption produced unrest and frequent, if small, rebellions. Administrators in the *daimyō* oscillated between imposing forced loans and writing down interest rates on loans. Some administrators, often samurai of humble origins, attempted heroic reforms in the decades before 1850, whether for the national or the domainal governments. Occasionally they resorted to setting up state monopolies for commodities. But reformers, whether in Edo or in the domains, could also be forced out by conservative samurai opposition.

Even before Commodore Matthew Perry arrived with his black ships in 1853, the Japanese old regime faced fiscal difficulties and social unrest, although without foreign wars as a source of crisis, which suggested that indigenous development in its own right destabilized societies of legal privilege and rank. Incidents of tax protest rose in the market-oriented domains, where new crops, especially the cultivation of silkworms, were increasing, while Samurai control remained stronger in the less commercially developed *han;* and the divergence characterized the choice of sides in the civil war at the end of the Tokugawa order in the 1860s.[38]

Pause for a moment of skeptical interrogation. Was the world from 1810 through the 1840s really in an epoch of coordinated transition? This historical account argues that world civilizations had arrived at some parallel rhythms of development as they interacted more intensely and systemically. Still, the wary reader and the cautious researcher should distrust any effort just to select convenient parallels. States and cultures do present a persisting individuality, as does any community that can be identified for study, whether at the grandest level of empires, on a middle scale of nations and regions, or at the local level between counties and villages, often between enterprises, parishes, and families. The world the historian investigates is differentiated, so to speak, "all the way down." But it is also fractal, in that at each scale similar pressures and similar rifts can be detected. The historian has to decide the relative importance of what is similar and what is different; these are not measures inscribed in the societies themselves. But he or she must make a persuasive public case for these judgments, which ultimately have to be validated by the critical reader.

We have made the case so far on the basis of fundamental and encompassing transitions: the century-long dissolution of hereditary and ascribed relations in the countryside; the growth of sufficient wealth to reward the growth of commercial agriculture as long-distance markets thrived for wheat and rice, for tea, coffee, naval supplies (timber, hemp, resins), and opium; the accumulating technologies that allowed coal and steam to magnify the energy at the disposal of labor; the denser networks of trust that let payment for investment and trade be postponed and reassigned to distant sources of savings—and the progressive casting of land itself into the maelstrom of the market. The case for the global history rests further on the ever-widening pressure from the West, whether through the unsettling presence of Enlightenment ideas or the capacity to draw on and transfer capital, and to move effective military units to far-flung shores. Europeans and North Americans pressed their demands no longer just on tribal societies (although this pressure continued remorselessly), but on the ancient states of Africa and Asia. Whether demanding that the rulers of East Asia open their realms to trade, or calling on the Islamic territories around the Mediterranean to protect their Christian subjects, continuing to intervene militarily in the republics of the New World or moving to control wider provinces of South Asia, Europeans encroached to an ever greater extent. Where they did not directly take over new territories (as the French did in Algeria in 1830), they pressed capitulary treaties on Asian and African rulers, insisting that their own nationals face trial only in their own courts and that Christian subjects enjoy protected status.

But finally, there was a worldwide blowback that constituted a global response—the mobilization of religious loyalties throughout the globe in large part as a reaction to the tendencies described above. Precisely as the traditional structures of the global old regime became unhinged, religious impulses emerged to offer a compensatory vision. As the West encroached, and traditional rulers seemed powerless to resist or even wished to emulate the new techniques and ideas, prophets and saints emerged to resist. This is not to say religious beliefs were ideological responses to social unrest. They were genuine and sprang from deep convictions. But they erupted as powerful organizing and missionary forces as long-term expectations of economic and political stability melted around newly exposed communities. Caught in the currents, conservative elites would deploy the traditional authorities and congregations to keep control, while the marginal elements of society more vulnerable to social dislocation or wedded to territorial autonomy would flock to doctrines of direct inspiration and leaders who demonstrated it. And subsequently, as states were reconstructed, women would assert their own historical role by establishing a presence in significant sectors of religious and charitable activity.

In their implicit claim to reintegrate emotional wholeness that imperial religious bureaucracies had deadened or market society corroded, all sorts of religious congregations arose to contest the new trends and sort alternative values. Thus, religious activism played a role in the great uncongealing of global society that was occurring. One consequence of the turbulence in the countryside was the generation of new messianic cults. But commodification was not the only incitement. The stirrings of imperialist pressure also contributed. Religions arose from the margins of settlement: whether Wahhabism in eighteenth-century Arabia or Mormonism in the "burnt-over district" of eastern New York state. Similar movements were created every few generations in movements characterized in the American colonies as Great Awakenings, more generally as revivalist: new revelations, new and unlikely prophets, often women or erotically charismatic male preachers. These would develop as faiths that tapped an outpouring of emotional energy, whether cathecting on other members of the community or on the deity.

It is not making any judgment on the doctrinal content of religion to analyze its this-worldly functions. Certainly these varied, as did political programs. Most religions could accommodate those who lived in compliance with the secular order and whose values of orderliness, family transmission, and ritual served to strengthen it. As in other epochs, religion could serve as a buttress for social hierarchy as it existed. In particular those sects or faiths tied to secular authorities served programs to reestablish authority. Whether the *'ulama'* of the Ottoman Empire, the appeals to Neo-Confucianism by conservative Chinese political leaders seeking to restore the empire's defensive capacity against the West and domestic rebels, or the so-called union of throne and altar and the reactionary appeals of the Holy Alliance among the European courts, political programs of monarchical restoration and imperial strengthening found support among the upholders of orthodox religious establishments or rites.

But at the same time the sects of the periphery, or those of the popular classes, fused faith and collective appeals. Their rites seemed destabilizing and subverted hierarchic authority even as they sometimes promised to reenergize outworn creeds. Their prophets, whether Christian or Hasidic, or Muslim Sufi holy men, preached austerity and inwardness or communal love, sometimes intense rigor, sometimes the emancipation from tiresome rules and structures, in either case a return from encrusted formalism. Their adherents sang hymns, danced, flocked to shrines, sometimes enlisted in the armies of prophets and used the inner convictions of the faith to conceive a world of far greater emotional energy and equality. Everywhere they offered an alternative collective vision of individual as well as communal fulfillment. The city of God might become manifest only later, but meanwhile the villages of God enlisted tremendous nineteenth-century energy.

Religious rededication, however, was not just a response of the dispossessed. Older elites and communities turned toward renewed faiths—responding not with Pentecostal zeal, but a puritanical and intellectual rigor or quiet mysticism. Islam in particular—its faithful spread from Nigeria north and east in Africa, to the Balkans and the Middle East, thence via Central Asia and the remembered domains of the Mughal Empire to the sultanates of Malaya and Borneo—was a faith in ferment. The difficulties of the Ottoman provinces of the Middle East were a revealing crossroads. As Constantinople's bureaucrats pressed forward with their secularizing and reformist Tanzimat edicts, the old elites of the outlying empire who had earlier been the agents of administration took contradictory paths. Some benefited from the new commercial activity tied in with European trading and became the local notables of the modernizing empire. Others resented the displacement of the traditional *'ulama'* and found new doctrines congealing that called for a purification of Islam. Whether Wahhabi currents from the Arabian interior, or the influence of Algerian exiles who had resisted the French conquest and penetration of the 1830s and 1840s, or old scholars, Islamic reformers called for a return to Quranic doctrine and the removal of centuries-old accreted practices—veneration of Muslim saints and tombs, the use of amulets, and such. The reform movement of Salafism took hold among the educated of Cairo and Damascus, somewhat as Calvinism had among Swiss and French urban congregations three centuries earlier. Salafism might tap energies similar to those that sparked the Wahhabi revival of the Saudi state in the Arabian Hejaz, but could also argue that Islam had called for tolerance and mutual learning from Christians, whereas the Wahhabi advocated religious war and the slaying of corrupt Muslims.[39] The contemporary reader, who reads about the recruiting by militant Islam in Pakistani madrassas or Asian immigrants in Hamburg or Birmingham, will be more familiar with this phenomenon in the early twenty-first century than one would have been fifty years ago. In the early 1800s no faith was untouched by the resources of radical communal fervor. The religion of the early nineteenth century could serve as a volcanic force.

Moreover, just as state rivalries kindled emerging nationalism, so the new religious energies stimulated and provoked responses from the other faiths contending for the loyalties of spiritual communities: British Protestants carried their message to the new domains being encroached on in South Asia; American Protestants followed the China trade with great energy. And as the imperial courts of East Asia sought to revive their fortunes later in the nineteenth century, successfully in Japan, less so in China, they tried to strengthen supposed national orthodoxies, Shintō and Neo-Confucianism. These religious energies were two-edged swords, however. Imperial rulers—including too the Ottoman sultans and the British in India—might sponsor religious academies and patronize spiritual authorities in the search for reliable intermediaries and propagators of their own legitimacy. But the energies they tapped into had their own crusading vigor and were not always to be contained within a pro-state program. Sufi prophets of spiritual renewal within Islam, for instance, organized their own quasi states in the peripheries of empire, whether the upper Nile or northern Nigeria.[40] As we reflect on the vigorous revival of Islamic practices today (or Christian, too) in the wake of what seemed like an unparalleled US extension of influence after 1989, we should remember that the extension of national and imperial authority across the globe in the later nineteenth century provoked some similar push-back from Islam and other religions. Those who render unto Caesar will awaken those who want to render unto God—sometimes by organizing their own purified state authorities.

Quasi-religious impulses flowed into secular doctrines as well. The transformations of global society could not take place without the most exciting of visions opening up to participants, both those who were enthused and those who were uneasy. Even as some social critics feared that trade, commerce, and the rise of industry and new technologies were debasing community life, others saw the possibility of new concepts of emancipation and fraternity. Socialist theorists and "utopian" projects marked the decades after the French wars. The Scottish industrialist Robert Owen preached the value of collectivist communities, and his disciples organized a few in North America as well as New Lanark in Scotland. The French writer Claude Henri de Rouvroy, count of Saint-Simon, who argued that factory owners and investors constituted a new elite that was far more important than the old upper crust of dukes and archbishops, inspired a movement that preached his doctrines. Remove the decorative nobility and no adverse consequence would follow; remove the productive elite (he termed them *industriels*) and society must stagnate. He was farsighted: it was the new fusion of commercial leaders, educated civil servants, and reformist landlords who would coalesce in midcentury—not only in

France but throughout the world—and create the institutions and states that were understood to be modern.

Saint-Simon and his followers were sometimes termed utopian socialists. In a European world where a new urban working class crowded into flimsy tenements, drank hard, often contracted the scourges of microbe-infected air and water, tuberculosis and cholera or typhoid, the "social question" was to become anguishing. The workers of Paris and London at this point were hardly disciplined trade unionists seeking respectability, but migrants from the country seeking work, often casual labor, sometimes reduced to crime and prostitution. Anarchic private development augmented the problem; did not the solution lie in a far greater effort at collective organization, whether by reformist entrepreneurs (as Robert Owen thought), or through workers' cooperatives themselves (as Pierre-Joseph Proudhon insisted), and finally by an encompassing working-class international (as Marx would argue)? Charles Fourier argued for reorienting family and social functions within the boundaries of "phalansteries." As these small but energetic movements recruited followers, they built on otherwise suppressed claims of erotic fulfillment (and in the case of some movements, erotic repression). Others were more strictly based on reorganizing capitalism.

Elusive Revolution

Rebellion is sometimes used as a synonym for *revolution,* but there are shades of difference. A revolution is a rebellion that succeeds in removing a given regime (or escaping from its jurisdiction) and installing another, even if the results are later reversed. Revolutions are supposedly carried out in the cause of an articulated program for government. *Rebellion* refers more to revolts, against rulers domestic or foreign, that ultimately fail to sustain their objectives even if they enjoy interim success. Rebellions can seek to institute radical and even utopian programs of equality, or they can seek to restore economic, political, and social orders that participants recall as less exploitative. Modern history in general has witnessed revolutions and rebellions great and small. In Europe and the Americas, the century after 1750 was an era motivated by a newly discovered discourse of rights and happiness. Its philosophers preached self-realization. Its Romantic sensibility glorified man's revolt against tyranny. All of this culminated in the 1840s and carried over into the 1850s, even as a new phase of state reconstruction got under way.

The era between the 1760s and 1860s concluded with two major revolutionary efforts, one in Europe, the other in China—and a third if the so-called Indian Mutiny of 1856–1857 is also counted. The uprisings of 1848–1849 in the West erupted after several years of difficult economic conditions, including rural immiseration and urban overcrowding, and growing impatience with the status quo on the part of frustrated elites who wanted greater political representation. It was not that reform would not have ensued: in Britain the tariff had been repealed; in Prussia a national parliament, or United Landtag, was finally being summoned; in Rome a new young pope seemed sympathetic to reforms even as nationalist secret societies, the so-called *carbonari,* called for unification of the peninsula. Partial progress only led to more impatient demands and agitation. A frightening peasant revolt against Polish aristocrats in Austrian Poland had taken place in 1846, and Protestant and Catholic Swiss cantons had come to the edge of warfare the year before. The Chartist movement in Britain managed a last active surge as it collected signatures for universal male suffrage, annual elections, and secret ballots. French leftists, in opposition to the complacent Orleanist regime, were organizing a campaign of political banquets. Revolution happened to be ignited in a state that was one of the weakest but had a reactionary ruler: the restored Bourbon monarchs of the Kingdom of the Two Sicilies or Naples. The parliament of Sicily, renewed during British occupation of the island in 1812, was not a popularly elected legislature, but an assembly of hereditary magnates. On January 12, 1848, they declared themselves in revolt against the monarch across the straits in mainland Naples. Revolution soon spread in the Italian states, and then to France and the Germanies with extraordinary speed. Monarchs quickly abdicated, or at least conceded constitutions and summoned liberal ministers to office, as if the governing powers realized how illegitimate they were held to be. These spring months of easy triumph were precarious in turn, however. They rested on a coalition between democrats infused with ideals of Romantic populism and the reform-minded among the civil servants and new bourgeois who had acceded to influence since 1815. The Romantic intellectuals provided the gestures and the rhetoric; the more solid men sought to build new institutions. But 1848 also saw the emergence of an urban proletariat whose demands and recurrent street demonstrations were frightening enough to alienate the liberals whom they had helped bring to power, and the coalition fell apart. Three days of street fighting in Paris, not in February when the monarchy fell, but in June when the working class threw up barricades, undermined the revolution. In the presidential elections scheduled for December 1848, Louis Napoleon, the nephew of Bonaparte, gathered many of the votes of the urban middle classes frightened by radicalism, and of the peasants who likewise wanted an end to months of demonstrations and liked the name of the emperor, whose reputation for victories and national pride was still powerful.

Elsewhere the process of rolling up the revolution took even less time. Military and tough-minded civilian advisers counseled the king of Prussia and the new young emperor of Austria to reassert their authority. Moreover, the moderates' national agenda failed. Whether in Italy, northern Germany, or the Austrian crown lands, middle-class moderates could realize their objective only by defeating Austria. This they failed to do. They remained concerned preeminently with defending their own cities, but not assisting their fellow rebels in other centers of revolution, thus could be successively defeated by Habsburg generals in their would-be national capitals: Milan, Prague, eventually Venice and Budapest. The German liberals had also sought to summon an all-German legislature in Frankfurt, but did not know how to solve the conflicts that existed among ethnic claims. The Habsburgs, who under the energetic minister-president Felix zu Schwarzenberg and a new, young emperor, Franz Joseph, recovered their nerve and authority by the autumn of 1848, responded to the Frankfurt liberals that if the Austrian Empire was to form part of a new German national federation, the monarchy must enter as an integral unit with its non-German nationalities, Bohemians and Hungarians. The Prussians did not wish to leave out their Polish subjects. The Frankfurt assembly would be suppressed before a "small German" alternative without the Habsburgs might be launched. Frustrated radicals revolted again in the spring of 1849, most seriously the Hungarians whose national militia defeated the Austrians. Now the Russians decided that the agitation must be calmed and, with Vienna's approval, intervened. The Austrians themselves extinguished the revived Italian national aspirations led by the king of Sardinia (whose kingdom, despite its official name, was based in Piedmont or Savoy) and Venice's own republic, while Louis Napoleon, newly elected as president of the French Republic, wooed French Catholics by sending troops to wipe out the Roman republic that had wrested power from the pope. A detachment of Prussian troops vacated the Frankfurt parliament and restored dynastic authority in Dresden and Baden. Richard Wagner, the composer, and his friend Gottfried Semper—later to design the grandiose Dresden opera house— fled from the Saxon barricades. The Austrian and Neapolitan dynasties were not charitable toward defeated revolutionaries, and their firing squads worked overtime.

What was snuffed out in 1849 was not the entire program, but the romantic elements—the belief that each national group might discover and build a state on its own *Volksgeist,* the genius of its people. Likewise the claims that personal liberty might motivate state building.

Some parliaments survived the repression. The Savoy or Piedmontese "statute" and parliament conceded by King Carlo Alberto in the spring of 1848 would become the constitution and parliament of the Kingdom of Italy in 1860–1861. The Prussian parliament summoned in 1847 remained in being, although the suffrage would be restricted and skewed in favor of the wealthy. The last measures of formal serfdom remained abolished in the Austrian Empire. France would never again become a monarchy under its traditional dynastic families. Governments would recognize the force of public opinion as represented in assemblies and the press. The "winners" would continue the program of bringing the market to the countryside—the Piedmontese liberals would embark on extensive secularization in the 1860s, as would the Mexican liberals, who passed the Lerdo Law, dissolving not only church holdings but Indian village communes as well.

There were some exceptions to the revolutionary ferment. Where representative institutions were already in place and public debate remained untrammeled, young, frustrated middle-class crowds did not tend to rush into the streets. The Americas were liberal enough that no revolutionary upheavals took place. The United States was busy absorbing its recent conquests from Mexico. The slavery issue precluded any coalition of radicals. Britain's institutions were sufficiently liberal—if its suffrage hardly democratic—that it could escape unscathed except for massive outdoor gatherings on behalf of the People's Charter. At the other extreme, Russia was still able to resist and repress any liberal assault before it went beyond salon chatter. Still, elsewhere in the West, the age of positivism, of realism, of solid moneymaking and middle-class aspirations was to begin—and the geographic boundaries of states would soon be transformed.

In Asia, though, the huge convulsions lay elsewhere. China was weakened by the outcome of 1842, and then the vast upheaval of the Taiping, which would cost twenty to thirty million lives. This was hardly a liberal revolution, but in fact a civil war that originated in the ethnic clashes, new endemic banditry, and eschatological protest. The fragmented gentry's capacity for ensuring the stability of the Yangzi region and the tradition of self-policing communities were badly frayed. The dynasty and its administrators faced multiple challenges—the continuing and humiliating pressure from Europeans for economic and legal privileges, the erosion of a precarious economic order among poor and crowded settlements, and the addition of messianic Christian ideas to the repertory of redemptive hopes that frequently inspired protests. The Yangzi region, as during the earlier White Lotus rebellion, was roiled by conflicts among new migrants, Han Chinese, and communities of non-Han peoples, by grievances at the Manchu leadership that had been humiliated in 1842, and by the pressure of taxes in increasingly scarce silver currency. Christian missionaries proposed a gospel that might fuse or confuse radical social ideas with promises of ultimate salvation. A leader emerged in Hong Xiuquan, born to immigrant peasant proprietors in 1814, studious but failing to pass the all-important civil service exams, and then converted to a millenarian Christianity by a Chinese missionary convert with a jumbled but austere doctrine of Chinese degradation and the need for redemption. The "Good Words to Exhort the Age" foresaw Chinese tribulations, such as also usually portended dynastic collapse, and left the concept of heavenly kingdom—imperial or supernatural—ambiguous. For Hong the "Good Words" were combined with denunciations of the Manchus and Confucian appeals to rectitude and good order and his own personal vision of having been transformed physically as well as spiritually by God during a serious illness after his third examination failure. With his own first converts he migrated inland from the Canton coast to preach in the hilly southwest of Guangxi and found a receptive hearing among the fellow Hakka, or northern Chinese migrants in the south. Over the next years branches of the God Worshipping Society metastasized in the province and brought forth new leaders, including a gifted military commander, Yang Xiuqing. Conflicts with locals and bandits under famine conditions during 1849–1850 led to the assembling of an army thousands strong and the proclamation of the Heavenly Kingdom of Great Peace in January 1851. A Manchu force sent to disperse them was defeated and its general decapitated.

Thereafter the Taiping army moved up the Yangzi, growing in size to a horde of over three hundred thousand, taking Wuchang, Anqing, then Nanjing in March 1853, killing all the Manchu inhabitants. Four kings were appointed alongside Hong, who claimed the titles "king of heaven," *Tianwang,* and "second son of God," and allowed Yang Xiuqing to assert his claim as third son, filled with the Holy Spirit. The Land Regulation of the Heavenly Dynasty decreed from Nanjing envisaged that the countryside would be divided into units of twenty-five families each. Wine, opium, and tobacco were prohibited, as were nonmarital sexual relations, which, as might be expected from earlier such utopian foundings, did not preclude exemptions and privileges among the hierarchy. From Nanjing the Taiping divided their forces to attack north and west. But the expedition to Beijing failed at Tianjin, and its remnants were wiped out in the spring of 1855.

The forces of order who organized to resist this wave of what they perceived as Christian radical barbarism were local gentry commanders who had raised ethnic militias since the White Lotus rebellion, the talented Zeng Guofan in the lead. They defended an ideology of puritan Confucianism, which stressed the traditional precepts of a well-ordered social hierarchy under the emperor but combined with a mastery of new military technology, a reorganized Chinese (and not Manchu) army, and a less oppressive tax system. They did not immediately prevail, however. The Taiping held a three-hundred-mile stretch of the Yangzi from Wuchang to Zhenjiang and scored important victories in 1855–1856. Nonetheless, conflicting ambitions and ruthless mutual jealousies were dividing the rival Taiping "kings," who murdered each other successively along with their families and thousands of adherents. Despite the bloodbaths, the Taiping reorganized and found a new gifted military commander and civilian administrator in Hong Ren'gan, who was a cousin of Hong Xiuquan and moved to turn toward a more orthodox Christianity and connections with the mercantile elements downriver in Shanghai. Still, the process of attrition became stronger even though the Beijing court distrusted Zeng's local initiatives and strength. The imperial forces moved to control the Yangzi above the Taiping and scored victories below them. The rebels failed to take the Wuhan cities to their west. Hong Ren'gan sought to assure the British in Shanghai that he would form a more orderly administration than the Manchu court, who had just lost another war against the British. But the British minister in China, Frederick Bruce, was convinced that the Taiping of any stripe were radical, unreliable, and inimical to the interests of commercial order. With French assistance the British helped ferry imperial troops upriver. In July 1864, Hong died, perhaps, so it was rumored, poisoned, and Zeng Guoquan, the brother of Zeng Guofan, conquered Nanjing, massacred its inhabitants, and burned the city.

The civil war had raged over an area equivalent to France and Germany for almost a decade and a half and had involved a million insurgents in military campaigns. Another vast civil war half a world away in the United States was grinding its rebel armies to defeat in the same months. Could the Taiping have prevailed and toppled the Manchu dynasty? They had engendered tremendous loyalties on the basis of an eschatological program. Nonetheless, their communities also remained outside the traditional society of the countryside. In this they differed from some of the other forces for endemic disorder in China, whether the ethnic uprisings of the Miao aborigines in the 1830s or the simultaneous rebellion of the Nian further north, who like the White Lotus and Triads in effect permeated peasant life. Anti-Manchu the Taiping might be, but they also remained outsiders among the Han Chinese majority. The local elites of the Yangzi region, moreover, were not prepared to see a Manchu dynasty toppled at the cost of unrest. In this, as we shall see, they resembled the forces of order, who would build new regimes conducive to reform from above throughout Europe, the Americas, Japan, and the Ottoman Empire.[41]

It was not surprising that the British had decided to join in the suppression of this persistent rebellion. Seven years earlier they had faced their own frightening uprising, the so-called Indian Mutiny of 1857, which in fact had threatened to develop as a major revolt against their thin presence in India. Ostensibly it had started as a revolt among the Muslim soldiers whom the English had recruited to police their growing acquisitions in northern and central India as they wove one native principality after another into their dominion, whether by displacing its ruler or having him recognize London's authority. But, as C. A. Bayly emphasizes, there was a long history of forcible resistance to Mughal taxation and then to the takeover of territory and financial rights by the EIC in the previous decades. "Revolt was inevitable in areas where more fluid, segmented forms of polities had been preserved by climate or terrain from the weaker pressures of Mughal centralisation."[42] The British presence meant new pressure to support the EIC's army and to extract crops for export. It was easier for the English to co-opt urban Indian elites than the diffuse forces of the countryside, which often were galvanized by religious reform movements. But no consistent socioeconomic background seems to have united the revolutionary forces; in some places they were hard-pressed villages squeezed by new taxes; in others, new peasant proprietors that the British had counted on as the basis for a new loyal class. Rural class divisions increased in the decades after 1857, not before. Those magnates who had done well in the preceding half century as the British moved in hesitated to throw in their lot with the rebels, as did civil servants and Indians in commerce.

Still, because the British were a numerically small presence in a massive terrain, the uprisings had the potential to destroy their position throughout the subcontinent. The revolt broke out when the British commander of a local garrison punished soldiers who refused to distribute new rifle cartridges greased with animal fat. The colonizers soon confronted frightening and widespread uprisings, which they believed were encouraged by the shadowy and hardly substantive authority of the Mughal dynasty in Delhi. The rebels held Delhi from May to September 1857 and besieged Lucknow until November. But the British never lost control of the Ganges valley and the trunk road between Delhi and Calcutta, nor of their base in Bengal. They retained the loyalty of the Sikh units in the Punjab and could march east on beleaguered Delhi. Once the British overcame the emergency, they would force the formal end of the Mughals and take over their position definitively, transferring formal power from the EIC to their own officials.

In China they finally threw their lot in on the side of the dynasty, recognizing a fundamentally different structure. The Chinese dynasty was weak, but the country was not built on a substructure of principalities that might be subordinated to London's governance. China remained a still-massive cultural and political entity whose government could grant them the concessions they needed. Between 1856 and 1860, the British gained additional territory for Hong Kong and further commercial connections in the so-called Second Opium (or Arrow) War, triggered by the Guangzhou police's effort to arrest Chinese crew members on an opium vessel, the *Arrow,* formerly—but no longer— under British registry. The move provoked the British admiral to bombard Guangzhou; the Whigs in parliament challenged Prime Minister Palmerston over the bellicose response, but were set back in new elections. Responding to the murder of a French missionary, Napoleon III threw in his forces alongside London's. The British and French attacked Chinese forts up the coast in Tianjin, forced an armistice that opened new treaty ports along the northern coast, allowed missionaries the right to travel, imposed reparations, and finally compelled the Chinese to legalize the domestic sale of opium, a move they had managed to resist after 1842. The right to exploit the opium commerce had been the longer-term objective of the London government. When the newly gained acquisitions proved difficult to enforce, the British commander, Lord Elgin, the son of the Elgin who had carted home the Parthenon's frieze, attacked Beijing, torched the summer palace (partly designed in French rococo style), extracted higher reparations, acquired the southern Kowloon territory around Hong Kong, and added Tianjin to the treaty ports. It was this debacle coupled with the evident weakness of the rulers that would finally compel reorganization of the empire—increasingly as a Chinese national state and less as a Manchu dynastic enterprise. Having secured the compliance of Beijing, the British decided that propping up their official source of their semicolonized regime was preferable to watching it succumb to xenophobic and unrestrained radicals.[43]

In any case, the end of the Taipings—like the extirpation of the Indian Mutiny seven years earlier, like the defeat of Polish rebels a year earlier in 1863, like the collapse and surrender of the Confederate States of America a year later, and the failure of the feudal Tokugawa forces in 1868 Japan—suggested that rebellion was a forlorn option. The long century of modern statehood would be built on the ashes of revolution, the reform of institutions not from "below"—not by the effort by peasant or national populists to bring about the millennium—but by programs of modernization and rationalization carried out both by farseeing conservative statesmen and middle classes, enthusiasts of the 1840s who had become the sagacious statesmen of the 1850s and 1860s. Their achievement, too, would require violence, but the measured and directed violence of warfare and repression, not rebellion.

CHAPTER TWO

Reconstruction on a World Scale

Developments from 1850 to 1880 wrought major transformations in
the organization of states across the globe. They constitute a genuine
"moment" of world history. Political jurisdictions changed as territorial states were torn apart from within and then reconstituted on a
more cohesive basis. Local leaders found that more distant authorities
had greater say over their power and their finances. The social origins
of men claiming public office and influence became more diverse.
Whether by virtue of their professional education, or industrial and
financial wealth, newcomers who came from outside the ranks of land-
owning elites, old families, or military office achieved a far greater voice
over public affairs. They hardly replaced the former ruling groups; usually they were recruited to serve alongside them in moments when their
exclusion threatened state survival or stability.

Long-distance communication, movement of peoples, and shipment
of goods became more rapid and dense. Global space seemed more of a
continuum, suffused no longer by divine transcendence but by vibrations of unseen energy. Paradoxically, for all the awareness of rapid communication, intellectual systems rarely became more cosmopolitan or
tolerant. Ideas of pervasive rivalry and conflict often replaced dreams
of fraternity. War "fulfills its cruel but indispensable role in the progress of the human spirit," wrote Italian observers of the Prussian triumph over France in December 1870.[1] The appeal to brotherhood
tended to relocate from patriots and poets to proletarians greeting
their supposed class brothers.

These developments pose two fundamental puzzles. The first is why so many decisive changes seemed to occur concurrently with such suddenness. The tempo of change is mysterious in many large-scale phenomena—"tipping points" can be modeled for many fields, but why they come when they do remains an issue for natural scientists and historians alike. The second riddle is why so many states and societies worldwide underwent analogous transformations at the same time. Compression in time and extension across space remain to challenge explanation. Why does history become global? The reconstruction of states became an imperative in the Western Hemisphere, whether in the divided and then reconstituted United States, a reorganized Canadian federation, a Mexico that lost vast territories to its northern neighbor but then went on to defeat a French invader, or an Argentina that threw off dictatorship. Europe, too, was reassembled at its center and at the edges. Italian and German nationalists achieved unification, Austria-Hungary renegotiated its ethnic balance of power; the Spanish monarchy was abolished, briefly pulverized, and then patched together, the Ottoman state redefined its constituent principles; while the military and bureaucrats of the Russian Empire sought to overcome what they recognized as the besetting impediments of serfdom. In East Asia ambitious Japanese samurai administrators determined to create an effective modern state that would challenge the ingrown shogunate; and frustrated Chinese officials endeavored to mobilize Confucian principles to reverse their polity's catastrophic experience of rebellion, floods, and foreign incursion.

No doubt the process was infectious. States exist in an implicitly competitive universe. Major initiatives in one must impact on others. But not just diffusion or contagion was at stake. Pressures for transformation arose from within many societies simultaneously. We can't rerun the course of history to test whether or not regimes in isolation would or would not have reconstructed their institutions. Before 1850 the Japanese state had been the large polity most insulated perhaps from foreign impact. It went into a fifteen-year crisis and transformation only after the outer world seemed finally to press determinedly at its gates, but there were certainly many pressures emanating from its own stratified society that were likely to compel far-reaching adjustment, and we cannot know how much change they would have compelled on their own. Did change, moreover, always emanate from "below"? Marx famously distinguished the "forces of production"—the levels of technology, and the social classes they brought to the fore—from the "relations of production" inscribed in legal and political institutions. He saw the pressures of the former leading to crises and revolutionary adjustments in the latter. Yet most historians are likely to describe a recursive process with many feedbacks, just as they envisage a recursive relationship between the realm of ideas and that of economic progress.

Many aspects of ordinary life, moreover, did not change qualitatively in the period, or changed at a less disrupting pace. This particular history follows the world of political transactions, not household existence and not the bonds of intimate loyalties. For masses of people the events recorded here did not seem to impact on their daily routines. The worker enclosed from sunup to sundown in a noisy textile mill, the domestic servant cleaning and cooking, the young man single-mindedly smitten by the young woman he passed daily on the street, the child savagely cuffed by a stepparent, the rural family facing hunger from drought and erosion, may not have sensed their lives were being transformed by a common sovereign for Naples and Florence, or a new German civil code, a new definition of Ottoman citizenship, or the burning of the Chinese emperor's summer palace by French and British soldiers. The chance to vote for a delegate to a national parliament hardly allowed the abused child to strike back, or the domestic servant to be impertinent, or, in many areas of the world, the young woman to follow her own inclinations in matters of the heart. Nonetheless, states would irrevocably touch even humble lives. They could expand educational opportunities, facilitate employment, encourage (or impede) inward and outward migration, insist on the ending of inherited personal bondage—if only to send the formerly bonded into the constraints of hard agricultural labor or long factory disciplines. States sometimes expanded and probably sometimes constrained the possibilities of personal fulfillment and household life. But then the pressures within millions of households had sent states careening as well.

The state was to be strengthened, but largely to remain viable in a world of state competitiveness, and only indirectly to cope with issues of poverty and income maintenance, except that order had to be maintained. Commentators tended to analyze the social costs of economic transition as a problem of individual or family difficulty, sometimes based on poverty, sometimes on moral failures. They organized charities, benevolent associations, educational reform, and later on, crusades for temperance and against sexual trafficking. Above all, serious-minded middle-class women, who could not go into politics, could devote their energy to these efforts on behalf of respectability and sobriety.[2] In the West, these reformist if sometimes patronizing attitudes had begun to emerge a decade or two before midcentury. The formation of reform associations, which took off in Britain and the United States in the 1830s, but marked the continent in subsequent decades, whether through the St. Vincent de Paul societies in France, or the Lutheran Church Diet in Germany, were part of the tremendous organizational effort that nineteenth-century society generated. Similar earnestness marked those in non-Western societies who responded to the Western challenge. Both Christian and Muslim intellectuals throughout the Levant and Egypt argued for the need to strengthen Eastern societies through urging them to learn about the scientific progress and discoveries recently made in Europe, and infusing them with a stronger sense of unity among "Easterners."[3] The extraordinary influence of the didactic tract *Self-Help* by the British author Samuel Smiles testified to the search for self-strengthening measures. The Scottish author began as a political reformer and a critic of laissez-faire, not the smug justifier of success or wealth. An Arabic translation was published in Cairo and Beirut in several editions as early as 1886, followed over the years by editions in Chinese, Punjabi, and Japanese, which sold a million copies.[4]

The poet Henry Wadsworth Longfellow, supremely talented in giving sentimental voice to middle-class pieties, wrote, "Life is real, life is earnest, and the grave is not its goal." Above all the midcentury world was earnest. Institution building reflected the earnestness. The personalist regimes of the 1820s and 1830s—led by such brilliant, reformist, but often autocratic generals as Simón Bolívar, "the Liberator" in Colombia and Venezuela, Muhammad Ali in Egypt and the Middle East, and, in some respects though under constitutional restraints, Andrew Jackson—seemed less suitable for the midcentury decades. Witness the repeated disasters incurred by the vainglorious Mexican general Antonio López de Santa Anna. Giuseppe Garibaldi, whose small expeditionary force ignited Sicily and southern Italy in 1860, was the closest to the Latin American model, but when he got to the midpoint of the peninsula he turned his forces over to the organizers of Italian unification from the north. The leaders who set their stamp on state building were serious and conservative, personifications of gravitas and patience—whether Abraham Lincoln, Benito Juárez, Otto von Bismarck, Itō Hirobumi, who was active in Meiji politics into the twentieth century, or the remarkable Zeng Guofan, the organizer of victory against the Taiping and continual advocate of Chinese technology and modernization. Chinese conditions, however, did not let such clear-sighted recommendations prevail.

The world of states that emerged by 1880 was a different one from that of a generation earlier—in Asia as well as the West. By then, despite the reluctance of some of its organizers, the state would have to engage with serious social issues—whether farm distress in Central Europe and western North America, factory regulation and even old age in

Germany, or opium addiction and military backwardness in China. It was a world of projects and work—the labor of organizing enterprises, of reforming education, of writing huge novels and large symphonies, pressing forward with ambitious political programs, uplifting darker-skinned peoples as well as working them hard for low wages, wagering on warfare.

Iron and Blood

Technological transformation was a critical input to the reorganization of states. Bismarck told the Prussian parliament in 1862 that the great questions of the day were being decided not by high ideals and lofty speeches, but by "blood and iron." He was correct. But the role of iron was newer than the role of blood. The British had achieved commercial supremacy, and built the financial leadership that came with it, originally on mechanized cotton and textile production (and indirectly slave and proletarian labor). The cotton mills erected in new industrial towns such as Manchester or soon thereafter in Lille, France, or Pawtucket, Rhode Island, were large sheds that grouped ingenious but relatively light machines powered by water or steam to spin and weave unprecedented quantities of fiber into textiles. So far as the organization of society was concerned, their epoch-making innovation was to induce a workforce to assemble together under a time discipline set by the proprietors as the condition for tapping hitherto undreamed of quantities of nonanimate power to apply to their labor. Textile factories and later iron-smelting furnaces brought new urbanization, as suggested by the sample of city populations in Table 2.1.

Hard upon this transformed productive process arrived a wave of innovation in transportation of people and goods, based on self-propelled steam engines that ran on parallel rails or were mounted on ships. James Watt had developed the decisive improvements that made the

TABLE 2.1

Selected urban populations

	1800	1850	1890
London	959,000	2,362,000	4,212,000
Paris	547,000	1,053,000	2,448,000
Naples	400,000 (est.)	415,000	463,000
New York	63,000	661,000	2,741,000
Chicago	—	30,000	1,100,000
Manchester/Salford	90,000	389,000	704,000
St. Petersburg	270,000	490,000	1,003,000

Source: Adna Ferrin Weber, *The Growth of Cities in the Nineteenth Century* (Ithaca, NY: Cornell University Press, 1967), p. 450, table 163.

modern steam engine possible as early as the 1730s. His design condensed the spent steam in a cooling compartment separate from the chamber in which the heated steam drove the piston, thus avoiding having to cool the engine between strokes. Watt had also devised the off-center fastening of the connecting rod that could convert the reciprocal action of the piston into the smooth rotary motion of a wheel. From 1803, the innovations were fitted to the paddlewheel boat that could travel upstream and propel a vessel no longer dependent on wind direction. By the 1830s steamboats were traveling intercontinentally. They did not displace sailing vessels right away but in fact led sailing ship designers to perfect the rapid clippers that expanded the China trade. As early as 1804 the steam engine was fitted to a vehicle that could run on parallel rails to haul iron, and a passenger steam train was installed in Wales in 1807. The first routes that had more than curiosity value were opened in 1830 in Britain and the United States— Manchester to Liverpool, Washington to Baltimore, Boston to its suburbs and then to Worcester, from Nuremberg to its suburb of Fürth in 1834, from Brussels to Mechelen in 1835, from the summer palace town of Tsarskoe Selo to St. Petersburg, and by 1851 in India, 1855 across

Panama, 1857 in Argentina, and 1872 from Tokyo to Yokohama. In the 1850s, mileage began to increase significantly: World railroad construction had amounted to 4,700 miles by 1840; then 19,200 by 1850; 43,299 by 1860; 63,300 by 1870; 101,100 ten years later by 1880; 152,200 by 1890. By 1850, US rail mileage was close to 8,600 miles; by 1861, 30,600, with 21,000 in the North (of which 11,000 in the midwestern states from Ohio to Kansas, Missouri, and Minnesota), and 9,500 in the South. By the end of the century world rail mileage was close to half a million miles, of which the United States had 185,000, while Britain, Germany, France, and European Russia had about 25,000 to 30,000 each.[5]

These were extraordinary developments, less because they displaced canal and turnpike traffic at first, but because they increased speed and incentivized technological breakthroughs. "Breasting the wind and light, the shower and sunshine, away and still away, [the steam train] rolls and roars, fierce and rapid, smooth and certain." "We believe that the steam engine, upon land, is to be one of the most valuable agents of the present age, because it is swifter than the greyhound, and powerful as a thousand horses, because it has no passions and no motive, because it is guided by its directors, because it runs and never tires, because it may be applied to so many uses, and expanded to any strength."[6] The technologies entailed in turn a vast expansion of iron (and later steel) production and fashioning—a far more power-intensive process than textiles required and one in turn calling for the extraction of huge amounts of coal and ore (Table 2.2). Britain would forge ahead into this era of heavy machinery and by the 1860s iron ships, developing new techniques for smelting iron and then purifying it into steel, requiring ever-larger tonnages of coal and coke. Britain, however, would increasingly share its economic preeminence with Germany and the United States. They increased the demand for coal, then for steel, which in turn required expansion of rail service to haul the coal and ore.

TABLE 2.2

Production of coal, pig iron, and raw steel (in millions of metric tons)

	UK	Germany	USA
Coal			
1830	22.8	1.8	
1870	112.0	26.4	0.8
1910	269.0	152 + 70 lignite	36.3
Pig iron			473.0
1830	0.69	0.11	
1870	6.06	1.26	0.17
1910	10.57	13.17	1.69
Raw steel			27.10
1870	0.334	0.13	
1890	3.64	2.10	0.77
1910	6.48	4.34	25.71

Sources: British and German Statistics from B. R. Mitchell, *European Historical Statistics, 1750–1970* (London: Macmillan, 1978), tables D2, D7, and D8. The German figures separated their significant lignite production from the aggregated bituminous and anthracite output *(Steinkohl)*. Anthracite and bituminous coals provide approximately the same range of BTU per ton; the calorific content of lignite ranges from about 30 to 50 percent of the higher grades. US statistics from *Historical Statistics of the United States, Earliest Times to the Present: Millennial Edition,* ed. Susan B. Carter, Scott Sigmund Gartner, Michael R. Haines, Alan L. Olmstead, Richard Sutch, and Gavin Wright (New York: Cambridge University Press, 2006). For coal, data has been aggregated from tables Db67 (anthracite) and Db60 (bituminous); pig iron data can be found in table Db74; and raw steel data can be found in table Dd399. The original figures for US coal and raw steel were given in short tons (2,000 lb) and have been converted, for purposes of comparison, to metric tons (1,000 kg or 2,200 lb).

Building railways required organizing large pools of investors. Coordinating rail lines over long distances encouraged decentralized modular management techniques as well as centralized supervision. The early short trains moved slowly but much faster than lurching coaches. Before the railroad, almost a week was required to cover the 380 miles from Pittsburgh to New York; by 1860 it was a day's journey. Midcentury wars—the large brutal combats that marked the seam dividing the first half the century from the second: Crimea, the American Civil

War, the German wars of unification—accelerated the technology of moving individuals, large groups of soldiers, and their equipment. Pullman sleeping cars became an attainable upper-middle-class luxury in the late 1860s, brought into American public consciousness by Lincoln's funeral train. Transporting dead cows or swine en masse was a greater challenge. The development of refrigerator cars during the 1880s enabled the railroads to move dressed meat to eastern centers of urban population from vast interior pastures and slaughtering depots (themselves now mechanized, with carcasses traveling on overhead chains to be butchered progressively at successive work stations). The invention of a practical compressed-air brake allowed these now longer trains to operate at higher speeds with their huge momentum under control from the locomotive.

The railroad influenced political organization in two fundamental ways—first by reinforcing the credibility of the nation-state as a cohesive arena of collective decision making, second by enabling and favoring new coalitions of historical actors to seize leadership within states. The future prime minister of Piedmont and the statesman instrumental in Italian unification, the liberal Count Camillo Benso di Cavour, understood the impact: "The steam engine is a discovery that can only be compared in terms of the magnitude of its consequences with that of printing or even better the American continent. The influence of railroads will extend itself throughout the universe. In those countries that have attained a high degree of civilization, they will impart to industry tremendous growth; their economic results will be magnificent from the outset and they will accelerate the progressive movement of society. But the moral effects must be even greater that their material effects in our eyes, and especially notable in those nations that are currently lagging in their ascent as modern peoples. For them the railroads will be more than a means of enrichment, but a powerful weapon with whose aid they will overcome the retarding forces that are holding them in a baleful state of industrial and political infancy."[7]

So, too, the Prussian state officials, contemplating their state strung from the Belgian to the Russian border across the plains and woods, understood that the railroad would knit together a geographical structure that had little inherent unity; and the military elite understood that it would allow troops to be moved from one frontier to another. By 1870 Prussia possessed an armature of railroad lines that complemented the institutions being created for greater state cohesion and potential leadership of an emerging German national unit. The Italians set to building lines from north to south as soon as they could after unification, although the fiscal burden bore heavily on the peasantry of the south and helped ignite an endemic rebellion. For Canada, the early railroads posed an existential dilemma. Business and political leaders had to either get the state to underwrite costs and link western settlements to Montreal and thence to the New York railroads and Atlantic ports, or let the fledgling Canadian nation risk separating into units that would be connected southward to the various US states. Because Britain had opened its markets to wheat from all sources and not just its own overseas dominions, the outlets were urgent. The first major decision came in 1849, when a railroad guarantee act facilitated the construction of railroad links to the New York Central, allowing Canadian grain to get to ice-free ports. The Montreal-to-Boston line opened two years later. For those countries that spanned a continent— the United States, Canada, and later the Russian Empire—national political and commercial ambitions led pro-railroad coalitions to advocate that tracks should span the immense distances from East to West (as for Argentina and Chile, north–south construction was likewise compelling). Once its Civil War ended, the United States sutured together its first transcontinental line in 1869. A decade and a half later, completion of the Canadian Pacific Railroad in 1885 could be celebrated as the great Canadian national epic. It may well have been a defensive response to the transcontinental US rail lines.[8] The Russian state laid down its trans-Siberian line only in the first years of the twentieth century, but the fiscal exertions that were required aroused strong opposition to the reformist prime minister, Count Sergei Witte, who determinedly pressed the project forward. In China, the railroad advocates could not find the same support. An early line in Beijing was removed; the 1876 British-built line from Shanghai to nearby Wusong offended the government's sense of sovereignty and was destroyed the next year. Reform-minded officials understood the stakes and outlined the consequences. Xue Fucheng despairingly reported that "all the European countries are competing with one another for wealth and strength and their rise to prosperity is rapid. What they rely upon are steamships and railroads . . . if the system of railways trains is not used, China can never be rich and strong." He understood the impact on prices: America built railroads whenever it opened untilled land: and one could travel from New York to San Francisco ten times as rapidly as one might under Chinese conditions and at one-tenth the price. But if China should adopt the railroad, "then distant areas could be brought near, the stagnant could be made to flow, the expense could be saved, and the scattered could be concentrated." And as other officials warned, Japan was following these policies with aggressive intent.[9]

Railroads appealed to private investors and rulers alike. Above all they appealed to investors when the state guaranteed the returns, as it did in Canada from 1849, and in France under the Second Empire, which struck bargains with the six major lines radiating outward from Paris, as did the Third Republic in the 1880s. Railroads were major investments, but they were immensely profitable because national governments provided indirect subsidies, whether through tax concessions, guarantees of interest on the bonds issued, or help in acquiring land. The United States and again the Canadians, in their second phase of development, offered alternate square-mile tracts along the right-of way, often with valuable mineral rights, but also designed to tempt settlers. As the rulers of imperial possessions, the British would build railroads across India for purposes of defense as well as development. Late developers imported capital and technology. Sultan Abdül-hamid II (1876–1908) in the Ottoman Empire, and Porfirio Díaz (his almost exact contemporary as authoritarian president of Mexico from 1878 to 1911), worked with the Germans and Americans, respectively.

Railroad construction shaped the internal political coalitions that dominated states that had representative institutions, or at least stock exchanges. With state guarantees, railroad consortia attracted both those groups that controlled financial capital and those agrarian elites who could mobilize the wealth of commodity production. Even before the American Civil War the outlines had emerged, as powerful railroad interests supported by Illinois Democratic Party senator Stephen Douglas bowed to Southern party members to secure the territorial administration in the West that was seen as the prerequisite for investing in further rail lines. The Kansas-Nebraska Act of 1854 sponsored by Douglas and eloquently opposed by Abraham Lincoln stipulated that local voters should be able to legalize slavery in their respective territories despite the earlier prohibition on allowing it to be instituted so far north. Douglas and the railroads won the issue temporarily, only to inflame the underlying national conflict over slavery. Within a decade the railroad sutured together Chicago and its agrarian hinterland but further divided the country. Ironically, the North's extensive rail development helped it prevail in the great war that Lincoln was to conduct against the secessionist South. Rail lines let the North project force into the central areas of Georgia, Tennessee, and the Mississippi Valley, and slowly choke the Confederacy. The great spurt in Southern railroads began in the years after 1865, although the crisis of 1873 interrupted the progress. When it resumed, Northern capital played a far larger role, especially the Illinois Central Railroad's domination of the Mississippi Valley.

The planter class slowly learned a lesson. Plantation owners teamed up with Northern industrial interests to extend railroads into the ex-Confederate states and simultaneously to undermine the Northern commitment to Reconstruction and subject the African-American workforce on the land to new modalities of subjection. As in many countries, railroad investment opportunities would draw together "old" elites from the land and the "new men" who had risen in industry. This was true in Europe, North and South America, and Europe's colonies. Political elites (some elected and some career bureaucrats), landed magnates and city bankers, and a great mass of smaller investors swept by enthusiasm for profits and technology formed a new iron triangle that would dominate politics.[10]

Of course, at the local level, men of property and wealth usually controlled the labor and conditions of life of those who depended on them. In villages the world over, the major landowners enjoyed power, and deference—by which is meant that general respect their tenants or village residents showed them without continual compulsion. Alexis de Tocqueville relates how in 1848 in France—a country, after all, that had had a major revolution, and repeated minor ones—the peasants on his land came to solicit his advice on exercising the new right to vote. Fifty years later the Italian Marxist theorist Antonio Gramsci would develop the concept of ideological "hegemony," by which he meant the general acceptance of law and private property and the existing social structure on the part of even those who were at the bottom of the economic pyramid, which was the true cement of domination—"soft power" applied to class relations. US conditions probably allowed the least deference, at least outside the coercive framework of African-American slavery. Eastern European, Balkan, and Ottoman societies incorporated more. Peasants touched their brows or kissed their landlord's hem. In Japan until the Meiji "revolution," ostentatious bowing before noble samurai was expected of peasants, and consequences could be severe if it was not provided. The intervention of peasants into East Asian politics remained confined to periodic upheaval and resistance.

Power at the regional level (whether in American states, French departments, German duchies, and so on), and at the central level, rested with traditional elites, but it had been challenged in the 1830s and 1840s by the new men of substance, whether of industrial and commercial wealth, professional degrees, or bureaucratic employment. European analysts then and since termed them bourgeois, or sometimes middle class, although that designation often described a more modest stratum. The 1848 revolutions had seen these elements try to seize power, but retreat with their own internal divisions. The politics of the 1850s and 1860s, however, became transformational but along new lines. Where political parties had become important they became less ideologically coherent. British Tories split on the fundamental issue of tariffs, American Whigs on slavery. Even where there were no parties, political elites would divide over issues of industrial modernization and political centralization—whether in Mexico, Japan, Italy, or Prussia. This would create the worldwide alignments that struggled to remake or preserve the societies in the decades that followed.

Wars of National Reconstitution

The reconstitution of states was not a peaceful process. It entailed violence and warfare on all continents, although to a lesser degree in Africa as of midcentury. In some cases long-constituted nations took up arms once again. Whereas in Central Europe political publics felt that their nations already existed on a spiritual plane—"The nation exists in the same way that the individual does, and has no need of a people or a Parliament to proclaim the fact," Francesco Crispi wrote the venerated Italian nationalist propagandist Giuseppe Mazzini in March 1865[11]—in Latin America the long struggles for independence in the 1820s had left armies, churchmen, planters, and cattlemen yet to form coherent republics. This was a process that emerged from warfare rather than preceding it.[12] Between the mid-1850s and mid-1860s, the British were fighting in Russia, struggling to suppress a major rebellion in India, engaging in combats on the coast of China, and sporadically intervening in Latin America. The French were fighting in the same war in Russia, the same campaign in China, and then in a major expedition in Mexico. The United States, which had invaded Mexico in the 1840s, was sending military expeditions throughout Central America, landing forces in Uruguay and Argentina, and then consuming its men and energies in its Civil War. Many of the wars were national, as state builders consolidated their new territories through armed struggle, whether to overcome foreign resistance or forge sentiments of unity at home. Other conflicts were internal or "civil," contests of force over crucial issues of who would rule at home and on what principles once compromise had broken down. Some wars had aspects of both sorts. The old landed empires—Habsburg and Ottoman—proved particularly vulnerable as aspirations for national state building became more intense among subject populations. These geopolitical assemblages were embroiled in recurrent conflicts in which foreign states joined indigenous nationalities in campaigns against the imperial center. Russia fared better: after initial defeat in the Crimean War against Britain, France, and Savoy, it could expand at the expense of the Ottomans and Central Asian khanates.

Historians of Europe sometimes downplay the importance of the wars of reconstitution in comparison either with the twenty-five years of warfare that involved the French Revolution and Napoleonic expansion between 1792 and 1815 or with the two world wars in the first half of the twentieth century. It is true that warfare abated for a generation after 1815, although the contests for independence in Latin America and European portions of the Ottoman Empire flared anew in the 1820s and 1830s. Armed conflicts that might best be termed wars of European expansion led to the French conquest of Algeria from 1830 and the Anglo-Chinese clash of 1840–1842 in the southern Chinese river deltas—the so-called Opium War. At the same time that the

British took up the Chinese challenge to their commercial rights in Guangzhou, they were pushing toward the Indus River valley in the states of western India, although they penetrated by a politics of alliance with local princes and rajas as much as by any show of force. Nonetheless, the politics of expansion led them into the first Afghan war of 1846. Wars of European or "white" expansion against the indigenous confederations of the Americas, Africa, and Central Asia would resume in the 1860s and 1870s, far from the capitals of their own home territories. They represented a transitional sort of conflict—wars in part to expand the power of the encroaching states, but simultaneously campaigns that suggested a new genocidal type of assault that would flourish in the twentieth century. Increasingly wars of national reconstitution were also wars of tribal destruction.

Of course, there was tremendous variety in terms of size and scope, troops committed, and duration. But these wars involved efforts to change the bases and organization of class and national solidarity. Dynastic claims, which had been so prominent in European conflicts through the eighteenth century, still played a role in the Carlist civil war in Spain in the 1830s and served as a pretext in the Franco-Prussian War of 1870 but otherwise were superseded. Some wars arose from rebellion or efforts at secession; others involved efforts at annexation or sought centralization of territorial authority. Not that they were always conceived of in those terms, but these became the implicit or explicit stakes.

The critic can object: are not all wars in some sense wars of national reconstitution? Certainly the wars of the French Revolution and Napoleon involved great changes in the management of Napoleon's satellite states, as many learned from the advantages that French national mobilization seemed to confer. The wars in Europe and the Americas from 1792 to 1830 wiped out a great deal of territorial administration by the Church, enlisted new educated elites in administration, opened up the higher military ranks to talented commanders, let the British

A climactic war of national unification: An illustration of German troops bombarding Paris in the fall of 1870. After the American Civil War, the Franco-Prussian War was the largest of the nation-building conflicts that marked the middle decades of the nineteenth century. The Germans' rapid victory startled observers and allowed Otto von Bismarck to complete the architecture of the unified German Empire, while the defeat led the French to replace their Second Empire with a besieged Third Republic. (Library of Congress)

wrest decisive maritime hegemony, and mobilized large armies. Still, they were often conceived of as consequences of radical and revolutionary upheaval or later of Bonaparte's insatiable ambition; and at their conclusion there would be a major effort to restabilize a hierarchical order based on the class and constitutional equilibria of the late eighteenth century and a somewhat patched-up balance of power. The rulers who finally won on the continent even envisaged a restoration based on strengthened Christian principles, the Holy Alliance. Only in the Americas could self-made military commanders such as Andrew Jackson or Simón Bolívar challenge the imagery of a restored agrarian order in favor of populist republics.

The wars of national reconstitution from the late 1840s to the late 1870s shared some of these traits. But there was no would-be hegemonic emperor at their center and no radical ideology. They became wars for or against an encroaching nation-state order, efforts to complete the work of secularization and to challenge multiethnic empire. They were wars to survive in a world of war and of warring national states. Insofar as they led to international efforts designed to mitigate the violence, such as the organization of the Red Cross of 1863 (and shortly thereafter the Red Crescent), they primarily laid down the ground rules for future war. Some of these struggles are listed in Table 2.3.

The European conflicts and the American Civil War represented armed struggles to impose—or to oppose—the construction of states built on reconstituted national or imperial principles against forces that defended a traditional social and political organization. They might also be called wars of modernization in that regardless of their intent or motivation, they resulted in societal arrangements closer to ones that prevail today. They would be followed by several decades in which the very nation-states consolidated in midcentury would turn their mobilized energies and technical prowess out to the "periphery." These produced the defensive struggles by nomadic confederations at the perimeters of white settlement that were mentioned the introduction, but other confrontations as well, through the 1880s and continuing until the end of the century, struggles marked by savagery on both sides: the American Indian resistance against US control of the Missouri Valley region, and the Apaches' battles in the Southwest in the 1880s; the British suppression of the Zulu state's resistance against British control in South Africa; the doomed effort by the Central Asian khanates against Russian control of Central Asian steppes and highlands; thereafter the quasi-genocidal Argentine conquest of Patagonia and the ongoing sporadic resistance in Yucatán of the Maya against the Mexican national authorities. But there were also wars of conquest

TABLE 2.3
Wars of national reconstitution

1845–1847	War of Swiss national consolidation (Sonderbund War).
1846–1848	US-Texan-Mexican war for control of northern Mexican territory.
1848–1849	War for the control of northern Italy: Piedmont and volunteers against Austria.
1849	Austro-Russian war to suppress Magyar rebellion against Habsburg rule.
1850–1864	Yangzi Valley war between secessionist Taiping state and Chinese Empire.
1853–1855	Anglo-French-Piedmontese war in the Crimea to limit Russian power in the Black Sea and Ottoman arenas. Settlement at Congress of Paris.
1856–1857	British suppressions of military insurrections in India and enhancement of colonial control.
1856–1860	Second Opium or Arrow War: Britain and France extract further Chinese acceptance of extraterritoriality regime.
1858–1860	Civil war ("War of the Reform") in Mexico.
1858–1860	Rebellions in Ottoman Near East; sectarian strife in Mt. Lebanon, Beirut, Damascus.
1859–1860	Franco/Savoy-Austrian war to remove northern Italy from Austrian control, carried out in conjunction with Garibaldian intervention to wrest south Italy from the Bourbon regime.
1860s	The "Brigandage" in southern Italy: continuing guerrilla attacks against the new Italian administration/occupation; finally suppressed with fierce reprisals by the new Kingdom. Unsuccessful Garibaldian campaigns against Rome in 1862 and 1867.
1861–1865	US war to repress secession of Confederate States.
1863–1866	Mexican civil war ("War of Reform") and unsuccessful French invasion.
1864	War of German Confederation against Denmark over nationality of Schleswig. Leads to 1866 Austro-Prussian war for leadership in German Central Europe and Prussian-Italian-Austrian war to remove Austrians from Venetia and Alpine regions.
1864–1870	War of the Triple Alliance: Paraguay loses 80,000 inhabitants, or half its male population, age 13–60, and 40 percent of its territory to Brazil, Argentina, and Uruguay.

TABLE 2.3 (CONTINUED)

Wars of national reconstitution

1866–1869	Unsuccessful Cretan (Greek) revolt against Ottomans.
1867–1868	Japanese civil war: Tokugawa adherents defeated by Meiji national forces.
1870–1871	Franco-Prussian war for territorial rearrangements and to unify North and South Germany under Prussia.
1875–1878	Russian defeat of Ottomans in support of Bulgarian independence struggle. Treaty of San Stefano and, later, a revised general European settlement at Congress of Berlin.

Source: Brian Holden Reid, *The Civil War and the Wars of the Nineteenth Century* (New York: Harper-Collins / Smithsonian Books, 2006).

Note: The list is partial and omits some secessionist episodes, as in Spain (1873), but includes China's unsuccessful efforts to resist European pressure.

against the small states of the perimeter. The War of the Triple Alliance against Paraguay included elements of racialized warfare that may have led to the highest national death rates of any modern war, perhaps 50 percent of the prewar population. Paraguay, though, was still a well-organized state with diplomatic representation.

Once the conquest of the perimeter and its peoples was largely accomplished—a result that US citizens called the closing of the frontier—the twentieth century would begin with the great wars (1894–1923) between contending imperial states—some ascending in power, others confronting once again, as they had a generation earlier, difficult internal crises.

Although they mobilized less manpower and exacted a lower level of casualties from participants (except for the Taiping uprising and American Civil War) than the Napoleonic wars or the First World War, the midcentury wars of national reconstitution could become protracted, often involving wars of position, sieges, and long fronts. Bismarck was correct about the iron as well as the blood. The victors in these struggles drew on the resources of the Industrial Revolution:

breech-loading rifles and the early versions of rapid-fire repeating guns, more-deadly artillery, ironclad ships, and the gunboats that proved decisive in river fighting. Prototype submarines and the early torpedo (invented by a British engineer in Austrian Trieste) made their appearance. Most important was the development of the railroads, which could move masses of soldiers with relative speed. This signaled the difference between the American Civil War and the wars of German unification, on the one hand, and the great Chinese civil war, the Taiping rebellion, which, though it began much earlier, would be settled in the same years of the 1860s. The Chinese fighting, though it featured massive sanguinary massacres, saw units of five to fifteen thousand troops ferried east and west on the Yangzi; the American fighting brought armies of over a hundred thousand to bear by means of the railroad, as well as sea and river communications.[13]

Clear-sighted military attachés sent to observe these great conflicts or sometimes seconded to assist in them could discern another fact: although railroads might deploy armies more rapidly and in greater numbers, and modern artillery might reduce old-style fortifications, the defense could tenaciously dig in, as did Confederate General Robert E. Lee in Virginia. In some respects the brilliant victory of Prussia over Austria in the summer of 1866 was misleading. Although it was decisive for the ascendancy of Prussia and the German national state, the Prussian triumph at Königgrätz (Sadowa) in Bohemia resulted from relatively old-style tactics of a line offensive that was successful against a decrepit adversary. As the most astute observer, Archduke Albrecht of Austria, observed, the Prussians devolved responsibility on corps officers whereas his own imperial army organization impeded responsibility at all levels.[14] Encouraging small-unit initiative remained the key to battlefield success from earlier French victories under Napoleon to later German triumphs in 1940, and the approach would deeply influence Israeli doctrine long after 1945.

Just as fundamental a lesson was that that modern war was often decided away from the battlefield, in those organizations required for the state mobilization of power. The Prussians had pioneered the general staff, a military think tank whose officers served both as a central planning office and as operational consultants with the battlefield units. The very grinding nature of the warfare also meant that state agencies—to procure matériel, supervise transport, supply and arsenals, organize credit and finance, and develop medical services—had to be organized or enlarged. The toll taken by projectiles led to reorganization of military hospitals: Florence Nightingale's work for the British army in Crimea, and the US Sanitary Commission's tending to Northern wounded in the American Civil War.[15] And armies had to promote their gifted organizers and engineers and not only dashing horsemen or those who had family connections. For countries (including the British) that had clung to older methods of recruiting their officer corps—such as the purchase of commissions—it was realized that professional training and accreditation had to be stepped up.

Most crucially, perhaps, the wars of national reconstitution reintroduced ideas and practices that suggested unarmed citizens were participants in the armed conflicts. Previous wars had never lacked for the deliberate burning of buildings and ports, and, unofficially at least, pillage and rape. And the great wars of 1792–1815 had mobilized civilian levees—most notably by the French after 1793, but then in imitation by the Prussians in 1813–1814. Warfare must, it was realized outside Great Britain, place young males under the obligation to serve their countries. As part of this democratization of warfare, however, the idea emerged that the civilian population had a responsibility for causing or continuing war. Again the French Revolution had evoked the nation in arms, but the corollary idea of the nation as a target was never made explicit. General William Tecumseh Sherman decided that economic devastation in a prosperous keystone region of the Confederacy would shorten the North's struggle to defeat its adversary. Germans invading France in 1870 were convinced that French civilians would take up arms as irregular forces or *franc-tireurs,* and faced considerable guerrilla activity after subduing the official armies of Napoleon III.

In short, warfare was central to the reorganization of states, nations, and empires in the mid-nineteenth century. British North America (Canada) was the one exception, perhaps, and it had gone to the brink in the 1830s. One cannot conceive of the modern nation-state, in the form that has prevailed since the 1850s or at least from the 1850s into the 1970s, without taking into account the applications of armed force—the use of explosives, lethal flying metal splinters, maiming of young bodies, and destruction of property—that accompanied it. Nineteenth-century liberal nation builders as well as the generals, who could themselves be moved and dismayed by the suffering, were willing to pay that price. Others, less sensitive, seemed positively to welcome the exercise as a manly exercise. Wars that were a path to empire were simultaneously struggles to reaffirm a gendered supremacy at home. Certainly that was part of their result, until, at least in the twentieth century, one had to enlist women in too many related efforts. In any case, the indispensability of violence can be ignored no more than one can leave out of account the role of at least localized genocidal policies in the maintenance of empire. In that sense the nineteenth century would flow into the twentieth, as we shall see subsequently. And of course, most of those taking the initiative in these policies believed the price was necessary and worth paying. To understand the bargains, we must avoid imposing our humanistic scruples of the late twentieth century. Just as terrorists today still remain convinced that individual lives cannot be allowed to get in the way of higher principles and loyalties, for the mid-nineteenth century, history increasingly was seen as a providential juggernaut: a steamroller of civilization and higher cultures that had to triumph over lower ones.

For God *or* Country

Open the era with an almost comic-opera civil war of three weeks in November 1847, in which seven of the predominantly Catholic cantons of Switzerland, who had formed their own "separate alliance" or Sonderbund to resist what they saw as Protestant centralization, were invaded and defeated by the Protestant forces. The victorious invaders lost 60 dead and 385 wounded; the defeated Catholics had 26 dead and 114 wounded. The Sonderbund forces had coalesced in 1843 against the efforts by the Protestant Radical party to strengthen the constitution of the confederation as well as to close and secularize Catholic monasteries. When the canton of Lucerne invited Jesuits to establish a center, Protestant irregulars had taken up arms, the Catholics organized their internal alliance, and the war finally erupted four years later. Swiss unity and neutrality had been inscribed in the European order at Vienna in 1815, so secession was hardly an alternative. The Protestant victory, however, led to a strengthened confederation and the ascent of commercial and secular forces.

The alignment of forces in the struggle was not new. Loyal Catholics had felt on the defensive against the secularizing state since the Enlightenment and the French Revolution. In Spain the liberals who had pushed through a constitution at Cádiz in 1812—to be abrogated by the restored Bourbon monarch, Ferdinand VII—returned to influence with the accession of Queen Christina as regent for her daughter Isabella in 1833, provoking the Catholic traditionalists of Navarre in the Pyrenees to take up arms on behalf of the brother of the late king. The resulting Carlist War lasted six years and became a major issue in European diplomacy. Loyal churchgoers in the former Catholic archbishopric of Cologne, under French rule after 1795, then assigned to Prussia's Rhine Province in 1815, had demonstrated against Berlin's effort to secure a compliant archbishop in 1840. The division was indicative—state supporters of secular or Protestant policies provoking a pro-papal resistance on the part of Catholic traditionalists (so-called Ultramontanist, because of the adherents' alleged loyalty to the religious authority across the Alps).

Did the emerging nation-states and the Catholic Church have to go separate ways? The greatest and most inspiring prophet of nationalism in Italy, Mazzini, had seen the nation as a divine association that might coexist with religious institutions. But over the next two generations the continental European nation-state—in Prussian Germany, the Third Republic, the Kingdom of Sardinia (Savoy or Piedmont), and then united Italy (which occupied the papal territories in 1870)—would be reconstructed, centralized, and secularized at the expense of a papacy that increasingly set its standard against modern liberalism and state education. In Mexico the same conflicts would be enacted on an epic scale. Monastic lands beckoned state treasuries and would-be bourgeois purchasers at repeated intervals: originally in Iberia and Ibero-America in the 1760s, then in France during the Revolution, and in the Germanies, Naples, and Spain during the Napoleonic occupations, in Spain again during the 1830s, and in Piedmont under Cavour's liberal auspices in the 1850s. But it was not just land that was at stake. Despite a few romantic populists such as Félicité Lamennais, the Roman clergy was increasingly boxed into conservative stances, especially under the papacy of Pius IX (1846–1878), who had been forced to flee Rome during the revolution of 1848, and then found the papal states (stretching across central Italy up to Bologna and the Romagna) progressively annexed by the new Kingdom of Italy. In 1864 the papacy's "Syllabus of Errors" would insist that it was wrong for Catholics to accept the teachings of liberalism; in 1870–1871, the Vatican Council would insist that the pope was infallible in issues of faith and morals. There was no room for democracy within the Church or in the wider world. The French authoritarian Catholic Louis Veuillot admitted that the Church wanted freedom of speech to propagate its doctrines but believed in denying it to others. Rome saw the new world of nineteenth-century statehood as a force for despoliation—which it often was—and the indoctrination of children in atheism. Protestantism was just as bad, given Prussia's campaign against Austria—the natural protector of the papacy, unfortunately ejected from Italy after 1859—and then Bismarck's war against the Church in the 1870s, one he christened as a struggle for civilization *(Kulturkampf)* and that involved the dissolution and expulsion of monastic orders, including the Prussian Jesuits. In Iberia, Freemasons supposedly threatened the Church as the occult center of the secular network, a belief that remained powerful through the dictatorship of Francisco Franco until the mid-1970s.

From the other side of this epic squaring off, state officials and liberals beheld a reactionary special interest seeking to block the rights of conscience, the freedom of the press and speech, and modern financial administration. Educational systems would become the battleground after 1870. Suffering as a "prisoner in the Vatican" after the Italians took Rome as their capital, smarting from the eclipse of Catholic loyalists after the establishment of the Third Republic in the same year, out of power in Mexico, prosecuted in Germany (until Bismarck shifted his allies in 1878–1879), beleaguered Catholics would establish votive churches, such as the basilica of Sacré-Cœur on the hill of Montmartre in Paris, to atone for the transgressions of their impious polities. (Emperor Franz Joseph would erect a neo-Gothic specimen on the Ringstrasse in Vienna, to atone for an anarchist's stabbing of his beloved wife, Elisabeth, known as "Sissi.") The secular state, defiantly male and aggressive, would face a Church that, as during the Catholic revival in Ireland, increasingly reconstructed its parish life around the role of women. And not just women nuns, but middle-class women who would tend to charities and good works, and occasionally adolescent girls of rural milieu, who, moved perhaps by the political martyrdom of their Church as explained in their Sunday homilies, claimed to see and speak with the Virgin—at Marpingen in the

Rhineland, Lourdes in the French Pyrenees, and later Fátima in Portugal.[16]

But if the blessed mother of Jesus could cure thousands of afflicted pilgrims who came to these sacred sites, she could not really roll back the advances of the liberal state and its administrative and commercial reforms. Her new churches memorialized the inexorable setback to her claims within the nation-state, just as the brief tribal victories at the Little Bighorn or the Zulu battlefields were in their way monuments to the defeat of the resistance at the frontiers of its expansion. Protestant or secular, male and militant, restlessly commercial, building railroads and buying new and improved artillery, rifles, and naval vessels, the nation-state advanced. Whether its commercial energies would ensure that these politically divided territorial units would vie in peace, or whether their military instincts (strengthened by the wars that had accompanied their creation) would lead to catastrophic combat, had yet to be decided. Certainly there were commentators who predicted each of these dénouements.

It is correct, but too simple, to group the new loyalties that were to prevail as those of nationalism. Nationalism—an idea originally of elites in search of a primitive and vital people who would be summoned to take on political form, establish a territory and government—had been placed on the European agenda by the French Revolution and then the Napoleonic wars. By midway through his period of rule, Napoleon I, the emperor of the French, was provoking opponents speaking the language of nationalist resistance. The Spanish partisans of the exiled Bourbon dynasty, the constitutionalists of Cádiz, and the popular forces or ex-Bourbon soldiers in the guerrilla movements that mobilized in the peninsula formed one manifestation. The philosopher Johann Gottlieb Fichte, lecturing in Berlin under French occupation, claimed to address a German "nation." The Italian writers aspiring to political independence for their lands began to advocate the reform not just of Austrian Lombardy, or Naples, but of Italy as a political unit. Some of the intellectual and military leaders from Prussia and smaller states envisaged not just a Prussian revival (although that might serve as a beginning for their aspirations), and not just a revived confederal organization for Central Europe, but a German nation. The Americans who went to war against the British in 1812 and thought of annexing Canada, or a few years later Cuba, struck a new chord of national truculence.

Of course the emerging ideas went back further. Concepts of the state as an international actor, as a force that must liberate itself from Church control, were intense since the Renaissance. The eighteenth century restored notions of the *Volk* as a vital people who had collectively formed languages, inspired epic poems (in one celebrated case, the supposed Scottish epic "Ossian" simply invented), and gathered folk and fairy tales, most famously those collected in the post Napoleonic years by the Grimm brothers, who also incurred political persecution for their democratic sentiments. The Romantic sensibility of the era just strengthened the appeal of this new sentiment, which could be nourished by literature, poetry, and opera as well as inspiring oratory. Students and other activists formed associations of Young Italy or Young America by the 1830s. In Germany, angered at the repressive censorship that eventually culminated in the Carlsbad Decrees of 1819, students celebrated the tercentenary of Luther's original challenge to Roman Catholic authority in 1517 with a patriotic gathering at the Saxon castle where the reformer had found a sanctuary.[17] Further protests followed in the early 1830s.

But it was easier to dream a nation than to form one. The Italian effort failed in both 1848 and 1849. Theorists had proposed schemes for the pope to become president of an Italian federation; others just called for federation. The young monarch of Savoy, Charles Albert, envisaged that he might take the command of the revolutionary agitation that swept the cities of Italy under Austrian rule; he raised an army, crossed the river border into Lombardy, and was soundly defeated.

Rebels in Venice had better luck and could declare a republic and maintain it within the city until August 1849. But the Habsburg court recovered from its indecisiveness by the fall of 1848 as the young Franz Joseph took the throne under the tutelage of determined aristocratic political advisers and generals. Austria was still large and powerful, held the key north–south river routes and their fortifications in northern Italy, and was not prepared to relinquish the provinces it had held even before the Congress of Vienna. In the spring of 1849, Charles Albert took up arms again, and was defeated anew and compelled to abdicate. Habsburg troops forced the surrender of Venice. Facing a renewed Magyar revolution, the Austrians got help from the Russians to suppress the revolutionary and secessionist regime in Budapest. Liberal nationalists had to bide their time. Many, including Lajos Kossuth, Carl Schurz, and Richard Wagner, fled permanently or temporarily into exile. Others accepted the straitened limits of populist politics and would join the new middle-of-the road forces willing to compromise with the post-1848 leadership, whether liberal as in Piedmont, or pragmatic as in Prussia. Many devoted their energies to supporting railroad development and agricultural improvement societies. Scientific agriculture as much as any rising industry looked to the soil as well as the territory. Cavour was a gentry farmer. The horse fairs and annual exhibitions of scientific husbandry and agriculture offered in effect a form of surrogate politics in contexts where national politics was either not yet or no longer an option—as in Ireland, Poland, and Italy during the 1850s.[18]

The reactionary aftermath of 1848 was bitter, but it would be relatively brief. Counterrevolutionaries, whether in Paris after the June Days of 1848 or in the recaptured territories of the Veneto, Hungary, and revolutionary Vienna, would shoot their opponents generously, but might pardon them by 1850–1851. Radicals changed their mentality. In 1849 the Russian revolutionary exile Alexander Herzen wrote to his son and readership in Russia, "I see the inevitable downfall of the old Europe and mourn nothing that exists, neither the heights attained by her education nor her institutions." And he rhetorically asked, "Why then do I stay *here*? I stay because the struggle is going on here. Here in spite of the blood and tears, social problems are being worked out and painful and burning as the suffering here is, it is articulate. The struggle is open and above board. No one hides. Woe betide the vanquished but at least they will have given battle." Twenty years later he wrote his erstwhile co-radical Mikhail Bakunin, who was still a partisan of revolutionary upheaval:

> You have not changed much, though sorely tried by life.... And if I have changed, remember that *everything has changed*. We have seen the frightful example of a bloody insurrection which, at a moment of rage and despair [he was referring to the June Days of 1848], took to the barricades and only then realized that it had no banner.... But what would have happened if the barricades had triumphed? Could those formidable combatants, at the age of twenty[,] have given voice to all that lay in their hearts? Their testament does not contain a single constructive, organic idea, and economic errors unlike the political ones which have an indirect effect, lead directly and deeply, to ruin, stagnation, and starvation.... Even if our whole bourgeois world were blown to bits, some sort of bourgeois world would arise after the smoke had dissipated and the ruins had been cleared away.[19]

And so it did.

Controlled Transformation

The national agenda was far more widespread than in Europe alone. In 1853 the American naval commander Matthew Perry anchored his squadron of four ships outside today's Tokyo Bay to open negotiations with the Japanese government, which had no naval force to counter the Americans. Washington demanded guarantees for the safety of shipwrecked sailors and commercial access to the largely self-enclosed society. With the acquisition of California from Mexico and recognition of the Oregon claims by Great Britain, the North American republic was a Pacific power by the end of the 1840s. Its vessels plied a vigorous commerce with China; Japan offered coaling stations and its own goods and lay athwart the trading route. Perry's visit followed several unsuccessful attempts to win access; for since the early years of the Tokugawa shogunate Japan had been shut down to the world with the exception of a Japanese outpost at Nagasaki at its southern tip.

Perry's menacing visit exposed what would become a fifteen-year crisis for the Tokugawa regime (the so-called *bakufu* or military administration), named after the warlord Tokugawa Ieyasu, the last of a string of three strongmen, who by 1603 after incessant campaigning had imposed a new sort of settlement on the ancient monarchy wracked by civil wars and feudal disaggregation. The imperial line, preserved with its feckless court nobility at Kyoto, had ensured ideological cohesion but little else. Policy was dictated by the shogun at Edo (later Tokyo), an office that had remained in the same family for 250 years. The realm was divided into about ninety autonomous domains or *han,* each ruled by a *daimyō* and a class of military and bureaucratic retainers or samurai entitled to bear arms and to exact visible deference from town merchants and peasants. Blood relatives of the Tokugawa line and those *daimyō* who had joined forces with the ascendant shoguns before 1603, the *fudai,* controlled the inner domains proximate to Kyoto and Edo. Those who submitted after 1603, the *tozama* or outer *daimyō,* were allocated about 40 percent of the lands farther north or south in the archipelago. In return for their domainal autonomy the *daimyō* were required to keep close family members at the shogun's court at Edo and reside there for half of each year with many of their samurai retainers. These great and frequent processions of the *daimyō* back and forth from their domains filled the roads of Japan, made Edo into a center of trade, personal services, and consumer goods, a lively theater and pleasure scene, and at perhaps a million permanent residents (estimates vary) by the eighteenth century, a rival to London, Paris, and Constantinople. The residencies consumed up to half the revenue that the domainal lords could raise from their peasantry. But the more consequential action was taking place within the further domains such as Tosa, Chōshū, and Satsuma, where European technologies and administrative methods were being studied and emulated without the resistance of a conservative court bureaucracy such as paralyzed equivalent initiatives in China.

Where reforming *daimyō,* such as Mōri Yoshichika of Chōshū and Shimazu Nariakira of Satsuma, could prevail, they prepared their domains to challenge the conservative forces of the shogunate. The reformist *daimyō* efforts to modernize these territories and a more strident resistance to the threat of foreign encroachment went hand in hand.

The American visit of 1853 thus crystallized the division between the conservative forces of the shogunate, who sought to preserve the old regime, and the impatient nationalists of the outer *han,* who believed that the kingdom must modernize to withstand the foreigner and forestall the regime of extraterritorial possessions that the British and French were imposing on the Chinese. The diaries of the fledgling British diplomat Ernest Satow reveal the growing violence of this confrontation as young, impatient samurai resorted to assassinating political leaders they thought too compliant toward the foreigners.[20] By 1867 the reformers of Chōshū, Satsuma, and Tosa had gained domination at the court. After marching on Edo with their armies, they forced the shogun to renounce his offices and "restore" governing power to the young Meiji emperor, who would henceforth speak for their policies. There would be further resistance in the northern island of Hokkaidō in 1869 and a doomed rebellion by diehard conservatives (one of whom, Saigō Takimori, enjoyed popularity as an honest and faithful reformer) in 1877.

The Meiji Restoration was in fact a controlled transformation from above, but with a radical impact. Japan entered one of those intense periods of rapid absorption of successful foreign models that periodically marked its history—whether centuries earlier with respect to China or later after defeat by the United States in 1945. Within a few years of 1867, the new oligarchy decreed a sweeping series of reforms. They eliminated the samurai class as a legal order and prohibited the traditional right to wear short and long swords. They transformed the old *han* into new provinces, each of which was to be governed by an imperial appointee as governor (prefect), and they fobbed off the old *daimyō* by placing them in a house of peers. Feudal dues were ended, and the *daimyō* landlords compensated by issues of government bonds that provided revenue from interest. (Russia had chosen this method of compensation when the state eliminated serfdom in 1861 and placed noble lands into the control of village communes.) They started to develop shipyards and arsenals and began a more intensive program of sending bright students abroad for technical and medical education. Within a generation the country transformed itself, determined not only to avoid national humiliation but to play the imperialist game itself, seeking enclaves in China and predominant influence over the Korean court. The Japanese state entered the nation-state system as a determined and successful participant.

Only by 1890, as the Japanese elite began to claim an assertive role in the East Asian arena, would they broaden the national project by instituting parliamentary representation. Scrutinizing European constitutions for guidance, the now-aging Meiji reformers chose the German model, not the British, American, or French patterns that granted a broad role for elected legislatures. The new Meiji constitution allowed the monarch and his civil servants a strong role in keeping parliamentary institutions within bounds: the new prime minister held his office at the pleasure of the emperor; the military leadership was given key cabinet roles as ministers of war and navy, and the army remained immune from parliamentary scrutiny. The Imperial Rescript on education of 1890 envisaged that the imperial state would in effect breathe life into an imperial citizenry through patriotic education and state-sponsored piety.[21]

Historians and sociologists have long groped for ways to characterize experiences such as Japan's, just as they had for revolutionary upheavals such as the French. For over a century Marxist theory seemed to offer a plausible, if often contested, framework. Marxist-derived explanations tended to view the agents for change as exponents of a bourgeois or middle-class world that advocated economic development, market forces, and universal legal norms against the feudal and agrarian elites of the past. The growth of commerce and early industry generated new group interests, which demanded and ultimately attained a greater political and legal role, not smoothly but through a series of revolutionary upheavals, just as ultimately, proponents often believed, it would bring the working classes to power in a new era of collective property.[22] Those who contested this historical description emphasized that often members of older aristocracies led the reform effort and pointed to the conservative aspirations of those taking up arms. This is not a debate to be resolved in a brief historical chapter. Marxian analyses serve perhaps most usefully to reveal the similarity among radical transformative processes, but less persuasively as detailed explanations for their individual trajectories. They have often been most insightful when their advocates, including Marx himself and his collaborator, Friedrich Engels, had to account for events that did not follow their early templates, such as the French and German revolutions of 1848.[23] Faced with the decisive role of the Japanese nationalist samurai (or the Prussian elite), analysts have often sought to describe the late nineteenth-century transformation as modernization from above. "From above" is correct in that national leaders, sometimes ministers, sometimes monarchs, pushed through important reforms that undermined the "feudal" institutions of an older regime.

Nonetheless, broad-based popular agitation and stubborn loyalties to village and local rights were never absent. The Japanese leaders themselves engaged in hard and vigorous debate over their policies, even if outsiders rarely saw the hard infighting in these years (in contrast to the assassinations that marked the 1850s and again the 1930s). Modernization from above, in fact, was perhaps the most widespread strategy for preserving state viability in an era whose statesmen understood that collective existence required fiscal efficiency, industrial and military modernization, and a dedication to competition. Thus, military challenges often advanced administrative centralization, as in earlier centuries they had compelled fiscal centralization. Other examples of this approach took place—with less decisive results, however—in the Ottoman Empire, in Egypt, later in the Russian Empire, for a period in Mexico, and in Thailand. Sometimes the term is applied to the new unified German "empire" that Bismarck worked to make a powerful German nation-state.

In fact, modernization from above is a rather loose term and, as we shall see, can be applied to at least two or three varieties of experience. The classical model of this process referred to a strategy for old empires and states that relied heavily on the traditional structures of religion and landlord domination over peasants, but found themselves threatened from abroad, especially by the most corrosive social force loose in the mid-nineteenth century: British financial and industrial capitalism, along with the burgeoning trade of energetic entrepreneurs (and their supportive regimes) in Europe and the United States. To respond, the determined and ambitious administrators of these states believed they had, in effect, to create citizens by edict and to harness their productive energies with state-sponsored industry. This meant in turn linking families and individuals directly to the state and diminishing the control of their landlords. Religious authority might remain useful in the process, but the political autonomy of religious authorities was to be subordinated to the secular administration with more or less success. Japan, Russia, Turkey were all examples. In late imperial China, the reformers who attempted such endeavors after 1860 tended to be outweighed by the residual power of traditional court policies. The ancient Chinese state claimed too much conservative legitimacy. It would take a revolution to clear away resistance, and even then the emerging reformers confronted very resistant patterns of popular inertia and entrenched privilege.

But modernization from above is a term that can also describe a more temporary recourse of states that had less powerful or venerable regimes in place. Several major states with robust traditions of popular participation in legislatures and at the local level resorted to a few decades of rapid industrialization and military reforms as a consequence of the civil strife and war of the mid-nineteenth century. If in the first category summarized above, civil servants attempted to compensate for an underdeveloped civil society and little democratization at the national level, in this second group they attempted to overcome the policy stalemates that resulted from regimes already democratic, but deeply divided over fundamental issues. Naturally enough, this second set of experiences included significant varieties of transformation. In France the population accepted the downgrading of the national assembly by Louis Napoleon (soon crowned as Napoleon III), who helped to superintend almost two decades of economic development and ambitious foreign interventions, which finally brought him down. In Mexico another developmental dictator supported by a national elite (and foreign investors) emerged out of midcentury conflicts over reform, invasion, and the influence of foreign capital. In the United States, the Republican Party pushed through the end to slavery, opened the western lands to free homesteading, and encouraged industrial development from the end of the 1850s into the 1890s.

Such a recourse to controlled transformation was compatible with regimes that already gave a large scope to electoral participation. In the United States the transformations resulted from the challenge of war, which in turn derived from the deep conflicts over which system of labor and economy would prevail in the gigantic acquisitions of land at the time of the Mexican War. The founders of the American Republic had compromised on the issue of slavery when they created their constitution in the late 1780s. They had agreed to let the institution continue—otherwise there would never have been a United States—but prohibit the importation of slaves after twenty years. This prohibition helped make the breeding of slaves for use in the newer states of the Gulf a lucrative commerce in its own right. But what was to be the regime in the lands opened west of the Mississippi? The effort at a stable compromise in 1820, which would have allowed slavery to be installed in Missouri, but otherwise only in territory south of Missouri's latitude (36°30′), proved unviable.

Northern farmers and laboring men could not tolerate the expansion of a system they felt threatened their own livelihood and national future. The economic stakes became higher as the factory looms of Lancashire and the American North multiplied their demand for raw cotton, even as the ideological and moral issues were sharpened. Southerners felt their peculiar institution was under threat from the new parties that were emerging from the development-oriented Whig coalition of the 1830s and 1840s, whether the dissenting antislavery Democrats, or the "conscience Whigs" in 1848, such as Abraham Lincoln, or the Free-Soilers in 1852 and the Republican Party in 1856. The older veterans of the Senate, Henry Clay, Daniel Webster, and John C. Calhoun, had engineered another compromise in 1850, which would let slavery exist in Texas and the District of Columbia, but not in California. Most objectionably to Northern adversaries, it required the return of escaped slaves and provided a fee for their recovery. The Free-Soilers and then the new Republicans saw a militant South demanding an unlimited extension of slavery—a conclusion strengthened by the Kansas-Nebraska Act and then by the US Supreme Court's 1857 *Dred Scott* decision, which ruled not only that Scott, a slave, had not gained a claim on freedom through his master's having brought him into a free state, but that persons of color had no claim on the constitutional rights provided for white Americans. Antislavery senatorial candidate Abraham Lincoln and incumbent senator Stephen Douglas squared off in a series of fundamental debates on race and the frayed territorial compromises on slavery in the Illinois campaign of 1858; Douglas won reelection, but Lincoln emerged as the Republican nominee for the presidential contest of 1860.

The race took place against the threat of growing sectional violence. A radicalized midwestern farmer, John Brown, already a participant in the Kansas skirmishes over slavery, attempted to seize a federal arsenal and ignite a slave revolt in northern Virginia in 1859 and was executed in December. Excited Southerners declared they would leave the Union if the Republican candidate, Lincoln, won the presidential election of 1860, which he did with 40 percent of the popular vote but a clear electoral-vote majority, in a four-way race. Advocates of secession opened debates in the legislatures of the Southern states, where the firebrands of South Carolina in the lead urged establishing an independent slave-holding republic. They bombarded the federal military base at Fort Sumter in Charleston, South Carolina, when Lincoln sent a flotilla to supply it in April 1861. The armed clash swayed the debate in Virginia, and eleven states voted to join the secession as units of the Confederate States of America.

The ensuing four-year war, which would cost the two sides together about 700,000 dead—a percentage of young men comparable to later casualty rates among Europeans in the First World War—sealed the transformation of the North American nation-state. The war itself was a slow and ponderous affair. If one measured the resources each side brought, the Union was clearly superior in population, industrial power, and railroad resources. It possessed the legitimacy of almost seventy-five years of statehood. Lincoln's call for troops brought an enthusiastic response. Nonetheless, the Confederacy was a large region and it had apparently only to keep the North at bay to secure its independence. However, a protracted war would also devastate its economy and reduce it materially. Its major cash crop, whose British sales had enriched the planter class in the 1850s, would probably remain bottled up because the Northern navy could blockade its major ports. The Union must be discouraged sufficiently to make it cease its effort to compel Confederate surrender.

The fighting began on the East Coast. The Southern capital at Richmond was only 150 miles from Washington. Initial combat revealed that the Southern armies were well led and resourceful. The attempt to land troops on the James Peninsula and then march inland toward Richmond failed because of the excessive caution of the commander, General George B. McClelland. The central valley of Virginia and the upper Potomac hills became an area of frequent combat but inconclusive gains. A major bloody victory in Antietam in western Maryland in September 1862 let Lincoln issue the Emancipation Proclamation, which declared slaves under Southern control to be free men. But this was a promise to liberate precisely those over whom the North had no control.

Heavy fighting also took place during 1862 and 1863 in Tennessee. The tributaries of the Mississippi that flowed through Tennessee would allow the Northern troops to penetrate the cotton states of Georgia, Alabama, and Mississippi. But again the battles oscillated. Border states that did not secede—Kentucky, Maryland—still had Southern sympathies but remained under the military thumb of the North. By 1862 Union forces occupied the coastal islands of Georgia and took New Orleans from the sea, imposing an occupation regime on Louisiana. A year later General Ulysses Grant secured Northern control over the Mississippi Valley by compelling the surrender of Vicksburg, which meant that Texas was separated from the main body of the Confederacy and the north–south transportation axis of the western confederacy was closed. The Southern wager on advancing in the east into

Pennsylvania (and further) had initial promising results—precisely at a moment when antiwar sentiment was becoming strong among the immigrant working class of New York, now feeling the grip of conscription. But the defeat at Gettysburg in July 1863 meant that henceforth the South must fight on the defensive.

Still it took almost another two years to force the surrender of an increasingly devastated Confederacy. Lincoln finally found a determined, tough commanding general in Grant, but Grant advanced slowly. The 1864 fighting in Virginia was immensely costly. More promising, General Sherman swung from Tennessee into Georgia, purposefully laying waste to the countryside as he advanced. He captured Atlanta, then moved toward the coast at Augusta, then headed north through the Carolinas. His army converged with Grant's near Richmond in the spring of 1865 and forced the remnants of the Confederate armies to surrender. The South was impoverished. Its black labor force was now legally free, and many were fleeing from their plantations. Food was meager. Railroads, industry, and farms were destroyed. Marauding bands of looters terrorized parts of the countryside. The war devastated the Southern economy; reduced the influence of its formerly slave-holding elite, but expanded the role of the reestablished central government and eventually united Southern and Northern industrial leaders in their determination to extract wealth from technology as well as cotton and wheat.[24]

Unfortunately the outcome of the war solved neither the issue of racial prejudice nor that of economic viability. Although they were legally emancipated, the black families of the South did not receive title to land, but continued as tenants where they had labored as slaves. Compelled to turn to their former masters for credit to plant their yearly cotton crop, much of which had to be surrendered to defray their debt and rent—the American "sharecropping" version of a rural pattern widespread at many times and places—many were reduced to an unremitting cycle of debt dependency. For about a decade Northern

troops occupied the South, enforced voting without racial discrimination, and seemed ready to impose a regime of racial equality. But blacks
were poor, the legislatures were resented, and white vigilantes often
imposed local tyrannies based on nocturnal terror. The Republicans
in the Congress tired of the conflict, and to secure victory in the dead-
locked presidential election of 1876 agreed to remove the remaining
troops. Within two decades the blacks were largely excluded from the
ballot, intimidated by the white-hooded Ku Klux Klan, and reduced
to subservience. Efforts to unite poor whites and blacks against the
"Bourbon" white elites were usually trumped by racial demagogy. By
the 1890s the former Confederacy would join such Eastern European
regions as Hungary and Romania as one-party landlord-dominated
states, where legalized servitude had been replaced by ethnic coercion,
peasant impoverishment, rigged voting rights, de facto peonage, and
exaggerated ideologies of national purity.[25]

The large geographical units to the south and north of the United
States—Mexico and Canada—also underwent major transformations
that combined institutional transformation, settlement of their vast
territories, economic development, and consolidation of a new elite.
The Mexican Republic was fated to develop, as one of its leaders
quipped, so far from God, so close to the United States. Of course, it
began from a different starting point: three centuries as a colony of a
Catholic monarchy with a powerful church and centralized monastic
settlements; an Indian population that recovered demographically during the long seventeenth and eighteenth centuries; and whites proud of
their Spanish descent even as many intermarried and produced a large
population of mixed or "mestizo" ethnicity. The independence movement was ignited by a radicalized clerical leadership in 1810 but was
soon suppressed by the Spanish. It was successfully resumed a decade
later by ambitious military leaders—some claiming traditions of a
populist and decentralizing left, others pressing the centralizing and
briefly (under Augustín de Iturbide) imperial claims of the right. Itur-

bide, who had helped Spanish forces defeat the revolutionaries of 1810, led the new rebellion when Madrid fell under the control of the liberals in 1820, claiming the title of emperor until exiled and ultimately executed. However, the continuing turbulence and warfare undermined the prosperity achieved at the end of the era of Bourbon reform. Catholic conservatives and liberal anticlericals replaced each other in power as the cynical and populist military strongman, General Antonio López Santa Anna, repeatedly switched sides, claimed the presidency, or pushed forward candidates he hoped to control.[26]

As the strongman in charge of a pro-Catholic conservative dictatorship in 1836, the general could not prevent the secession of Texas, but he fended off a French expedition to Veracruz in 1838 and briefly restored some of his luster. He returned to lead a weakened state that still claimed vast territories in the American Southwest although it only nominally controlled Anglophone Texas settlers and the feared Comanche federations of the borderlands. The Comanches' devastating raiding, carried out both to secure livestock and to exact vengeance, exposed the fragile hold of the Mexican state over its northern territory, including the contested area in today's southern Texas that led ambitious Texans and American nationalists—President James K. Polk in the lead—to press extensive border claims. Santa Anna's recourse to war in 1846 was an abject failure, and the Republic of Mexico had to surrender large swaths of territory to Washington.

This war on the margins of the settled world had profound ramifications for both republics: for the United States it undermined the 1820 Missouri Compromise on the extension of slavery; in Mexico, following another conservative coup by Santa Anna, it opened the way to the Revolution of Ayutla and the great liberal anticlerical government under Benito Juárez of the second half of the 1850s. The constitution of 1857 outlined the constitution of a liberal and secular state with constitutional liberties and civil marriage. The Lerdo Law of 1856 pushed through a rigorous secularization of church properties and other forms of corporate and collective ownership, even if it spared the collective *ejidos* that still prevailed in many rural and Indian communities. In effect they carried through the last of the eighteenth-century revolutions, deeply dividing the country and igniting a three-year civil war, the War of the Reform, followed in turn by French invasion. Napoleon III believed he might take advantage of the turmoil (and of the United States' great internal conflict in the 1860s) to try to set up an imperial state under a Habsburg cousin, Maximilian of Austria. Maximilian found significant support among those resentful of Juárez's reforms, but the Juárez government rallied, and after the Battle of Puebla the French withdrew, leaving their well-meaning creature to be defeated and then executed. Liberal government meant an end to the threat of military dictatorship although not to the periodic warlordism that would grip the country from time to time.

Liberal government, even when headed by an Indian, too often meant incomprehension, not of the almost mystical pre-Columbian legacy, but of the social and economic organization that many still chose. The ramifications made themselves felt in the southeastern corner of the republic, the Yucatán Peninsula. Yucatán *ladinos* (including creoles and mestizos but not Indians) had attempted to secede from the republic following the turmoil of the late 1830s, but had to come to terms in the early 1840s, only to have the port city of Campeche (vulnerable to US gunships) seek its own independence, which was then followed by a renewed secessionist uprising in the interior. In January 1847 the Indians, economically hard-pressed by the country's attack on communal rights, including water claims, staged an uprising soon seen in the most lurid images of race war and cannibalism. *Ladino* Yucatán seemed lost to the Indians by 1849–1850, but Santa Anna ground down the Mayan rebels by 1855. The liberals who ousted the general had no more tolerance for the indigenous vision of government and common property, and suppressed renewed revolt, even selling some of the defeated insurrectionists into Cuban slavery. Still, rebellion continued to smolder beyond the *ladino* cities, rooted in own quasi state of "the Cross" through the rest of the century.[27] Indifferent government gave way to the tightening control of the president chosen in 1876, Porfirio Díaz, who would subdue the opposition and rally a group of *científicos,* or business elites, who worked with American and British investors to lay down a modern railroad system.

Díaz would rule for almost 35 years, until a new generation threw off his autocratic regime. During that period Mexico would advance industrially, although with firms dominated by foreign capital. It would remain poor (in fact it had regressed in comparative economic terms since the late eighteenth century), but less poor; Catholic, but secular in its institutions; recognizing in theory its indigenous heritage, but indifferent to its current condition. The elements its history wove together—wars of national consolidation, hardheaded leaders who dominated politics and simultaneously the channels for capital, and the new railroads and industry; the persistence of popular religiosity at the village level, but the secularization of church lands; reform of the educational system to take it out of Church hands; a free market in land that undermined any residual collective rights of the indigenous population; the use of railroads to knit together a vast, if largely arid, territory—were in fact the ingredients that transformed the mid- and late nineteenth-century state. But like other Latin American states, it had to rely on British, and later on US, capital and its elite had fundamentally divided over ideological alternatives.

Further to the south, the dream of a unified South American republic had fallen apart during the wars of independence led by Bolívar and José de San Martín. But all the Spanish-speaking lands remained with powerful armies, underdeveloped national or local assemblies, and a tradition of military strongmen and powerful landlords. The era of the independence struggle also tended to divide the successor elites into conservatives who wished to preserve relatively strong "centralist" institutions with respect for the Church, and "federalists," who saw themselves as liberals and supporters of decentralization and access to British capital. In effect, the Latin American republics froze, until deep into the nineteenth century, in the kind of confrontation that briefly separated American Federalists and the Jeffersonian Democratic Republicans in the late 1790s—but with the confusing difference that in South America the term *federalist* signified the decentralized option that Jefferson and Madison defended toward 1800. And no Latin American statesman could have said, as Jefferson said of Republicans and Federalists in 1801, we are all centralists, we are all federalists.

In Argentina the dictator Juan Manuel de Rosas had drawn on the backing of the independent cattlemen of the pampas, the vast grazing lands around Buenos Aires, to intimidate the liberals in the port city, who sought to maintain their leadership of the republic and their commercial connections with the British. Nominally a federalist, Rosas and his provincial supporters established a dictatorship during the 1830s and 1840s that depended increasingly on violence and terroristic elimination of his enemies and was ousted only in 1852. Like Andrew Jackson to the north, Rosas made his reputation fighting the indigenous inhabitants. But unlike the US president, he never had to contend with the former colonial power's armies. Nor did he ever have to come to terms with an emerging popular democratic movement as Jackson did. Finally he estranged even his own rancher supporters, who had benefited from his grants of little rural despotisms, by the costs of his wars and the conflicts with France and Britain over control of Río de la Plata trade. The victory of the *porteño* (Buenos Aires) British-oriented liberal elite under Bartolomé Mitre, Domingo Sarmiento, and Nicolás Avellaneda in the 1860s and 1870s brought the victory of liberal principles, British investment and railroad development, and an agrarian-export prosperity, followed by a massive immigration of southern European labor. A generation of cohesive state development followed, but Argentina remained a polity where a reactionary military and *cau-*

dillo legacy remained a jagged ideological alternative. In Colombia, too, a conflict between military and liberals set the pattern for decades of civil strife. Army officers and churchmen who had sought to continue the Spanish ruling institutions described themselves as centralist; the liberals tended to speak for states or provincial rights. Politics seesawed between the two.

Brazil's economic and ideological conflicts were softer. The legacy of the Portuguese court and the presence of Braganza dynasty heirs as emperors from 1822 to 1889, as well as the unity needed to maintain a slave population, helped form a coherent oligarchy. So too did the coffee boom and the common intellectual formation of many in civil law and then as state administrators—a contrast with the theological and anticlerical conflicts inherited elsewhere in the Catholic Americas. The state cohered although its project remained administration, not development. The liberals' moves in the 1870s toward abolition of slavery did mobilize the conservative opposition of the coffee provinces in the south, but the liberals included sugar interests in the northeast and no major confrontation of economic interests compelled either political extremism or grand state wagers on one sector or another. The landed elites fed the state bureaucracy.[28]

The United States completed its first east–west railroad line four years after its Civil War ended. For Canada the equivalent epic accomplishment followed in the 1880s with the building of the Canadian Pacific. The history of its railroads and its political federation had been intertwined for a generation. Following rebellions in 1837 against the British colonial government in French Lower Canada and the Anglophone Tory oligarchy of Upper Canada, the British mission of Lord Durham recommended self-government and unification of the two provinces into a Canadian Union. The financial strains of building the Grand Trunk railway designed to link the Saint Lawrence's goods to US ocean ports, and US revocation of free trade for Canadian products, caused financial strains and exacerbated the tension between the linguistic communities. A series of conferences and negotiations in the mid-1860s produced the British North America Act and the creation of the self-governing Dominion of Canada under the Crown and comprising a new federation that redivided the old Upper and Lower Canadas and attracted the maritime provinces, and provided a basis for adhesion of the western lands. The Anglophone elements saw the hope for national domination; the Francophones secured control of a provincial unit, including the cities of Montreal and Quebec.

It is instructive to think of the alternatives that might have been. Suppose Lee had won at Gettysburg in July 1863, for example, then marched toward New York, discouraged the North and allowed a peace-minded Democratic Party to eke out a victory in the presidential election of 1864 and negotiate a settlement that allowed at least de facto autonomy within a regionally decentralized United States— united though in name only. A secessionist Confederate States would have had a social structure more akin to that of Brazil. It would have formed in effect part of a Caribbean geopolitical unit based for several decades more on plantation agriculture and servile labor. The southwestern territories won two decades earlier from Mexico would have remained dependencies of this southern slave republic, and California might ultimately have been divided between its once-Hispanic south and its Pacific-oriented north. Far-fetched? That depends upon whether we believe all counterfactuals are far-fetched by the very fact that they did not come to pass. Some historians, myself included, are more willing to live, so to speak, in the hypothetical or subjunctive mode. The point is that the political and social units that shaped global institutions in fact rested on particular outcomes that came together in a decisive series of events. As the poet Robert Frost wrote, the road not taken made all the difference. From 1850 to 1880, alternatives were progressively shut down by virtue of the advance of evolutionary ideas, the progress of technology based on iron, steel, and coal, the emerging social groups that grew in tandem within these innovations, and the military decisions that these impacted.

Given the variety of experiences that revolution or modernization from above can refer to, I prefer the very loose term *controlled transformation*—a process in which a group of ambitious and powerful men, whether political leaders or economically powerful, or often both, attempted to direct policy to achieve a more vigorous national development. They could attempt this within the shell of ancient empires (where they encountered fierce conservative resistance), or under the ground rules of popular elections. Without the new opportunities of railroad and communications, and rapid-fire weaponry, they would have found their moments less favorable. Without the widespread belief in the inevitability, and even the "hygiene" (as one Italian imperialist termed it), of military conflict, they would also have played a less obtrusive role. And of course they reinforced the charged ambiance of war and industrialization that made their policies seem so essential and natural. Bismarck was right: the great issues of the day were to be resolved by blood and iron—and by strong and determined national strategists such as himself.

In the Middle of Europe

From at least the Treaties of Westphalia in 1648 through German reunification in 1990, the state structures of Central Europe have been, in effect, part of an implicit European constitution, central to issues of war and peace and the representation of ethnic communities. The Habsburg empire rested on two dominant national groups—its German-speaking west, then including today's Austria and the hilly perimeter of Bohemia and Moravia (today's Czech Republic), and, to the east, in the kingdom of Hungary, the Magyar-speaking landlord class who dominated an extensive countryside through a county organization with courthouse politics, not so different, as noted, from the plantation class in the American South. Instead of black slaves, the Magyars drew on peasant laborers—in some districts Ukrainians, Poles, Slovaks, or Romanians—who were still enserfed until 1848. Even in the second half of the nineteenth century, after serfdom had formally ended, they constructed a voting system that ensured that the Slavic groups and Romanians would not capture significant political power. Geographically the kingdom of Hungary contained today's Slovakia, western Romania, and today's Croatia. Outside the kingdom of Hungary and its Austro-Bohemian heartland, the dynasty also ruled Lombardy, with its capital Milan, and Tuscany, and, from 1797 to 1866, Venice and its hinterland. To the northeast the Habsburgs ruled today's Slovenia and beyond the Carpathians the plains of southern Poland or Galicia with the city of Lemberg (later Polish Lwów and today's Ukrainian L'viv), taken during the Polish partitions, and even the region of Czernowitz, taken from the Ottomans. When the remains of the Holy Roman Empire had been dissolved under Napoleon's pressure, the Habsburg rulers had reconstituted their diverse territories as the Austrian Empire, not as a unified unit but with different constitutional arrangements. All in all there were about ten different linguistic units, not including the dense Yiddish-speaking Jewish populations in Galicia. Between then and 1945, the Jews would emigrate or disappear in the Holocaust, and the three million Germans of Bohemia and Moravia would be expelled at the end of World War II, as would millions of Germans from the then eastern territories of Prussia further north. But major territorial and border changes would take place earlier, in the late 1860s and at the end of World War I in 1918–1919, as well.

The Habsburg empire thus comprised many linguistic groups. Increasingly they would feel the attractions of nationalism, the notion that they each should be able to govern their own communities in a national state. Or at least their intellectual and political leaders had this conviction. In fact many of the population spoke two or more languages—the local vernacular at home and in the village, but German or Hungarian in the more public world of officialdom, and in the armies. And forming new states would not be easy in areas where populations were mixed. It was in the interest of the rulers to hold back the belief in nationalism, which would tear apart this patchwork into a welter of contending peoples and places. And even if the dynasty was a German one, it would survive only by leading a multiethnic unit; its rulers learned Hungarian and Italian as well as the French so current in European diplomacy. The Austrian chancellor from 1810 to 1848, Prince Klemens von Metternich, understood the potential vulnerabilities of his state, large with respect to its population of fifty million but vulnerable in its site and its multiple ethnicities. But he also understood how to leverage Austrian power. The tsar of Russia and the king of the major state in northern Germany, Prussia (which had a significant Polish-speaking minority in the east), shared a common interest in social and territorial stability in the early years after the Congress of Vienna. They signed a common program of religiously based stability, the Holy Alliance, consulted together with British and French in periodic "congresses" on the state of Europe, and through 1849 agreed to act in common against revolutionary outbreaks. And they established a German Confederation—a loose structure that included the German territories of Austria and Prussia as well as the smaller German states that emerged from the Holy Roman Empire. Austria and Prussia alternated in the presidency of this unit. And the whole geopolitical machinery was in effect anchored by the implicit power of Russian armies, which supported Metternich's program of conservative stabilization. Notably, in 1848–1849, when the Hungarians had threatened to successfully wrest their independence, Russian armies had intervened to help the Austrians suppress the revolt.

But within a generation of 1815 the structures were increasingly fragile. The sentiment of German nationalism and Italian nationalism grew among the growing middle-class elements of the region, in particular among young literate students. Demonstrations on days of historical significance, monuments of national allegorical figures—a Germania, for instance—celebrations of Italy or Germany in literature increased. Moreover, the Prussian kingdom's officialdom grew restive with the deference to Austria that the system entailed. The western parts of the kingdom grew as coal and iron production increased. They had inaugurated basic education for their village population in the eighteenth century. The monarchs' policy of religious toleration helped attract qualified Huguenot and other persecuted minorities. After defeat by Napoleon, they had adopted a French system of universal military conscription. They recovered and augmented their territory in 1815 as a member of the coalition against Bonaparte. Smaller in population than Austria, Prussia had a vigorously growing economy and its cities, including Berlin, were increasing in size. As early as 1819 its civil servants designed a customs union, or Zollverein, for their own state of Prussia that eliminated the internal tariffs, and in the decades to come they signed up the other midsize states in this free-trade area. The Habsburg realms not only faced internal tensions; increasingly their claim to control the German Confederation was under challenge.

So too the Italian territories in Lombardy and Venetia increasingly chafed under Habsburg rule, and many of the middle-class elements in central and northern Italy developed schemes to unite an emerging Italian nation. Many intellectuals, poets, and writers took up the cause, which was still suppressed by the Austrian authorities and other conservative rulers in the divided peninsula. But the ferment of ideas and discussion was to become known as the Resurgence or Risorgimento. Memoirs of anti-Austrian agitation and schemes for unification crystallized discussion. Nationalism was increasingly chic—British Romantic poets wrote lyrics for the Greek rebellion of the 1820s. Poles, too, had national aspirations, and soon the Czech-speaking intellectuals of Bohemia would as well, as would various southern Slav groups. But they were more directly under Habsburg control. German nationalism could prosper because of the divergence between Prussia and Austria, and the growing attractiveness of nationalism to the elites of the other states.

How was national unification to be achieved? In 1848–1849, the revolutionaries had tried and failed. The mass uprisings and demonstrations in Italy, Central Europe, and Paris threatened a social revolution and soon alienated the socially respectable middle classes. Moreover, the Habsburg court rallied and its generals suppressed the uprisings in the various cities—Vienna, Prague, Budapest, and Venice—one by one. As noted in Chapter 1, the king of Sardinia, who took up the national cause, was defeated twice, first in 1848 and then in 1849. When the Hungarian revolutionaries took up arms again in 1849, the tsar's troops obligingly intervened, and their leader, Kossuth, was left to become a salon hero in America. The Roman revolution, in which Mazzini served as one of the three triumvirs, frightened the pope and was suppressed in 1850 by the newly elected president of the French Republic, Louis Napoleon, who wanted to please Catholics at home. The Frankfurt Assembly could not solve the conundrum of Central European organization—the reviving conservative forces in Austria, led by the tough-minded prince Felix zu Schwarzenberg, brusquely told the Frankfurt liberals that Austria would enter a Germanic federation only with all its territories, including the Hungarian and Polish domains, or not at all. The Prussian monarch, approached as a second-best alternative, refused to offend the Habsburgs and take a crown that depended on popular legitimacy. The nationalist and revolutionary enthusiasts of 1848 were scattered and suppressed after their second wave of uprisings in 1849. Prussian troops dissolved the remnants of the Frankfurt National Assembly in early 1850.

But nationalist aspirations were quieted less than a decade. By the 1850s, Central Europe was in flux anew. First of all, economies rebounded vigorously: railroad construction and industrial development surged ahead, in Prussia and in France, as in the Americas. Even the

Prussian court was prepared to adopt a more assertive policy. The tsar vetoed early plans in 1850 and 1851 for a Prussian-led union of North Germany as potentially too unsettling; St. Petersburg did not want to undermine Austria's conservative presence in Central Europe. But within Prussia the Zollverein and railroads advanced; now, too, there was a Prussian legislature since 1848, which allowed middle-class liberals a forum. In Piedmont, with its capital in Turin, the new monarch was willing to abandon the sleepy clerical conservatism of previous decades, and under the constitution of 1848 (the "Statuto") a vigorous liberal elite, under the leadership of Count Camillo Cavour, sought to emulate British parliamentary practice and French anticlericalism. The kingdom secularized Church and monastic lands and pressed forward with various reforms. Increasingly Piedmont became the hope of the Italian nationalists for leadership in unification. Earlier republican ideas, or the notion of an Italian federation under the presidency of the pope, were abandoned as unrealistic and juvenile. Moreover, Pius IX, who had begun his papacy in 1846 as a possible liberal reformer but was scarred by the Roman revolution, would gravitate toward condemning liberalism and nationalism. The Italian National Movement that was founded in 1859 united a determined cohort of middle-class and aristocratic supporters in the northern and central towns of the peninsula. No longer students or activist members of the secret *carbonari,* they were now a bourgeois movement. Similarly in Germany, the national enthusiasts confessed that they had been too generous and idealistic in 1848; they must accept the states that existed as a basis for action and work with the princes. The restored state structure of Central Europe was cracking open and the initial repressive reaction loosening up in the late 1850s. In Prussia the restored monarch Frederick William IV—who had refused a "crown from the gutter" (that is, from the Frankfurt parliament)—was removed as insane in 1858, and his brother was made regent (to inherit the Prussian throne as William I in 1862). No liberal, he did, though, appoint a new cabinet that backed off from the harsh approach following the revolution and called for new Landtag elections, inaugurating a period of renewed political discussion, the so-called New Era.

With respect to ideology and social origins, nationalists were prepared to abandon republicanism and find monarchical patrons, whether in Turin or Berlin. They were certainly not prepared to embrace socialism. But how should they solve their geopolitical dilemma of Austrian power, seconded by the tsar and prepared to intervene in Germany, Bohemia, and northern Italy? Cavour's strategy was to persuade Bonaparte (now after a coup d'état in 1851, and a plebiscite the next year, governing as Napoleon III, emperor of the French) to take up the Italian cause. Napoleon III fancied himself the champion of nationalities, but he was also preserving the rule of the pope in the middle of Italy.

It was the Crimean War of 1853–1855 that transformed the international political possibilities. Ostensibly this was an arcane struggle, fought by the French to protect their influence in the Levant and the Roman Catholic religious guardianship of Jerusalem against Russian Orthodox claims over the same holy places. But for London the underlying preoccupation was Russian pressure on the Ottoman Empire, weakened by earlier losses in its European territory, the earlier campaigns of Muhammad Ali, and probably by the ramifications of its own effort at reforms, the Tanzimat. St. Petersburg aspired to military hegemony in the Black Sea and the Straits of Marmara, and free entry into the Mediterranean; London saw a threat to its own maritime role and was determined to keep the Ottoman Empire a viable structure. As discussed above, the war—largely fought for control of the ports on the Crimean Peninsula—turned out to be a protracted and messy struggle, revealing the weaknesses of both sides. It also revealed the overextension of the Austrian Empire. The Russians expected that Vienna would repay its help in suppressing revolution in 1849 by interdicting any Anglo-French military movement in the Balkans; instead

Cartographic teleology: The advance of the modern nation-state, as seen in Italy, 1815–1870.

the Austrians occupied the Danubian provinces the Russians agreed to vacate. But Cavour in Turin threw in Piedmont's forces with the British and French, hoping that in the peace settlement to follow, London and Paris would compel Austria to surrender its hold in northern Italy. Fearing the loss of its Italian provinces, the Austrians sought to appease the French and British by "tilting" toward them and threatening the Russians with intervention unless they accepted their enemies' peace terms. Cavour would be disillusioned at the 1856 Congress of Paris that concluded peace; he received no concrete commitment from Napoleon III or London to take up the question of Piedmont's aspirations to unite northern Italy against Austria. On the other hand, Russian policy makers were angered by Vienna's apparent ingratitude. They had to accept that the clauses kept them from reconstituting a naval force in the Black Sea; the Straits to the Mediterranean were closed to them. If challenged anew, Vienna could not count on St. Petersburg's help. Prussia's star rose instead. Under the young Bismarck's forceful advocacy, Prussia adopted strict neutrality and made it clear that France could not intervene in Russian Poland across its territory.

Although Cavour was disappointed at Paris, events were in the sort of flux that occurs only once a generation. Within three years Napoleon would align himself with Savoy. The emperor wanted a dynastic marriage with the princess of Savoy for his heir. The groom was unattractive and brutish; King Victor Emmanuel would not compel his daughter to the union, but she accepted her patriotic duty. In addition an assassination attempt on the emperor by an Italian radical, ostensibly frustrated by the opposition to unification, raised issues of personal security. By early 1859 the French pressed Vienna into war. The two major battles, Magenta and Solferino, were bloody confrontations, signaling the shape of the new warfare. Napoleon concluded a quick peace; the Austrians conceded Lombardy (the province around Milan) to Paris, which retroceded it to Italy. Venice was to remain Austrian until 1866, when it would be joined to Italy as a result of Prussia's

A nationalist icon: A depiction of the "handshake of Teano," the meeting between Giuseppe Garibaldi and King Victor Emmanuel of Savoy north of Naples on October 26, 1860. Garibaldi, originally an advocate of a republican unification for Italy, had forced the withdrawal of the Bourbon monarch from Sicily and Naples, but he agreed, for the cause of unity, to recognize Prime Minister Camillo Benso, Count of Cavour, and Victor Emmanuel's monarchical framework that was being extended southward from Turin. Five months later, Victor Emmanuel was proclaimed king of a (mostly) united Italy. (Private Collection / The Stapleton Collection / The Bridgeman Art Library)

victory over Austria. And in return, the kingdom of Savoy ceded to France the region of Nice and the area around Lake Geneva that had been part of its own territory. Cavour won more than Lombardy, however. By this time the pro-Piedmontese liberals throughout Italy— men of substance and socially conservative, though usually liberal advocates of parliamentary politics—were organizing a movement in all the small states of the Po Valley and Central Italy; and a wave of plebiscites ratified uniting these states with Savoy into a new Kingdom of Italy. Napoleon III's troops still prevented annexing the province of Rome, although the papal province of Bologna would join Italy, as would Tuscany. Once the Franco-Austrian peace was concluded, the big question remained the fate of the Kingdom of the Two Sicilies, that is, the Kingdom of Naples, encompassing all of southern Italy and Sicily. The Neapolitan Bourbons had been restored after the brief revolution of 1848; now in 1860 they were to fall definitively to a new revolution, supported by the dashing republican leader Garibaldi and his "Thousand." The question was, would the democratic republican leaders of the revolution in Sicily and Naples unite the region with the north? Cavour's Piedmont was a constitutional state, but with a limited suffrage and clearly conservative—Garibaldi and his lieutenants envisaged for a while a radical republic in the south that would oust the landlords, with feudal privileges and loyalties. But Garibaldi decided to yield control for the sake of a larger Italy, and in early 1861 the king of Savoy became the monarch of a united Italy. Venice would be gained in 1866, the province and city of Rome in 1870, the northern region of Trent and Bolzano, Trieste, only in 1918. Garibaldi would be disillusioned in the Turin parliament, would bitterly denounce the cession of Nice, and bitterly attacked Cavour, who although only in his fifties was ill and would shortly die. Garibaldi would attempt several invasions of Roman territory in the 1860s, only to be checked by Italian troops. Only when Napoleon III faced the Prussian invasion of 1870 would he remove his garrisons from Rome, which allowed the new kingdom to take the ancient capital.

Cavour and his close colleagues who brought about the unification of the Italian state were in effect gentry—largely gentlemen landowners, who admired Victorian liberalism and its ability for a public-spirited oligarchy to manage a country through a parliament and a moderate monarchy. The group of unifiers would become known in the early 1860s as the Right, and later the Old Right, but they quickly offered coalition privileges to those who termed themselves the Left, also middle-class men who sought a broader electorate but worked within the gradualist paradigm of state building. As of 1862 they formed a "marriage" or *connubio;* by 1882, the Left would win the elections. The Left then invited their defeated adversaries from the Right to "transform" themselves into liberals like themselves, a process of glossing over ideological differences that would characterize the governance of the state into the twentieth century. *Trasformismo* had a cost. The Italian state remained perhaps too cozy; it viewed its peasant masses as sullen adversaries, and the 1860s were spent combatting widespread peasant resistance (the *brigantaggio*) in Sicily, which cost more lives than the wars of unification. A great inquest in 1874 revealed how impoverished the rural masses remained in the Po Valley lands as well as in the south. But the unifiers were, perhaps understandably enough, also preoccupied by making their new state a viable contender in European great-power politics. That meant completing the north–south railroad lines and having a military—both of which entailed heavy taxes on milling wheat, to be borne primarily by the masses. The more radical Left, those who flocked to Garibaldi and his southern lieutenant Crispi, remained outside the system until the 1880s. So, too, did the upper reaches of the aristocracy in both the north and the south: the novelist Giuseppe di Lampedusa memorably re-evoked their quasi-feudal world in *The Leopard.* And so, too, did the Catholic faithful, who were instructed by their clergy not to participate in the regime that had taken Rome and confiscated their properties, leaving only the Vatican territory. Until 1900 or so they remained aloof from politics, then gradually were allowed by the Vatican to vote for the Liberals and even to run "clerical" candidates to keep the socialists from power.

The Italian process contrasted with what was occurring in northern Germany. There too in 1858–1859, middle-class nationalism and Prussian administrators saw the chance to take up the German national banner with themselves in the lead. But whereas the Piedmontese monarchy accepted a British-style constitutional role, the Prussian monarchs were habituated to far more executive authority and drew on a stronger identification with the military, which had a more powerful role in government. The new king in fact wanted to strengthen his professional army and diminish the role that the liberal militia had come to claim. In 1861–1862, he urged an army enlargement and reorganization that the liberals resisted for ideological and fiscal reasons. Not having the votes to ram it through the Prussian Landtag, under the advice of his generals he summoned Otto von Bismarck to take the office of minister president. Bismarck was also a noble, a Prussian *Junker,* who in 1848 had been resolutely conservative and supportive of Austria's role in the Confederation. In the interim he had served as ambassador to Russia and as Prussian representative on the Diet, where he came to resent the Austrian leadership. Bismarck came to Berlin and was willing to collect the necessary taxes without parliamentary approval, in effect an unconstitutional recourse, although he found the legal authorities to justify it on dubious grounds. The Prussian Liberals were incensed, but within a few years Bismarck had managed national military victories that would reconcile them. The German-speaking province of Holstein with its port, Kiel, was nominally a fief of the Danish king, but concurrently a member of the German Confederation. The Confederation Diet deputized Austria and Prussia jointly to compel the new king of Denmark to renounce succession plans for removing Holstein from the Confederation so that he could preserve its traditional administrative unity with the neighboring Danish province of Schleswig. At the conclusion of the short war in 1864, Denmark had to concede both duchies to the Austrians and Prussians as agents for the Confederation, an administrative condominium doomed to conflict and one that enabled Bismarck to provoke a war with Austria two years later. By the mid-1860s Austria rightly understood that Bismarck wanted to expel Vienna from any significant role in the non-Habsburg German territories. Austrian forces, however, proved ill prepared and in the brief war that ensued lost decisively to the Prussians at Königgrätz (Sadová) in early July 1866. Austria sued for peace to avoid further losing battles on the road to Vienna.

Bismarck exacted no territories from the Habsburgs, but forced the end of the German Confederation in which they had shared power. Prussia won the right to organize the north German states in a North German Federation, with a parliament. The southern states of Bavaria and Baden remained outside, but were compelled to sign a military alliance that would subordinate their armies to Berlin's in case of another war. Bismarck did get to annex German territories within the North—the wealthy city of Frankfurt and the north-central city of Hannover, among others. His Italian allies were awarded Austrian Venetia despite having lost a naval battle in the Mediterranean. Just as important as the success in external policy, Bismarck won the retroactive parliamentary approval for his tax measures and the army expansion. The Liberals, enthusiastic supporters of a united Germany, saw the minister president as filling their dreams of 1848. Their voting bloc divided into those willing to approve his policies—known henceforth as National Liberals and including some of the ambitious members of the annexed state government of Hannover—and the smaller number of those who refused to support him, the so-called Progressives. Bismarck expected a rapid completion of German unification with the absorption of Bavaria, Baden, and Württemberg, states now outside any regional federation. But he underestimated the growing Roman Catholic resistance to his program. Catholics were concentrated in the south and Prussia's own Rhine provinces and Silesia in the southeast. The Catholics identified with Austria as a guardian of Catholic interests and they feared the triumph of a state identified with Protestantism.

But the chancellor knew how to exploit these divisions: Catholic hostility made Protestant Liberal support even stronger than it would have been, and within a few years the Prussian leader was willing to wager on a third military adventure, this time a risky war against Napoleon III's France. By exploiting various issues, the German leader made Napoleon appear as an enemy determined to block German unification and even conspiring to seize the duchy of Luxemburg. The French emperor was facing a rising tide of political opposition at home and felt he could ill afford to appear weak and indecisive. A pretext for war was found in a contest over Spanish politics. Spanish parliamentary and military forces were trying to stabilize a new regime after deposing Queen Isabella in 1868; the parliament rejected a republic and with General Prim sought to find a suitable monarchical candidate, inviting a cousin of the Prussian Hohenzollerns. The French objected; the Prussian royal family was willing to renounce the project, but Bismarck released a brusque edited version of the negotiations—the so-called Ems telegram—that aroused Prussian national feelings, and angered the French court. Goaded on by the hawks in Paris (whom his wife favored), Napoleon III declared war—and, to the astonishment of European observers, lost disastrously. A French general surrendered the major fortress in Metz; the emperor himself had to surrender an army on the battlefield at Sedan on September 2, 1870. The republican opposition in Paris declared the regime over and installed a de facto government that was divided among republicans, Bourbon monarchists, and supporters of the emperor—who, as a Prussian prisoner, was allowed to go into exile in London. As Prussian troops moved on Paris, the city itself rose again against the new legislature that was convened at Versailles, and for many months installed a revolutionary commune. The assembly, under a conservative republican, Adolphe Thiers, negotiated a peace with Prussia, which cost it an indemnity— soon paid—and the provinces of Alsace and Lorraine on the border, which Germany would hold until its own defeat in World War I, forty-eight years later. The Paris Commune remained besieged, cold, and near famine through the winter of 1871, until the Assembly finally retook it in the spring, executing thousands of the Communards and exiling others to New Caledonia. Only five years later would the provisional government formally recognize that it was a republic with a president as a chief executive (who was deprived of any real power) and a National Assembly that governed the country through a civil service.

Bismarck, however, knew how to exploit the victory and the rush of nationalist enthusiasm Germans enjoyed. The southern states were bound to Prussia by the alliances negotiated after 1866. In January 1871 the German parliamentary delegates, enjoying a victory session in the palace of Versailles, voted that the king of Prussia should become at the same time "German Emperor." Essentially Bismarck used the institutions he had designed for the interim North German Confederation in 1867, but with the addition of the south German states. The resulting governmental structure was a compromise amalgam of popular and executive instruments. Prussia and the other states retained their Diets or Landtags. The minister president of Prussia became the German chancellor. He alone appeared before the German legislature; there was no collective cabinet responsibility as in Britain, and he held power at the pleasure of the emperor, just as in Prussia he held power at the pleasure of the king. The military ministers were important members of the council of ministers (as would be the case in Japan), and the military budget was debated only every seven years. Nonetheless, Bismarck did agree that the new Reichstag (like the old Customs Union parliament and interim North German Diet) should be elected by universal manhood suffrage. (An upper chamber with restricted powers, the Bundesrat, was based on state delegates.) This meant that one organ in the German constitutional structure had a franchise as democratic as the American Congress and the new French Chamber of Deputies. But it could not vote to unseat the chancellor; all it could do was make his life difficult by paralyzing the budget process. Moreover, even as he sought to placate a Reichstag majority in which, over time, liberal and working-class representatives increased with industrial development, the chancellor–minister president had to pass a Prussian state budget a few blocks away in the Prussian House of Deputies (and a Prussian House of Peers) that had a far more conservative majority. For until defeat in the First World War, Prussia retained a "three class" suffrage that gave wealthy voters a far greater proportional share of the delegates than the nonwealthy.

Bismarck had the force and the prestige to navigate within the system, but his successors found the task a growing challenge. After the end of the Third Reich, historians tended to stress the autocratic side of the empire—the potential for a willful emperor and powerful military officers to intervene in politics—but recent scholarship has emphasized the vigorous quality of political debate that marked national and local life. Until the end of the 1870s it pleased Bismarck to work with the National Liberals and to rally them against supposed threats from the disgruntled Catholics and the emerging working-class Social Democratic movement. By the end of the 1870s, Germany unified its legal codes and its monetary systems; it retained conscription and the strongest army in Europe. Its industrial development, spearheaded by the coal and steel concentrations of the Ruhr and newly annexed Lorraine, rapidly made it the preeminent industrial power of the continent, and it would overtake Britain in steel output by the 1890s. Bismarck declared that Germany was a satiated state and wanted to be a force for stability, but the annexation of Alsace and Lorraine had made it difficult to win a real reconciliation with France.

The Austrian Empire underwent its own structural consolidation after its defeat in 1866. While the new realists among the Magyar nobility had (until 1918) shelved the goal of absolute independence from Vienna, its leaders under Ferenc Deák exploited the Austrian defeat to extract a large degree of autonomy under the terms of the 1867 Ausgleich or Compromise. Henceforth, the Habsburg empire would be a dual federation: the emperor "of" the lands in the west (Austria, Bohemia, and Moravia) would be king "in" Hungary, and the country would become the hyphenated Austria-Hungary or Dual Monarchy. Dualism brought a precarious degree of state consolidation to each half of the structure, but the two "historic peoples" each faced fractious nationalities in their respective regions. The Magyars would govern their large half the country through a rigged suffrage, much as white United States citizens in the former Confederate States of America would dominate their region. Within the kingdom, Croatia enjoyed its own partially autonomous status. Linking the two halves of the Dual Monarchy was a common foreign office, a common army and navy, with German still accepted as a language of command, and a commercial trade treaty, to be reviewed every decade, that connected the grain-growing lands of Hungary with the more industrial regions of Bohemia and Austria. Austria still retained Trieste as its port on the Adriatic Sea; Hungary held the ports of Pola (today's Croatian Pula) and Fiume or Rijeka on the Adriatic. The Hungarian parliament, restricted in suffrage until 1911, divided between more or less nationalist elements; the Reichsrat in Vienna, which united the western half, would break down into Social Democrats, Liberals, eventually Catholic populists (Christian Socials), pan-Germans, and strong components of Czech and Polish deputies who fought over the linguistic rights of their respective nationalities and the control of school budgets. Civil servants were expected to use German in reports to Vienna, the local vernacular with the citizenry dominant in the respective areas. Language issues for schools—perhaps familiar to Americans accustomed to disputes about bilingualism—continued to vex the Austrian half.

It was unclear what to call the western half: strictly speaking, Austria was only part of the unit; the emperor retained a confusing series of sovereign titles over the various provinces (of which Bohemia was listed as a kingdom and Upper and Lower Austria as Archduchies).

The designation "imperial and royal," *"kaiserlich und königlich"* or *"k. und k.,"* became the term applied to officials, flags, consulates, and so forth of the whole realm. The western half was sometimes unofficially referred to as Cisleithania—the lands "this side" of the little river Leith that formed part of the border with Hungary. Officially it remained the lands represented in the Reichsrat. As ethnic nationalism increased, the structure came under greater and greater stress, although the Austrian Social Democratic Party and the Jewish population, who understood the dangers of German and Magyar, Polish, or Romanian nationalism, remained the most loyal to the dynasty as the unifying and hopefully moderating force. Historians have often viewed what also became known as Austria-Hungary as a doomed state, but it fought for four long years in World War I before finally fracturing. Its armed forces were rarely victorious unless acting together with the German military, but they functioned as a unit despite their recruits' linguistic diversity. Its bureaucrats seemed addicted to a ponderous formalism, but they successfully represented the presence of the monarchy and its elaborate legalism. And curiously enough within this ramshackle compromise between modern prenational (and postnational) elements, likewise between parliamentary state and military-bureaucratic empire, the boldest experiments in music, philosophy, and psychiatry could flourish.[29]

The World of the 1870s

The world of the 1870s had been transformed—not by revolution, but by strong leaders, realists who believed in railroads, property, economic development, and national power, and the inevitability of conflict and competition. Of course there were major differences. The Italians who moved their capital to Rome in 1870 (after an interim six years in Florence, which had followed Turin) knew that they had chosen a course different from that of the Germans and Prussians. Their parliament was more influential; they felt the Prussians glorified war. But they too identified with a national state. The unifiers who were constructing the new Japanese national state felt a kinship with the Germans—like them, they saw the monarchy and its civil servants and its military leaders as crucial for their state, and they were emulating the industrialization as quickly as they could, sending their promising diplomats and generals to study in the West. The Brazilians and Argentines, who had cooperated (with the Uruguayans) in almost obliterating the Paraguayan Republic, which defied their access to the great rivers from the interior, depended much more on Britain's commercial influence. But they overcame the old conflicts to a degree, rallied (to use the Brazilian motto) around the Comtean ideas of "order and progress." Brazil, huge and decentralized under the emperors elevated from the exiled Portuguese royal line, slowly moved to abolish slavery and with it the empire. Canada was completing its railroad network and negotiating a united Dominion. Vigorous US growth came at a price. The Republican Party in the United States was determined to favor manufacturing with a tariff and open up the West to farmers, ranchers, and miners—thereby forging a coalition that would run the country for several decades once it had abandoned its radicals' effort to remake the ex-Confederacy. But in the opportunities that abounded for farmers, industrialists, and even southern landlords in the railroads and the trans-Mississippi West, blacks, Indians, and the contract laborers from East Asia would remain severely disadvantaged, if not victims. Even the French Republic, which had installed a powerful Assembly, would advance its railroad network and a state-run secularized school system, with a centralized prefectural system.

So throughout much of the "civilized" world—understood as Europe with its American outliers, the British dominions, and the ambitious Japanese—states were trump. The recipe for governing was to develop their territory, keep power in the hands of men of science, expertise, and property, and prepare for a continuing military rivalry. And to resist the archaic blandishments of communalism, dangerously close to anarchism and syndicalism, whether manifesting itself as a program to found government on village communes and collective property, advocated only by formerly servile peasants or indigenous tribes, and reject the new working-class claims to trade-union and syndical power. And to resist, too, any supranational claims to religious authority, whether from the Roman Catholic hierarchy in the West or the *'ulama'* in the Islamic world or Buddhist monasteries in Asia.

Of course, there were laggards in this process. China remained a victim: the British and French had gone to war again in 1860 and forced more concessions; the Taiping had sapped imperial strength—the power of the Confucian state and the growing impoverishment of its peasant masses prevented an effective response, though not the effort. The Ottomans, who had lost Egypt and most of their Balkan territories, faced the severest self-contradictions: if they adopted modern principles of secular Ottoman citizenship, they undermined the religious communalism that had been the basis of the Empire when it was on the rise. They found it hard to mobilize economic resources and extract revenues. As in the case of China, and to a degree Latin America, where mineral extraction, commodity exports, and the coastal port activities generated wealth, foreigners would control much of the process and slow down self-development. Britain revealed some of the same pressure to modernize a political and educational system that had not been compelled to reform by radical shocks or military defeat. Between the 1830s and the 1870s, Britain too would adopt crucial reforms—a less paternalist approach to poverty, the reform of its military (abolishing purchase of commissions), free trade, key municipal reform—and rationalization of its great Indian possession after suppression of the rebellion of 1857. So, too, the Russians proceeded less dramatically, but did abolish serfdom and started toward representative institutions in the 1860s and 1870s. The transcontinental Russian railroad would have to wait until the end of the nineteenth century, as would the loosening of the communal hold over village lands, and a national parliament came only in 1905. Britain, in effect, could modernize without radically transforming its state–society balance; in Russia the state remained powerful enough and its adherents conservative enough that modernization came slowly. But all these states were on a new trajectory by 1870, and so was their intellectual and cultural patrimony. With such transformations it was to be expected that the pressure to dominate and control would press even more drastically into the colonial peripheries, and the instrumentalities for control at home would rely even more on science and measurement, steel and steam and communication. It would be both gritty and glitzy, ferociously innovative, but factual as well.

But yet, the 1870s disclosed a collection of states still spread out in their institutional and ideological transformations. Some remained hostage to their continuing multicultural divisions. The old empires—Austro-Hungarian and Ottoman, Russian to a lesser degree—had to balance ethnic or religious diversity even as they sought to modernize for the harsh international competition that had threatened them since the late eighteenth century. The once opulent Mughal Empire had finally disappeared in 1858 at the hands of its feeble princes and persistently encroaching British adversaries after the collapse of the Indian rebellion. The so-called Raj—which after 1876–1877 became officially the Empire of India under the Empress Victoria—found it expedient to preserve its patchwork territories and diverse communities, including the approximately five hundred princely states preserved alongside the directly ruled presidencies and other jurisdictions represented in London by the secretary of state for India and administered from Calcutta by the governor general or viceroy. The Manchu state with its allogenic dynasty could hardly embrace an unrestrained

Chinese nationalism, but its loyal officials found Confucian traditions based on the classics and a virtuous gentry too limited to carry through a successful reform program. The Germans and Japanese seemed to understand that if they morphed imperial legacies into efficient military and bureaucratic government, they might retain the nominal trappings of empire. And countries formally democratic at home understood conversely that the currency of power in the world of states was to develop empire abroad.

Historians have always emphasized the violent confrontations between highly organized states as the material of traditional "diplomatic" history. But the contentious world of rival states was also united in its pressure on the fragmented communities at its edges, or sometimes within its territories, whom they perceived to be obstacles to progress and civilization. These alternative communities were often desperately poor, lived sometimes in a symbiotic relationship with their animals, and periodically renewed the religions of empire, whether Christian or Muslim or Hindu, with the voices of local prophets, dissident priests, austere Sufi mystics, and healers. They were remnants, but persistent remnants—the Maya of the Yucatán borderland; the *vaqueiros* or herders of the Brazilian scrublands of the northeast known as the Sertão, who resisted the new encroaching republic in 1896; the American Indian nations slowly compressed into reservations; the gypsies of Andalusia and Romania; the Chechens of the Caucasus; the Pashtuns at the northwest frontier of the Raj and other societies of Central Asia; the tribesmen of highland Burma; Uighurs of Xinjiang; and numerous other peoples. Some, such as the Tasmanians, were largely exterminated as early as the 1820s and 1830s; others later, as the Indians of Patagonia in the 1880s; still others, such as the Herero in German colonial territory, decimated in the early years of the twentieth century— as many had been in the earlier expansion of overseas empire after 1500. Many would be absorbed in encroaching cities and territories; still others managed to persist in jungle or highland sanctuaries too daunting for the victorious—waiting for chiliastic redemption or even later to be discovered and often called back to mediated life by anthropologists. Their fate caught the attention of novelists at the time and is being deservedly recovered by contemporary historians. But we must carry on with the progress of those who continually pushed out at their once immune domains.

CHAPTER THREE

The Human Zoo

Keep bad news in perspective. . . . Nine days after Custer's detachment faced swift annihilation at the Little Bighorn, the United States celebrated the hundredth anniversary of its original Independence Day. As part of the centennial year, Philadelphia entrepreneurs organized the largest world's fair to date, from May 10 to November 10. President Ulysses Grant and Brazilian emperor Dom Pedro, the last monarch resident in the Western Hemisphere, opened the celebratory exhibits of technology and agricultural bounty by switching on the immense Corliss Steam Engine in Machinery Hall. Steam and iron caught the imagination of the ten-million-odd visitors who came to the Exposition. Alexander Graham Bell's telephone, patented two months earlier, was also on exhibit. Two years later an even larger world exposition opened on the Champ-de-Mars in Paris, the meadow on which the Eiffel Tower would arise for another ever-larger world's fair eleven years later.[1] Again, marvels of engineering—but also a "human zoo" or "negro village," where four hundred indigenous peoples were put on exhibit in reconstructions of their supposed habitats.

The 1870s saw human zoos set up in cities throughout Europe, including Hamburg, Warsaw, Barcelona, and London—tribal specimens displayed in the most un-nomadic conditions possible: as objects for vicarious tourism and occasionally study. The zoos presupposed the hierarchies of civilization: spectators confirmed to themselves and their children that they were superior; exhibitors had to acquire, transport, and then supply and manage these arenas of domesticated encounter. What those exhibited thought is hard to know. We would be hasty to attribute humiliation or anger. They were in a service occupation, perhaps like actors, although the terms of their recruitment and service could be rigorous, as a recent historian of the world's fairs reminds us. They were on stage, not in a cage. Perhaps they retained their own sense of superiority to the elaborately clad visitors who came to see their miniature habitats.[2]

Confronting the Primitive

Establishing allegorical meanings is, of course, a cheap trick for historians as well as literary scholars. Seek and ye shall find. Still, controlling colonial and urban environments, keeping potential savages safely fixed to their own turf, ensuring minimal welfare for all while reinforcing the visible signs of hierarchy, finding appropriate rules for what a contemporary German writer has called today's "human zoo,"[3] marked the evolution of states and governments from the 1870s until the outbreak of the First World War. The zoos were reassuring; they suggested that the "primitive forces" of humanity—supposedly fundamentally differentiated by color and other racial characteristics, only semigoverned in their native habitats, untutored in the basic civilizing concept of private property—could be mastered and even made grateful for their subjection. The darker forces at home, whether racial in the Western Hemisphere or working class in the industrializing world, were more threatening. As late as 1871 they mounted a revolutionary regime in Paris, the Commune, established in the besieged capital of France by the radicals who resisted the new Third Republic's willingness to make peace with the German forces bivouacked to the east of the city. The Commune would soon come to represent, through both the suffering the city underwent and the hostages the regime would execute—the heart of darkness at home. In fact, within a few decades the major threat posed by the organized proletariat no longer seemed to be insurrection—the aging Friedrich Engels recognized that revolutionary aspirations would not prevail on the barricades—but the emerging Socialist and Social Democratic political parties throughout the West.

The peasant masses of southern and Eastern Europe also represented a reservoir of primitive and dark forces. Insofar as they could be woven into a social drama of integration and peaceful acceptance, analogous to the human zoo, it was through the appreciation of folklore and folk art, which flourished in this period. Human differentiation and classification also contributed to heroic scholarly achievements in the social sciences. Motivated in some instances by an assumption of inequality, in others by a cosmopolitan effort to understand difference without presupposing inferiority, late nineteenth-century anthropologists and archeologists acquired new knowledge of remote times and places. Whereas social observers a century earlier had traced curious customs and recognized that far-flung empires were as civilized as their own, the later nineteenth century pressed ahead with concepts of social structure, kinship, and religious organization. Empire allowed a collection of splendid artifacts—often entire architectural elements without parallel, to be accumulated in Paris, London, Berlin, St. Petersburg, and eventually New York.[4]

For the white middle classes of Europe and the Americas, technological angst and second thoughts about their destined global domination were usually remote through the 1880s. By the end of the century, darker preoccupations and an edgier awareness would surface as the "positivist" confidence of the previous generation yielded to critiques of empire, social activists exposed the squalid living conditions of the tenements, and the barely coded artworks referred to as "symbolist" suggested deep sexual insecurities. As the writer Rudyard Kipling understood, empire was precarious ("Lest we forget") and the perennially gloomy Henry Adams questioned machine civilization.[5] Still, the artists and intellectuals of Europe, the Americas, and Japan had not yet crossed Freud's threshold of frank insistence on Oedipal jealousy and infant sexuality. Some depicted hooded messengers of death; others, intimations of castration. Painters and composers had not entirely cast loose from the reassuring conventions of representation and tonality as they would after 1905; the world of art stood on the cusp of modernism. Intellectuals in China and India and the colonies had not yet developed sustained revolutionary critiques of imperialism. Massacres of stubborn peoples targeted by the hubris of empire—adherents of the Mahdi of the Sudan, the Armenians in the Ottoman realms in 1896–1897, the Filipinos who resisted US takeover of their islands from the Spanish, the Herero in German Southwest Africa in 1905–1906, the Formosans (Taiwanese) taken over by Japanese administrators in 1895—aroused some regrets and criticism but little effective counteraction. Anti-imperialists in the United States may have braked further territorial acquisitions by force after 1898 (although the Danish Virgin Islands were purchased in 1917); the difficulties incurred in subjugating the Boer republics sobered the British; and the German policies of genocidal suppression in the later Namibia provoked parliamentary opposition, but faits accomplis were not to be undone. The unfortunate excesses of violence amounted to what President Theodore Roosevelt called the "attendant cruelties" of progress. And TR did not even consider the reduction of forest to rubber plantation or slash-and-burn sugar cultivation.[6] They took place on the margins.

And yet—even if the macho statesmen of the late nineteenth century resisted making the connection—the "pacification," and sometimes massacre, on the perimeter was related to those triumphant displays of progress in the great expositions and the ever greater confidence in modern statehood. The late nineteenth-century state was a triumph of the positivist spirit, of the materialist forces of civilization, of the social-scientific counting of populations and measurement of territory, of progress and the future. Nonetheless, it often appeared hostage to potentially the darker forces of its own proletariat, the ignorant and church-besotted peasantry of its countryside, and sometimes threatened even by its own emasculating women. The issue of female rule produced a constitutional crisis in mid-nineteenth-century Hawai'i; was accommodated in late-Victorian Britain, in effect, by desexing the widowed monarch; troubled late-imperial institutions in tsarist Russia and Qing China; and also emerged in growing claims for suffrage. Before World War I women would get the right to vote in New Zealand in 1893, Australia in 1902, Finland in 1907, and Norway in 1913, as well as in the American western states. US women won the suffrage for national elections in 1920, Britain admitted women to the polls in stages from 1911 to 1928; the Weimar Republic from its beginnings in 1919. France finally consented after World War II in 1944, and the Swiss at the federal level in 1971.

How to master these encroaching claims for political representation and participation—whether through repression and arbitrary rule, or through progressive concessions and greater inclusiveness—was the great political issue that hovered over the late nineteenth- and early twentieth-century state.

Statehood and Governmentality

When Americans talked about states, unless they had attended German universities they usually referred to the territorial subdivisions of their country. In Europe the state was a collective abstraction, referring to the legal authorities that claimed the right to legislate, enforce, and administer. The British did not use the term instinctively; French and Germans did. Other cultures had rough equivalents that referred to polity or rule, such as the Hindi raj. Having a state in the nineteenth century was an attribute of an allegedly advanced people. Colonies were allegedly not ready to claim it, but it was perhaps the highest attribute of rationality. Revived in the early nineteenth century, above all by the philosopher Georg Friedrich Wilhelm Hegel, the celebration of statehood had become a Prussian juridical specialty, a doctrine that served a new sovereign unit constructed almost mechanistically across diverse German- (and Polish-) speaking territories. By midcentury, heavy treatises of *Staatslehre* and *Rechtslehre,* the doctrines of the State and of law, had become legal and constitutional specialties of German-speaking Europe. Friedrich Julius Stahl from the 1830s, Otto von Gierke and the Swiss jurist Johann Caspar Bluntschli in midcentury, Georg Jellinek by the end of the century, were among those contributing to the genre. Some attributed to the ruling agencies and to the law an ethical and philosophical loftiness, a spiritual reality that the associations and markets of civil society allegedly could not quite possess. "The state is a moral being and it has moral tasks in life," Bluntschli insisted.[7] Civil society, so the eighteenth-century Scottish philosophers, including Adam Ferguson and Adam Smith, had argued, remained associations of interests aspiring to wealth and public happiness. Continentals felt these aspirations remained inferior, whereas the state was an association of ideals, ethics, and law. Historians used to ascribe to these German thinkers some of the blame for Nazism (ironically, Stahl and Jellinek came from Jewish backgrounds), but in fact National Socialism—insofar as it could claim any intellectual pedigree—would draw on different theories, more attuned to national and ethnic celebration as well as to the gut belief that politics was war by other means. In fact, Jellinek, a liberal, denied any metaphysical reality to the state, insisting rather that the state was a legal creation that could play an active role in regulating society and the economy. States did what private associations could do—deliver the mail, build railroads, provide education, relieve poverty—but rendered these public functions.[8]

All these treatises took care to differentiate the legal structure that was the state from the bundle of historically or linguistically formed allegiances that comprised the nation. Conceptually they also separated the state from the society it regulated. But there were important dissenters by the late nineteenth century. The idea of society had moved beyond just the notion of either a politically oriented "public" or an undifferentiated "people." Society implied a population structured according to their interests and allegiances or what today might be termed identities. These might include religious preferences, regional and local loyalties, and class and occupational affiliations, which, it was implied, took shape independent of state action. Society was often depicted spatially: it was organized from the bottom up, not from the top down, or it constituted an intermediate layer of connections more extensive than family and kinship and less powerful than the state. By the late nineteenth century some legal theorists were suggesting that these functional groups should provide the basis of the legal order. Ideas of transcendent state sovereignty should give way to a compact among interests and groups, collectively endowed with legislative power. Dismayed by the revolutionary turmoil of 1848 and after in Prussia, German liberal Rudolph Gneist looked to political administration and the development of British parliamentary representation for pragmatic representation, while Otto von Gierke examined German medieval guilds to find models of self-government. A generation later Léon Duguit, the French admirer of Comte's earlier positivism, argued that an authentic legal order had to express the "interdependence" of modern social interests, not the abstract and fictitious notions of natural rights. "Yes, the state is dead, or rather what is dying is its Roman, royal, Jacobin, Napoleonic or collectivist form, which in all these diverse aspects, has been only one form of the state." What he saw arriving was not a state as traditionally conceived but a government of technical representatives based on professions and elimination of class conflict. The American "pluralists" of the early twentieth century argued similarly that politics rested on interest-group negotiations, not on constitutional forms.[9]

Social scientists have often tried to distinguish between strong and weak states. The strong state "penetrated" society and could allegedly shape it by extensive measurement and regulation; neither wealthy elites nor organized masses effectively challenged its authority: think Prussia. The weak state's authority might be extensively flouted, subverted, or ignored by families and associations: think Italy. But the dichotomy remains too clumsy. The relationship of state and society—insofar as these abstractions correspond with the messy anatomy of human institutions—is a crucial variable for understanding history and politics, but a robust state and a strong society could complement each other. No state protected accumulated family wealth more than Great Britain; the state could be strong because it so fitted the agenda of its great families. If social discipline was inculcated and family cohesion emphasized, as in China, state authority might thereby benefit at times but evaporate at other times. The same held for Russia. And then again, did a strong bureaucracy serve as the instrument for a strong state, or did it develop into a powerful special interest blocking any projects for the general interest? The relationship of state and society thus remains complex and often paradoxical—nonetheless, the authorities we routinely aggregate as the state did become more ambitious about shaping the everyday attributes of the societies they governed in the late nineteenth and early twentieth centuries. They envisaged a more encompassing and interventionist agenda, and the results they sought entailed a different sense of mission. The good ruler in the eighteenth century might define his objective in terms of felicity or happiness or the preservation of order. The good bureaucrat in the late nineteenth might think in terms of energy or hygiene.[10]

Masses of people had no provision if business cycles threw them out of work; they had no access to medical care; their old age was dependent on family support. Did not the state have constructive missions? Without the state, they would experience not picturesque village assistance, but misery. Without the state, their water and food supplies would be sources of disease. It was logical that American and some British social reformers admired the emerging welfare-state regulation of Bismarck's (and his successors') Germany. As Jellinek wrote, "The economic and spiritual life of the people is advanced by laws and legal compulsion, that is social results are brought about through governmental power. . . . Through their common rule, subjects become comrades. The advancement of communal purposes through social means has become the task of the state to an increasing degree. . . . The state has become the most powerful social factor, the strongest protector and advancer of the common interest."[11] They found in the German municipalities, Prussian state commercial ministries, and national Protestant church Diet, offices that claimed state power to limit child and women's labor and provide social insurance for the disabled and elderly, at a time when American courts struck down this sort of legislation.[12] Whether or not one judges the state today as an abusive concentration of bureaucratic interference with individual freedom, the historian must recognize that as states were melted down and formed anew from 1850 to 1880, they seemed to represent civilization and progress.

The doctrines of the state found receptive audiences in far-flung soils, certainly among the aging Japanese leaders of the Meiji Restoration, who in the 1880s and 1890s wanted to endow the regime they had constructed with lofty conservative principles, including constitutional arrangements borrowed from Germany, which limited the scope of the new Diet, entrenched the influence of the military leadership, and exalted the monarch with an Imperial Rescript of 1890.[13] Latin American conservatives and military spokesmen found the ideas congenial, for they prized the authority of the central state, which as a creation of colonial elites had often remained a precarious attainment. Roman Catholic authoritarians invoked the Church's mission to enforce authority, but they also liked the idea of an authoritarian state, as did right-wing nationalists in Italy who imported Hegelian idealists with enthusiasm at the end of the century. In the Ottoman, Russian, and Qing empires, the doctrines certainly found approval, but they were hard to nativize because the German concept of the state was so transcendent that it might undermine the very real institutional claims of the monarch. The Japanese emperor might fade into the abstraction of the realm that the new ruling elite wanted to strengthen. It was harder to bypass the Russian tsar, although his civil service and their authority (the *gosudarstvo*) might become the object of loyalty for some. The conservative Chinese reformers seeking to rescue the fraying Qing state translated Hegel but turned more readily to the ancient Confucian and Neo-Confucian ideals that aligned the family, the gentry, and the emperor in a cosmic sense of duty. And in the Islamic world, including the Ottoman Empire, the religious mission of rulers overshadowed so strict an emphasis on law, abstract and compelling in its own secular transcendence. The mission of the Ottoman clan (and later the Turkic ethnic core) also made their familial or ethnic claims too strong for the state as such to legitimize authoritarian rule.

After the twentieth-century experience of states (or parties that governed states) whose leaders claimed to have the knowledge and good intentions to wield great power over individuals and associations, the effort to apply legislative power for alleviating social inequality or enhancing environmental benefits—controlling floods, increasing the yields of agriculture and husbandry, and so on—suggests an enterprise that ran amok. The distortions that arose from state ambitions, even those benevolently intended, and of course those that single-mindedly sought to control and regulate inherently variable distributions of people, environment, and property, now dominate many of the historical narratives and political analyses. A large literature, exemplified by the work of theorist Michel Foucault (d. 1984) and the political anthropologist James C. Scott, now proposes that knowledge of society—whether codified in the form of censuses or cartography, or pursued for public health reasons or even public education—was not just the prerequisite of social control, but designed precisely to achieve it. Knowledge is power, Francis Bacon, the early exponent of scientific observation, had written in the sixteenth century, and by the eighteenth century "useful knowledge" had become the goal of the broad Western movement called the Enlightenment. The alternative to "reason" seemed to be prejudice, backwardness, and superstition, still too often institutionalized by organized religion. But critics then and since have emphasized instead that social knowledge leads to the abuse of power even if applied benevolently. Knowledge, in this view, provides not just power but domination.[14]

But from the mid-nineteenth century to the mid-twentieth, state power seemed hardly so suspect. Anarchists and anarcho-syndicalists might propose that local associations could replace central government and large corporations. They wanted to build organizations from the workshop or village "upward," delegating only a minimum of authority to national governments. For two months, from late March through late May 1871, exponents of anarchist concepts, alongside other radicals, played a role in the Commune that seized power in Paris, which had been besieged since the preceding fall, first by the Germans, then by the newly elected conservative National Assembly that convened in nearby Versailles. The Commune would leave a reputation for revolutionary misery and terror, but its violence paled before the massive repression exacted when the city was finally recaptured. In Spain, also racked by revolution from 1868, the briefly established republic of 1873–1874 went through a "Federalist" episode of decentralization, confronting, moreover, a wave of local "cantonalist" uprisings in the southeast that sought even more total autonomy.

Of course, there was no direct causality that linked the anarchist uprisings in Paris and Spain's cities of the early 1870s with the episodes of tribal resistance on the margins of European expansion a few years later, which we cited in the Introduction. Nonetheless, along with the nomadic struggles on the periphery of empire, these doomed spasms of spontaneity in Europe also demonstrated that in the world of the 1870s the organized national or imperial state was trump. Thirty years earlier liberals and radicals had aspired to create nation-states that would reconcile impulses of emancipation with collective self-determination. After 1870 they found that the states they had wished for served a different spirit of organization and national competition. Francisco Pi y Margall, the scholarly theorist of grassroots government who served briefly as president of the disintegrating First Spanish Republic in 1873, would spend the next quarter-century of his life as a historian and parliamentary deputy for the republican opposition and a defender of autonomy for Cuba. Sitting Bull lived out the post-Custer years on a reservation—each a surviving witness to a vision of collective life that the modern state had effectively rendered obsolete.

Anarchism did not go quietly into the night, however. After military restoration of the Spanish monarchy in 1874 and a cozy agreement for party alternation in the parliamentary elections, Spanish anarchists put their energies into organizing agricultural cooperatives and a union federation, the CNT (National Confederation of Labor), which patiently built its strength in the Andalusian countryside and eventually among the urban workforce of Barcelona. It sent delegates to the national parliament but refused to join any governing coalition until the second Republic, installed in 1931, was challenged by the right-wing military uprising of 1936. Spanish anarchism was exceptional in its embrace of patient and collective organization. Elsewhere the doctrine attracted impatient terrorists who believed in the power of "the deed." By the 1880s and 1890s, terrorist zealots were resorting to assassination to destroy the state, claiming the lives of Tsar Alexander II in 1881, the French and American presidents in 1894 and 1901, the empress of Austria and queen of Italy. Still, these violent gestures did not succeed in arresting the strengthening of central governments, and they were disavowed by most revolutionaries, Marxist or otherwise.[15] Other advocates of working-class advancement, such as the European social-democratic parties emerging by the 1890s, believed that "capturing" the state and using it to pass such reforms as minimum wages, enhanced social insurance, stricter safety measures, and limitation on factory hours, was a more promising strategy for advancing social justice. To be sure, faithful Marxist revolutionaries condemned this "reformist" stance at the congresses of the second Socialist International, but until the eve of World War I, it attracted increasing numbers of adherents, especially among trade unionists, who played a large role in socialist parties.

Nevertheless—let's get real. For all the recent histories that suggest the state became exponentially more ambitious and powerful in controlling its citizens, nineteenth-century governments still hardly "penetrated" society. Empires left administrative power in the hands of local notables; vast areas of sparsely populated countryside had virtually no police forces. Factory owners faced virtually no challenge to their power within their enterprises. Western states taxed their citizens extraordinarily lightly; liberals had rolled back the heavy burdens that the wars of the eighteenth century and then the Napoleonic era had necessitated. Above all, as we shall see, in those offshore preserves of arbitrary power—the colonies, formal and informal, of the British, French, Spanish, Dutch, Germans, Italians, Portuguese, and later the Japanese and Americans—remote states assigned coercive power to private agents. The extortionate loan, the power to evict and to fire, sometimes the lash, the knout, the switch, and the bamboo rod, not the rational state, ensured social order and the investment opportunities that would be one of the incentives for development. (The other remained the precapitalist motive of expanding strategic power for the home country and its state.) The development of European empire rested upon this happy compatibility of motivations.

But this fabric of local and non-state authority would be significantly encroached upon from the 1860s for the next century. Not entirely, to be sure, and often least significantly in those great imperial superstructures run by the Habsburgs, Romanovs, Ottomans, and Qing. Elsewhere, having rebuilt nations, the vigorous administrative elites of the late nineteenth century and twentieth, could rebuild states. To these efforts we apply a term proposed only recently: *governmentality*. Governmentality has become a fashionable concept in the social sciences and has begun to seep into historical accounts as well. Its recent use derives from the French social theorist Michel Foucault, who applied it to describe the growing administrative and pastoral capacity of the Catholic Church in the late Middle Ages and then post-Renaissance political units to regulate the behavior of those living within their borders. The Church had the mission of tending "souls" and providing the nurturing institutions that would ensure their salvation; the state would take over this welfarist mission. Foucault separated the pursuit of governability from that of sovereignty. Sovereignty, or state authority in the abstract, he suggested, was the concern of sixteenth-century thinkers, such as Machiavelli, but from the seventeenth and particularly the eighteenth century, officials were preeminently concerned with the health and prosperity of their populations. Tracts on national economies, epidemics, and trade displaced the disquisitions on the rights of the ruler. Statistics and measurement, and the regulation (or deregulation) of national economies, became the instruments for advancing the well-being of the population.[16] In effect the nineteenth century recapitulated the transition that Foucault described from the seventeenth-century theorists of sovereignty and power to the eighteenth-century Physiocrats, cameralists, and administrative cadres, who inscribed prosperity, growth, and health of their societies as preeminent state objectives.

The discipline of sociology emerged in part as a response to the recurrent threat of revolution and working-class mass action: ideology was supposedly to yield to science, or so conservative scholars argued. The Paris popular upheaval in June 1848 (and then again the Commune in 1870) led Hippolyte Taine to displace what he felt was destructive ideology with scientific management of society through sociology.[17] In Britain Herbert Spencer applied what he believed were the lessons of Darwinism to reject any efforts at what he insisted was collectivist interference with the healthy evolution of society. His disciple in the United States, William Graham Sumner of Yale, likewise condemned social legislation as disastrous interference with the market. Émile Durkheim was in a far more liberal political camp, but also insisted on "social facts" to be measured statistically; and one of the major facts he analyzed was "suicide," which he treated not merely as a psychological collapse but as a societal disease that testified to an underlying condition of social disintegration he termed anomie. Whether on the left or the right, however, the new state possibilities of intervention depended on postulating an organic society that could be measured and shaped. This new confidence in the measurability of social relationships took its name from Auguste Comte's doctrine of positivism—a confidence in the observability of natural and social phenomena that characterized the statesmen and intellectuals of the 1870s and 1880s but would erode and dissipate, at least in high culture, by the 1890s and the first decade of the twentieth century.

The new states, having been created and re-created by the 1870s, turned essentially to projects of modernization and the transformation of their societies. Numbers were the epistemological foundations of these projects. In itself this was not new. Whenever the accumulation (and avoidance) of old taxes had to be replaced—as early as the "Single Whip" reform of the Ming dynasty, or whenever a ruler acquired a new territory—property surveys followed (recall the Domesday Book of William the Conqueror). Romanovs, Ottomans, and other monarchs needed to know their boundaries and their resources. Abbatial and manorial administrators, the trustees of Muslim pious foundations, Chinese gentry, and thereafter Italian and Dutch cities had to provide for public works and military expenditures. William Petty had pioneered efforts by means of "political arithmetick" to measure the wealth of the British kingdom in the late seventeenth century. The politics went on unabated; the arithmetic became more detailed. The brilliant mathematicians of the Bernoulli family, along with the French Huguenot Abraham de Moivre and later the German Carl Friedrich Gauss, developed the theoretical groundwork for statistical inference from the seventeenth into the nineteenth century, although governments clung to counting and eschewed sampling until the US Census of 2000. Censuses had ancient roots—Jesus had been born in the course of one—but they became far more widespread and important.[18]

The censuses were numbers fixed to territorial locations—mapped quantities. The eighteenth century had seen a proliferation of cadastres—maps of landholding and domains surveyed with an eye toward imposing taxes more systematically. Trigonometry and triangulation underlay the new techniques of measurement on the global surface as it had for celestial navigation. Rectangular grids provided the representation for locating the resources of specific sites. The British in Ireland and India undertook major geographical surveys of their still-colonial spaces; the Mexican states undertook geographical surveys as well. In 1877, President Porfirio Díaz established a cartographic commission to establish a master map, and chose a geographer who had experience in cadastral and geographic surveys, but the enterprise was underfunded and subject to imprecise local knowledge, and generally lagged behind the equivalent work carried out in British India or France. Still, its ambitions corresponded to the positivist hopes of the Porfirian state: modernization from above, clarification of property, of lines of communication, goals that by 1896 had shifted significantly from the military considerations that dominated when the project was begun.[19] Half a world away, among a Chinese administrative elite beset by intimations of weakness and decline, the geographer's impulse also served the desire for state strengthening as the researchers interested in "practical statecraft" turned to learning about the western regions as a Qing achievement in which to take pride (especially because control over the maritime frontier was dominated by foreigners). But real differentiation of a geographic focus had to await the Republican era, when Japanese territorial seizures focused attention on the threat, not just to sovereignty, but national space.[20]

Fixing people in space was crucial for control as well as for taxation or military defense. Foucault again emphasized the trend in Western societies to discipline social deviance by the confinement of vagrants and the insane.[21] By the New Poor Law of 1834, the British would establish the Workhouse, not the parish or village treasury, as the recourse for those who had no other support. More generally the new states depended upon fixed population: recall the defeat of the nomad challenge of the 1870s. James Scott's paean to the evasive tribes of the upland colonies of Southeast Asia is a testimony to their powers to move physically; running away or melting into dense forests and high mountains was sometimes the most effective strategy of resistance.[22] When migration was no longer possible, collective ownership might preserve a sort of countercultural capacity to white colonizers or middle-class development, although at the cost of conventional economic development. The capacity of indigenous peoples to shift their resource base and resist tethering to agricultural allotments they had the right to sell individually remained a fundamental challenge to the modern state. The United States, which had established and progressively reduced tribal reservation land, decided on a policy of allotment to individuals and families by the Dawes Act of 1887. This allowed further reduction of "excess" reservation land, and then a disaster for tribal society once unrestricted sales could take place. But society as a whole was intended to be counted, located, and surveyed, a task that Francis Amasa Walker, president of the Massachusetts Institute of Technology, made his own with the 1874 publication of the *Statistical Analysis of the United States,* a compendium of positivist social information based upon the 1870 Census, which he had directed. Ironically, the project of fixing abodes seemed urgent at the moment when mass migration from Europe to North and South America multiplied, at a time, too, when Chinese poured into Southeast Asia and, along with the Japanese, crossed Pacific shores. The new instrumentality of passports and labor booklets, as well as the agencies set up to inscribe the migrants, was the states' response.[23]

But consider again the new cartography. Perhaps its distinguishing feature, derived from the spatial imagination of the late nineteenth century, was the assignment of potential resources to the territorial grids. In this sense it matched the new understanding of electromagnetic physics developed at the same time by James Clerk Maxwell. Every point in physical space was a point in an energy field and could be assigned a proportional quantity of energy potential. So too in the emerging statistical counting every point had a quantity of human energy resources linked to it. The surveys and the censuses both counted them and assigned them a location. Thus nomadism and even collective rights of ownership—American Indian migrations and reservations in the US case—threatened the rationality of the modern state. On the other hand, immigration and the westward movement of the population enhanced the energy potential of previously empty areas. The empty areas of the United States, the Arid Regions, would also find their great cartographic description.[24]

Walker recognized that Americans did not like to be questioned and counted, but expressed confidence that in 1880 they had "outgrown the little, paltry, bigoted construction of the Constitution, which, in 1850, questioned in Congress the right of the people of the United States to learn whatever they might please to know regarding their own numbers, condition, and resources."[25] By 1900 the American Economic Association elected as its president Richard Ely, who rejected laissez-faire sociology and admired Bismarck's nascent welfare state in Germany. He was in sympathy with the president of Johns Hopkins, who brought German graduate education methods—specialized research in laboratories and seminars—to the United States. They spoke for experts, for quantitative knowledge, and for the state. They also represented a heightened role for gender differentiation. The engineering profession, then like other specializations developing their credentialing organizations and claiming expertise and status, was a career for men, although the Census hired women, who would soon become highly represented in the clerical profession.[26]

The military experience of the mid-century wars of reunification had shaped many of these men in an almost existential way. It had put their lives on the line at a formative age, made them serious, and tested manhood. Manliness was a critical theme of the last decades of the nineteenth century and the first one of the twentieth. In a book on the state it may seem excessive to speculate on the roles of male companionship and homoeroticism, but the themes surface—whether in big game hunting, the French and British military excursions into the interior of Africa, the menacing females of symbolist fin-de-siècle painting or, to take an achievement of naturalism, the rowers of Thomas Eakins. But if a subterranean temptation, such gender uncertainty was vigorously suppressed by rites of passage from which men such as Roosevelt and Eakins emerged. The unexamined life is not worth living, but in a pre-Freudian era the excessively examined life could seem paralyzing. Imperialism and masculine vigor beckoned as a vocation; white manliness was critical—to be formed in sports and hunting large animals in remote locations. A French nationalist, Pierre Coubertin, would organize the 1896 revival of the Olympic games; Robert Baden-Powell would found the Boy Scouts and encourage military expansion.

Two later monuments to Theodore Roosevelt celebrate the diverse themes flowing together. The visitor to Theodore Roosevelt Island, in the Potomac in Washington, DC, will come upon the oversize bronze orator with his aphorisms on tablets behind him—one of which ("The State") offers his precepts for political life. The visitor to the Museum of Natural History on Central Park West in Manhattan will also find TR, again in imperial bronze but now on horseback being led by an American

Indian in tribal regalia and a black African—a 1940 rendition by
James Earle Fraser, most famous for his noble but exhausted Indian on
horseback *(The End of the Trail).* The tourist who contemplates the
1898 bronze statue of the Meiji generation conservative Saigō Takimori
near Tokyo's Ueno railway station encounters the robust nationalist in
Samurai garb with his beloved dog. Saigō, too, was a military expansionist, hoping to provoke a war to conquer Korea in 1874. But he was
also a dyed-in-the-wool conservative, sometimes supporting but often
opposing the reforms that were transforming Japan in his lifetime
and finally persuaded to lead an unsuccessful uprising in 1877 that
cost him his life. TR rode up San Juan Hill, sought to regulate laissez-
faire celebration of capitalism, and pressed for American entrance into
the First World War. A generation apart, the Japanese dismayed by
modernity, the American embracing it, both were fulfilled by militant
nationalism.

"Teddy" exemplified the synthesis of vitalism, reform, and frank
imperialism. For all the volatility of this mix, it was still compatible
with the reorganized state's emphasis on measuring human resources.
In an age of social Darwinism this meant categorization by type as
well as by quantity. Racial typology emerged; the nascent criminology
depended on profiling by body type—an effort made most notorious
by Italian statistician Cesare Lombroso, who felt that earlobes revealed criminal types. Measuring made sense because of underlying
"type"—a preoccupation that at the end of the twentieth century
might be refined as the idea of "risk" as supposedly determined by
genetic factors. Mass migrations and the arrival of diverse ethnic
groups—whether the Irish in England and the United States, Italians
and Spaniards in France, southern and Eastern Europeans (including
the Jewish migrations from Russia and Galicia) in the United States,
Italians in Argentina, Chinese and Japanese in the American West,
the contract labor recruited for the colonial plantations of Malaya and
southeast Asia, or the Indians relocated to South Africa—meant a

confrontation with groups that sometimes seemed to bring unrest and crime and different physiques. In an era of economic expansion and industrialization, migration could not be halted, was necessary—but it required control and counting, and intensified inter-ethnic prejudices. Anti-Semitism became more virulent as one consequence, increased too by the economic adversity encountered by agricultural producers from 1873 to 1896, when deflationary pressure meant that financial interests—banks and ostensibly Jewish creditors—led to openly anti-Jewish agitation in Central and Eastern Europe, France, and the United States, as social discrimination became more prevalent. Wherever there were sizable numbers of middle-class migrants and merchants, vulnerability increased. Not that these prejudices halted the trends toward the mobility of peoples and capital; rather, they provided evidence that, short of major war, the geographic and social mobility would not be reversed. Migration and measurement increased together; the modern state could not halt the flows but it sought to classify them.

Time measurement was another project for the modernizing agenda. The development of east–west railroads made the problem critical. Sun time meant that watches had constantly to be adjusted for travel. Paris was 9 minutes and 20 seconds ahead of London, Bombay 41 minutes behind Madras. In 1884, representatives of governments, railroads, and organizations concerned with standardizing time met in Washington, DC, and Paris and demarcated the twenty-four time zones (each ideally 15 degrees of latitude although with variations for local land masses), within each of which the same time would prevail. All but the French agreed that the Greenwich Observatory near London, which served to anchor the Meridian or degree zero of longitude, might serve as the midpoint of Greenwich Mean Time, and twenty years later the French gave in. But stubborn reluctance persisted, worldwide, to abandoning the local time, usually reckoned by the sun's zenith, for the uniform hour imposed across the time zone. Local time was long-standing, governed working hours, and often was conspicuously displayed on public clocks. Where religious exercises, such as the five calls to prayer for faithful Muslims, were keyed to the divisions of daylight, which varied with the seasons, the coexistence of old and new time became even more complex. But to impose standard time was seen as modern and progressive. The effort preoccupied Sultan Abdülhamid II (1876–1908), who erected clock towers in key cities designed to send the empire's message to his "Well Protected Domains," a measure perceived by traditionalists as another example of his despotic centralization of power.[27]

Governing by Party

Governing was different from governmentality. The French said, "to govern was to choose." Ultimately decisions had to be made or fudged, which meant, as it still does, essentially postponed until they were resolved incrementally. Today's neologism, *governmentality,* curiously enough, has sometimes implied that to govern wisely was not to have to choose. Such prized public outcomes in the early twentieth century as "national efficiency" or "the one best way" might emerge as a result of knowledge, not electoral contests. Science, technology, or the psychology of human manipulation would allow a painless form of government that was self-justifying. Legitimacy supposedly would flow from the wisdom of the result, not from the process by which it was enacted— the old dream of rule by philosopher-kings, but now philosopher-technicians. But despite this dream, continually refreshed by different generations of social thinkers—even today, as we shall see in conclusion— policies had to be decided, states had to be governed. Would railroads be built? Were armies and naval forces to be expanded? Until what age and under whose auspices would children be schooled? What prerogatives might traditional religious establishments retain? So how were choices made?

In theory at least, the new states created at midcentury, like the ones constructed earlier, were countries in which representative assemblies played a large role. Piedmont and Italy, Austria, Germany, and Japan had introduced them between 1848 and 1890. Other old empires were holdouts: Russia claimed to be an autocracy, and a parliament was introduced only during the revolutionary turmoil of 1905; the Ottoman Empire established a parliament in 1908, Iran after its revolution in 1906, China in 1912. With few exceptions only males could vote on the national level before World War I. Until 1885 in Britain, property qualifications narrowed the suffrage, and varying forms of tax requirements helped keep peasants and proletarians from exercising any sort of proportional voting rights in many areas of Europe and the United States. In the kingdom of Hungary, the suffrage was rigged to keep non-Magyars (and poor ones too) from achieving parliamentary representation. So too the American South excluded black voters by virtue of poll taxes and literacy requirements (also used in Italy until 1912). Southern Europe, parts of Latin America, and the southern United States might best be described as areas in which political argumentation played itself out within a racially pure ruling class that dominated regional and sometimes national legislatures. Sometimes, if even this pattern of privileged parliamentarism seemed too fragile to prevent the advance of popular claimants, private violence could easily be organized: atrocities against Armenians in the Ottoman Empire, lynching in the old Confederate states, and Cossack pogroms against Jewish settlements in 1890–1910 might ensure that challengers to newly refurbished "traditions" were cowed into submission. Thus reinforced by occasional exemplary violence, the structures of domination allowed a parliamentary oratory to flourish, replete with glorious defenses of liberty, appeals to national and regional pride, and defense of the highly inegalitarian social status quo.

The discrepancy between words and deeds also afflicted those parliaments that more adequately reflected popular classes and opinions, as in France and the United States. No matter how broad the suffrage, the parliaments were dogged by corruption. The public financing of railroad lines, the speculative real estate booms in the expanding capital and industrial cities, the fusion of old agricultural elites with the new wealth of industry and finance and their search for compliant legislators meant that the parliamentary politics of the late 1870s through the 1890s was riddled with scandal. Typical disorders included Tammany Hall—the Democratic Party "machine" in New York—and other US political cliques, the French corruption associated with the selling of honors from the president's office and with the bribery used by the Panama canal development company, bank scandals in Italy, and payoffs by colonial interests.

The institution that dominated the systems of government was one that written constitutions would not explicitly mention until the mid-twentieth century in Germany, that is, the competitive political party. (Single parties inscribed themselves earlier.) The party was an association of individuals and the groups who stood behind them dedicated to governing on the basis of shared principles, material interests, and just for the sake of holding power and keeping opponents out of office. "Party" interests existed in the ancient world and in the city-state republics of medieval Europe, but they often could not agree on policy without proscription, assassination, and civil war. In the modern era, the point of parties was precisely to settle affairs, often by a principle of alternation in power, without the need for repeated imprisonment, exile, and political murder. In its modern career, party originated in the postrevolutionary regimes of Britain in the late seventeenth and eighteenth centuries and in the former American colonies in the 1780s and 1790s, sometimes as rival associations of elites who claimed to be the legitimate heirs of a profound historical transformation. Rulers and those who felt excluded from such associations often saw the constellations of adversaries as cabals or conspiracies. Distinguishing party from conspiracy was perhaps the signal achievement of Anglo-American government in the hundred years from 1720 to 1820. That distinction meant that men might disagree over policies—war or peace, favoring of landed or commercial interests, defending or diminishing the claims of religious institutions, imposing taxation or not—without seeing each other as traitors or usurpers.

This distinction did not come easily: in periods of acute turmoil it was hard to accept that the opposition did not intend to betray the state and its vital interests. A war for independence, as in North America, usually created a body of "patriots," and when their common adversary was no longer present and they differed among each other, suspicions of sell-out and betrayal were hard to overcome. The United States overcame a major hurdle when in 1800 it was recognized that one group of former revolutionaries had emerged to challenge another, and took over major offices without a protest or civil strife. The French Revolution got to this stage only after an interval of dictatorial rule by violence (frankly called Terror) in supposed defense of democratic principles against domestic and foreign enemies. The weakened institutions established to prevent such a recurrence—the so-called Directory from 1795 to 1799—suffered repeated coups and canceled elections until finally overthrown by military conspiracy that installed Napoleon with increasing dictatorial prerogatives. The British rulers of the same period used political trials to establish conservative conformity and subdue those sympathetic to the French radicals with whom they were at war. The United States seemed ready to go down that route briefly before the elections of 1800 arrested the process. Gradually party was seen as the key instrument, not only of achieving political rule, but of limiting political violence. It was a key invention of the modern state.

Party as an instrument of government advanced in a major way in the late nineteenth century, and the United States seemed to be the key innovator. Whereas in the mid-nineteenth century in Britain or the early years of the French Third Republic, parties seemed to fission and dissolve, certainly between elections, by the 1870s and 1880s they developed into continuing associations, managed often by professionals with permanent offices, and as important for local politics as for national politics. Political "machines" came to be the major force for organizing arenas where the suffrage was wide and cut across diverse classes and interests. Tammany Hall was renowned as the Democratic Party machine that organized the immigrant vote in New York City. The Birmingham Caucus of Joseph Chamberlain emerged by the 1890s. Sociologists such as Max Weber and the Russian Moisei Ostrogorski studied the American political machine with great interest. The party manager and professional appeared to be a new type; the American primary or British "caucus," a disturbing nonconstitutional innovation that had the potential to corrupt disinterested government. Roberto Michels, a German-Italian student of Weber, argued that parties of the left were all the more prone to entrench oligarchies within their own ranks.[28]

The British- and American-style parties spread to the continent. By the late 1860s party was becoming important in Bismarck's Customs Union Parliament (Zollparlament) and North German Confederation—his institutional way-stations between the defeat of Austria in 1866 and the German Empire founded in 1871. Catholics, concentrated in Bavaria and the Rhineland and Prussian Silesia, feared being dominated in a Protestant state once Austria no longer had a voice in Central European government. They coalesced and soon formed a "Center Party" to defend their interests. Although persecuted by anticlerical legislation, they would soon become a mainstay of government in the German Empire, thereafter the Weimar Republic, and even the German Federal Republic after 1949. Ideologically flexible, they could form coalitions with conservatives to their right or liberals to their left. On the left of the spectrum, German Social Democrats had diverse origins. Ferdinand Lasalle founded the formal party in 1869 to compete in the Bismarckian state; Marxists comprised one strand, but not the only one. Swinging from his decade-long hostility to Catholic political organization (the so-called *Kulturkampf* or struggle over civilization), which had been combined with a reliance on nationalist liberal support, Bismarck decided to outlaw the Social Democrats in 1878, after an assassination attempt on the emperor, and to govern on the basis of a coalition of Catholics and Conservatives. Only after the old chancellor's dismissal by William II in 1890 could the Social Democratic Party (SPD) reemerge legally—to become by 1912 the largest group in the Reichstag—intent no longer on revolution in the streets but on capturing power in the parliament. Austrian Social Democrats followed suit. French Socialists remained divided between different ideological strands, but were urged by the International to merge and did so as the French Section of the Workers' International Party (SFIO) in 1905. Meanwhile the French non-Socialist left had organized itself as the Radical Socialist Party in 1901 (it was fairly centrist) as a consequence of the Dreyfus affair. Parties usually had an official daily paper or at least a newspaper that tended to support their views and interpretations. Increasingly candidates for office had to be approved by the central office or, as in the United States, by a system of conventions.

The reality of political parties was disturbing to many. Again Weber made a contrast between an old style of politics where eminent leaders offered their services at elections *(Honoratiorenpolitik),* and the new one of mass politics where party government with its backroom deals and professional organization really took government in hand. By the first decade of the new century, party government seemed to be the inevitable product of modern "mass society," by which was meant not a revolutionary or socialist movement, but the dominance of the anonymous urban citizenry, working often in clerical and retail jobs and swayed by irrational appeals to national glory. Corruption seemed to go naturally with this view of a mass society governed by highly organized political parties. Was it democracy?

Parties could function in different ways. In Latin America they perpetuated some of the divisions that persisted after the wars of independence from Spain. Confrontations of centralist conservatives and liberal federalists (the advocates of limited centralization and more extensive regional powers) often produced coups d'état (*pronunciamentos* or *golpes*) and periods of harsh violence. The presence of strong military leaders fed this tendency. Political parties, whether in Chile, Colombia, Mexico, or Argentina, in sum remained frozen in a situation of continuing potential civil war, as had obtained long ago in the Roman Republic. In most other arenas, however, parties were content to share out the spoils of governing. In this case parties might be nominally distinct but rather similar in terms of ideology and social support. In Spain, for instance, Antonio Cánovas, the conservative prime minister who finally brought the civil wars and coups d'état of 1868–1873 under control, helped work out a monarchical restoration under whose terms liberals and conservatives agreed to alternative power with each four-year parliamentary session. This *turno politico* really meant politics was directed by a rather narrow governing class. Italy remained committed to parliamentary government; it was accepted that the monarch would choose as a prime minister only a leader who could assemble a majority in the lower house—a consensual arrangement challenged before the advent of interwar fascism only briefly from 1898–1900. The heirs to the unifiers, the expansive Liberal Party, had leaders and wings respectively more or less committed to suffrage reform and broadening the tax base, who held power at different times. Ideological challengers on the left (originally republicans and radicals and later socialists) or on the right (new strident nationalists) were largely marginalized. In Hungary, after the great constitutional settlement that provided autonomy in 1867 (the Ausgleich), liberals also dominated although conservative challengers were important in debate. Japanese constitutional government was imported gradually by the aging Meiji oligarchs (the Genrō). In 1890 they adopted a

German-style constitution that bestowed a limited role on a new Diet. After an unruly beginning, the emerging post-Meiji generation produced a rudimentary political differentiation among the elite and two party associations, Kenseito and Seiyukai, that were oriented around rival leaders.

Such systems functioned as oligarchies, good for sharing patronage in normal times but prone to breakdown. The elites in Hungary, Italy, and Argentina tended to envision themselves as a sort of idealized mid-nineteenth-century British ruling class, cultivated and deferred to. But like their counterparts in Britain, they found their cozy politics challenged by bitter personal rivalries and the emerging challenges of working-class demands, and the popular passions of foreign policy that they sought to manipulate in their favor. Systems of nominal alternation (as in Spain), single-party electoral domination (as in the American South), or continued absorption of earlier opposition groups ("transformism," as in Italy), required large reservoirs of consistently loyal voters responsive to favors, personal fealty, or ethnic allegiances. American Southern Democrats and Hungarian or Italian liberals were thus hardly liberal—they were the leaders of political oligarchies who hoped to preserve power without wrenching changes. Early welfare legislation, such as that introduced by Bismarck in Germany in the 1880s and then advanced by the left and many occupational groups, became a major cause for political division, though more so in other countries where it enjoyed less conservative patronage, as did new land and income taxes. As controversies over social legislation grew, the issue of widening the franchise became important. Italian politics functioned because masses of the southern peasantry could not vote because of the literacy requirement. England faced harsh issues of whether Ireland should achieve home rule. New and ambitious political leaders decided they could prevail by more-ideological appeals to the masses. The mayor of Vienna, Karl Lueger, was successful in building a machine of Christian Socials, who claimed to govern Austria for the popular classes against the reactionaries and the nefarious Jews. Anti-Semitism and other ethnic appeals became more strident.

The difficulty was that toward the end of the century in the West, the old politics seemed increasingly under stress. On the one hand, the spread of industrialism—of labor in mines and factories and with machines—created an activist working class. It moved all sorts of occupational safety and pension issues into the forefront of politics. Even more disturbing was the emergence by the twentieth century of parties with new total claims, who did not believe they should share power, such as the Committee for Union and Progress in Turkey and the Russian Bolsheviks. After the revolution of 1908 in the Ottoman Empire, the Young Turks, as the revolutionaries were dubbed, preached a restoration of ethnic Turkish domination. It was hard to organize the slow-moving, clientelistic decentralized empire with such a force.

But even when parties seemed to function smoothly, the contrast between the rhetoric of liberal parliamentarism and its shabby reality ensured that a harsh critical analysis would emerge. By the 1880s trenchant critiques of democracy were emerging from the European Right with Italian writers taking the lead. (The term *Right* is chosen because the writers scorned government by liberalism or discussion in favor of rule by elites and also believed that an emerging social democracy was really just another hypocritical claim to exercise bureaucratized power.) These new critics from the Right no longer invoked the old traditions of the Church or praised paternalist and wise elites, as had conservatives almost a century earlier. Instead they pointed to the discrepancy between liberal ideals and corrupt reality to suggest that elites had always and would always rule, no matter what the nominal form of the government. Pasquale Turiello argued that the continuing poverty of the Italian south proved that liberal government had failed the masses; Italy needed instead a great new national cause, perhaps a new war, to ensure national solidarity. Gaetano Mosca's *Theory of the*

Governed (1881) argued that the masses could never rule; elites would always be in charge. Vilfredo Pareto, teaching economics at the University of Lausanne in Switzerland, and known today for his statistical concepts, was the most cynical: his *Socialist Systems* (1902) argued that for all their claims on behalf of democratic reform, the Socialists were just a new elite advancing a Marxist ideology designed to ensure their own narrow rule. Mussolini briefly attended his lectures. The once republican poet Giosuè Carducci attacked the supposed reality of the new state and evoked the vultures flying over Rome.[29]

French writers also contributed to the new antidemocratic critiques and added to them an extreme nationalism and anti-Semitism. The French Right learned that even in an age of mass suffrage, a populist nationalism could win them votes: General Georges Boulanger at the end of the 1880s ran and won in several of the parliamentary districts. His adherents wanted him to seize power, but he lost his nerve and fled to Brussels, where he committed suicide. Still, the episode testified to the role that nationalism could play. The success, too, of Edmond Drumont's rabble-rousing anti-Semitic newspaper revealed the power of prejudice and demagogy. The Panama Scandal of the early 1890s, and the Dreyfus affair—in which a Jewish army officer was repeatedly prosecuted for espionage even after it was clear that he had been framed—ignited a broad-based distrust of Jews. Maurice Barrès suggested in his novel *The Uprooted* and other writings that the Republican system and the influx of foreigners, among them French Jews, were corrupting the village virtues on which French history had been built. Charles Maurras's Action Française, a movement and a newspaper, violently attacked Jews, extolled military nationalism, and urged that an authoritarian monarch replace the Republic, which he habitually referred to as "the slut" *(la gueuse).* Although the Right lost national elections in 1898 and 1905, they became fashionable purveyors of doctrine among students and made many inroads in the national capital.

By the late 1870s nationalism manifested itself as a doctrine aspiring more to territorial aggrandizement than to linguistic or communal self-determination. This transformation of an ideology that had accompanied liberal and revolutionary aspirations into a set of xenophobic attitudes by which antiliberal leaders sought to organize mass constituencies was a fundamental development of the late nineteenth century. Poles might aspire to recover a national state wiped off the map a century earlier. Within the Austro-Hungarian Empire there were still champions of ethnic self-determination and even secession. But nationalism no longer manifested itself in Western Europe as a romantic enthusiasm for grouping the members of a language group or an ancient territory. After all, Germany and Italy had already achieved unity and Romania, Bulgaria, and Serbia were recognized as sovereign nation-states. Their imagined communities were no longer imagined; they (or their nationalist elites) were merely dissatisfied with the territory they currently held. Even Austria-Hungary seemed to settle into a constitutional equilibrium that satisfied Hungarians as well as Germans.

The economic strains of the era from 1873 to 1896 also intensified national competition. The growth of grain imports from the Western Hemisphere—the United States, Canada, and Argentina—after the American Civil War and the expansion of continent-wide railroad systems meant stagnant or depressed prices for farmers and intensified the sense of national competition for markets. The absence of new gold discoveries between 1849 and 1896, in an age when currencies were being keyed to gold and the United States was "redeeming" its paper currency from the Civil War, meant a deflationary pressure on prices for over two decades, which in turn made credit dearer for farmers. National tariffs imposed on imported grains, and on behalf of domestic manufacturers, seemed the logical answer and also allowed logrolling bargains between the spokesmen for farmers and for industry. The Republican Party in the United States had urged and inaugurated tariff protection since its inception in the 1850s; Bismarck instituted a tariff in 1879, and it was significantly raised under his nationalist successors in 1897. The duties provided needed revenue at the national level, but also facilitated cooperation between rye growers and industrialists who were often arrayed in hostile parties: Conservatives and National Liberals. But not only the Right passed tariffs: the incoming coalition of the Left in Italy sought to confirm its power by passing a protective tariff in 1882, and the centrist coalition in France would pass its first tariff on foreign grains in 1892. Only Great Britain resisted tariffs in the last decades of the nineteenth century; and Britain certainly did not resist the other great trend that intensified the sense of national competition—the search for exclusive colonial domains.

The Colonizing State and the Colonial State

What does the great scramble to partition Africa and Asia and seize exclusive territorial domains overseas tell us about the state? We discuss the pattern of domination established overseas, the colonial state, below. But was the state of the colonizers decisively impacted by the experience of imperialism? How did acquisition of an overseas empire change the European, Japanese, or American regime? The question is not easy to answer. Max Weber asked in the 1890s what significance German political unification would possess if the country did not go on to develop an overseas empire.[30] Late nineteenth-century expansion followed upon the satisfaction taken throughout Europe in national success and power that followed the preceding period of nation-state construction but then seemed necessary to confirm it. For a few decades at midcentury, acquisition of overseas territory seemed less compelling than earlier or later. The British had acquired the Cape Colony at the Congress of Vienna. The French invaded Algeria in 1830. At midcentury British policy makers expressed no great urge to expand their political domains, since their economic prowess as bankers and manufacturers seemed to ensure their easy superiority in markets and states overseas. By the 1870s, competition—political and economic—was perceived as harsher and pervasive, so that by the 1880s and 1890s remaining territory was quickly arrogated.

Historians a generation ago could easily demonstrate that there was no master plan, no timetable, and even, they suggested, no intention. The British Empire was supposedly created, so John Robert Seeley had written in his influential 1883 lectures, *The Expansion of England,* in "a fit of absence of mind." Hardly: the tracks were laid—empire had been the aspiration of large states throughout history; the wars of 1850–1870 showed that power and territory were important. Napoleon III was muscling into Vietnam and even seeking to conquer Mexico. Disraeli and other conservatives signaled the need actually to control land masses (and the people that went with them). Seeley cautiously affirmed the imperial vocation and its beneficial impact on the lands London ruled, and vast areas of Asia and Africa beckoned. The great rivers that ran from their remote interiors to the sea—the Nile, the Niger, the Congo, the Zambezi in Africa, and the Mekong and Irrawaddy in Southeast Asia—allowed European gunboats to penetrate far inland, just as earlier the Saint Lawrence, the Hudson, the Mississippi, Orinoco, and Amazon had opened up the Americas, and even earlier the oceans had allowed overseas exploration. Against his supposed intention, Prime Minister Gladstone intervened in Alexandria and Cairo in 1882 to enforce the claims of British bondholders who had financed construction of the Suez Canal. By the 1890s British troops were conquering the Sudan hundreds of miles up river ostensibly to quell the disorder that always broke out beyond their last line of penetration.

A year before the British seizure of Egypt, the French moved east from Algeria to take over Tunisia—nominally a remote province of the Ottomans, but in fact a quasi state where Jewish and Italian traders lived among the Bedouin and Arab populations—and the competitive consuls of France, Italy, and Britain sought to interest their governments in seizing control. The French moved first, from Algeria, and established a protectorate by the Treaty of Bardo in 1881, which angered the Italians, who had their eyes on this prize across the Mediterranean. French expansion in Africa depended less on river routes. Like the Muslim conquerors of earlier centuries, they knew how to expand across the vast dry lands of the Sahara and Sahel, relying on oases and a tough corps of mercenary soldiers—the French Foreign Legion—as well as their own colorful detachments of Zouaves. In the decades from the 1830s to 1890s they took over a large Central African domain, from Senegal and the Ivory Coast to Chad, then turned toward an "inkblot" strategy of penetrating the sultanate of Morocco in the new century. The Russians also penetrated an inland terrain: the khanates of the Caucasus and of the Oxus River highlands of Central Asia. Ultimately by the 1880s the Italians would establish a foothold on the East Coast of Africa, first in Somalia and Eritrea, and then would endeavor unsuccessfully (until 1935–1936) to subjugate Ethiopia. Ambitious Meiji statesmen eyed the poor and isolated Korean kingdom as well as the Manchurian littoral. American overseas ambitions excited the owners of sugar plantations in Hawai'i and fruit plantations in Central America (as before the Civil War they had stimulated cotton plantation owners in the deep South) and the fervent Presbyterians who wanted their gospel spread and women educated throughout Asia.

The years 1882–1885 comprised a crucial period of commitment to "the scramble." The stories of remote missionaries in the interior or ambitious national claimants on the coast helped create a favorable opinion for intervention at home. Bismarck, always a continental thinker, had little use for African colonies but decided it was easier to yield to the nationalist enthusiasm and his explorers' faits accomplis. Germany moved into Togo and Cameroon on the West Coast, the large territory of Southwest Africa (today's Namibia), and a swath of East Africa (today's Tanzania). The Berlin Conference of 1884–1885 also adjusted boundary claims for the coastal colonies and in effect confirmed the partition of coastal black Africa as a European cooperative project, just as the Congress of Berlin seven years earlier had established the recognition of states at the expense of the retreating Ottoman Empire as a project under Western European tutelage. Whereas the 1878 Congress of Berlin had sought to regularize the claims of newly emerging nations at the expense of a weakened but venerable Ottoman sovereign, the 1884 Berlin Conference was an effort for Europeans to expand without internecine warfare in a region they deemed to be devoid of sovereign claimants. The later National Socialist legal theorist, Carl Schmitt—we will return to his cold-blooded lucidity later—was at least partially correct when he described the international law that arose from the conference (as it had earlier from other colonial arbitrations) as a project designed to ensure European despoliation without conflict. What happened in the vast interior escaped control. Vast territories, supposedly ceded to European agents by indigenous chiefs, fell into a hazy legal status between commercial control and state sovereignty. In the months before and after the conference, Leopold II, king of Belgium, won American and then British recognition to transform his Association Internationale Africaine (AIA) into the Congo Free State, which his uncontrolled managers transformed into a gigantic tropical gulag devoted to the excruciating harvesting of rubber from the tall vines of the jungle. This scandalous behavior in what was virtually Leopold's personal colonial domain finally led the other European powers to compel its takeover by the Belgian state in 1908. In the interim the French and British carved up the huge regions of West Africa, Germans established colonies on both coasts, the Portuguese pressed inward from their old coastal outposts, and British settlers and generals reached the central great lakes from north and south. Thousands of miles of frontiers were drawn and adjusted. Leviathan 2.0, so laboriously reconstructed in its ancient, settled habitations, could allow itself fantastic windfalls of appropriation.[31]

At the same time the French, who a century earlier had withdrawn from India, now under Napoleon III pressed for outposts in the wealthy Southeast Asian states of today's Vietnam. Vietnam had a stormy history of kingdoms that at times recognized the nominal overlordship of the Chinese emperors, but then had revolted and insisted on their own independence. Consider for a moment the welter of states around the Indian Ocean, the Bay of Bengal, and the South China Sea. Here lay the region of the globe that, from the fifteenth century to the twentieth, was most saturated—or at least on a par with the middle of Europe between France and Russia—by claims of sovereignty, sometimes overlapping, sometimes fiercely exclusive, usually contested. Mughal, Portuguese, British, and French imperial claims impinged on a succession of sultanates and monarchies and overlapping religious loyalties—Muslim, Buddhist, and Christian. Mughal sovereignty decomposed during the eighteenth and mid-nineteenth centuries; London's claims expanded in the West and East as British agents pushed from India into Singapore, Malaya, and lowland Burma by the 1840s, and into the highlands by the 1880s, all the while consolidating their hold on the west of India (today's Pakistan) and its northwest territories. Between the late 1850s and early 1860s, the French secured new extraterritorial enclaves in China and took over Cochin China (southern Vietnam), then in the 1880s absorbed Annam in the center and, after war with China, Tonkin in the north, as well as Laos and Cambodia in the western interior of the Mekong River watershed. Thailand preserved its independent monarchy because it served as a buffer between the two expanding European powers and perspicacious monarchs pushed through a sustained course of institutional reforms. The Dutch, who had outposts in Sumatra and Java (including the settlement of Batavia, today's Jakarta), pressed east across the Indonesian archipelago, finally subduing the Bali monarchy in 1906.

Meanwhile the United States opted for a course of annexations from the late 1890s: American sugar planters helped engineer a takeover of the Hawai'ian monarchy between 1893 and 1900, and although Democratic president Grover Cleveland resisted annexation, William McKinley supported the local planters. The 1898 war with Spain yielded a protectorate over Cuba and the cession of the Philippine archipelago as well as island bases on the routes to China. China was too huge and developed to be taken over, but Europeans and the ambitious Japanese secured territorial enclaves with rights to impose their own legal jurisdictions. Rivalries moved to the northeast Pacific region by the mid-1890s, in part because the feeble Korean state became the objective of Chinese, Japanese, and Russian ambitions. China viewed Korea as a tributary kingdom; Japan moved to claim trading rights and undermine Beijing's residual suzerainty. By the summer of 1894 a familiar escalation of incidents led to war between China and Japan, with the surprising victory of the latter. As a result of its victory, Japan annexed the island of Formosa (Taiwan), imposed a massive indemnity upon Beijing, and secured recognition of their rights in Korea, which it would add formally to its overseas possessions in 1910. Their initial annexation of Port Arthur and the Liaodong Peninsula had to be renounced in the face of French, German, and primarily Russian pressure, the so-called Triple Intervention. St. Petersburg would itself "lease" Port Arthur in 1898; the British and Germans would secure new enclaves on the Shandong Peninsula, Jiaozhou and Weihaiwei. These events hastened the anti-foreign turbulence in a beset China, where the nationalist societies known as Boxers mobilized in Shandong and by the summer of 1900 besieged the foreign legations and missionaries in Beijing. The Dowager Empress Cixi, who had reversed reformist initiatives and imprisoned the young emperor in 1898, threw in her lot with the Boxers, but the Chinese and Manchu generals divided over what stance to take. An eight-nation expeditionary force of up to about 50,000 European, Japanese, and US soldiers crushed the revolt, suppressed the societies, and imposed another indemnity on the hapless court. Who might represent the nation in this huge but possibly decomposing polity: a Manchu court torn between traditionalists and reformers? or nationalists angered by a feckless dynasty and apparently rapacious foreigners?

These were momentous developments that came thick and fast and of course provoked major debates about causation as well as policy. Within a few decades, European states joined by Japan and the United States had claimed the right to rule hundreds of millions of people throughout Asia and Africa. The area they enclosed and bordered was many times the size in area of their own national territories, and it was often ceded in dubious and coerced claims. From one viewpoint, colonial territories were acquired as strategic resources for their imperial states in the struggle against other imperial states. Until recently those who wrote that history had not paid much attention to what was happening within the societies being subjugated and reorganized. They have focused on the confrontations and transactions among the colonizers, and for generations they have argued as to whether economic or political causation was fundamental.

Marxian notions in particular aroused efforts at refutation from diplomatic historians who stressed either traditional political rivalries or sometimes the role of missionaries—a dispute that was caught up in the greater ideological confrontations of the Cold War. Marx, and after him Rosa Luxemburg and other theorists, maintained that the falling rate of profit at home led to the search for more profitable investment abroad in areas still predominantly nonindustrialized. Thereafter, states or monopoly enterprises—sometimes combinations of banks and industry fused in what Social Democratic theorist Rudolf Hilferding called finance capital—would press their states to establish exclusive zones for their own advantage. After the outbreak of

Foreign penetration of China, ca. 1900.

World War I, the Russian Bolshevik leader in exile, V. I. Lenin, claimed that imperialism was in fact just the highest stage of capitalism and would have to lead to a major war.[32]

A related view suggests that governing elites adopted programs of imperialism because their societies were increasingly racked by social division at home and they calculated that expansion might divert domestic conflict into foreign adventures. Hans Ulrich Wehler's study of Bismarck's imperialism a generation ago argued that the chancellor's acceptance of colonialism placed his licensing of colonies in the framework of a German state under the stresses of industrialization.[33] Certainly many advocates of empire, some of them on the right but not all, looked to empire precisely to counteract doctrines of class conflict. British Tories, such as Alfred Milner, wanted a program of social imperialism, as did charismatic pastor Friedrich Naumann of the German Progressive Party. Italian imperialists and nationalists such as Enrico Corradini suggested that their own working class should recognize that Italy was itself a proletarian nation and fall into line behind the industrialists and intellectuals who wanted to advance the agenda of empire and military preparedness.

Not all Marxist theories had to lead like Lenin's to the notion that such imperialist rivalry had to culminate in a great war. Karl Kautsky proposed that imperialist powers might arrive at a "super-imperialism" or peaceful partition of the colonial world. Kautsky's argument suggested in fact the perspective that has become the major approach in the last few decades' study of colonial empires, namely, that we should interpret imperialism not as the extension of European rivalries but as a common European confrontation with the Third World. This point of view suggested that colonialism could be understood as a common enterprise of the advanced states and economies in the Northern Hemisphere with respect to the less resistant states in Asia, Africa, the Caribbean, and the Pacific.

The notion that the colonizers confronted the colonized in some encompassing global binary relationship, more important than the nationalist rivalries that divided them, has in fact emerged as a dominant interpretation of the imperialist era. Social segregation, sexual exploitation, and political disenfranchisement lay at the base of the colonial relationship, in this view. But not only in the colonies: European institutions, concepts of citizenship, gender relations, and labor, it has been argued, were shaped decisively by Europe's experience as colonizer, just as the world of the indigenous inhabitants was structured by the experience of being colonized. To expand from the Indian historiography of "subaltern studies," all relationships were supposedly stunted by the experience of colonial subjection. Subsequent scholarship has suggested that this framework perhaps involves too radical a confrontation of colonizer and colonized and thus perhaps makes the experience of the colonized too passive and homogeneous.[34] The colonial territory offered the colonizing power natural resources, minerals, and agricultural goods, and specifically tropical assets that his constricted and colder territories at home could not provide. And the colonized subject essentially offered labor power at costs far below what domestic workers imposed and sometimes with less quarrelsome attitudes. Eventually they could bargain with their masters and extract concessions that by the mid-twentieth century would undermine the colonial relationship.[35] But that stage was hardly anticipated in the late nineteenth century.

Beyond the resources of territory and inexpensive labor, beyond any pride in a civilizing mission, the colonizing state provided status and prestige. Small powers along with large powers felt a sense of mission. The architecture of an imperial capital made aesthetic claims. The massive ministries of Justice and Foreign Affairs in Brussels testified to the fact that a small power controlled vast overseas resources. In the case of Belgium, moreover, the overseas mission helped cement the two linguistic communities: the French Walloons staffed the colonial bureaucracies at home; the Flemish took up office in Africa. Empire did provide a dividend of cohesiveness and grandeur as long as one did not have to fight a long war to preserve it. Britain and France did extract from their dependent populations loyalties they could draw on in the two world wars ahead. For better or worse the colonizing state could never be just an agency for providing domestic services at home. Whether this was valuable or instead the source of needless violence and illusory grandeur cannot be decided by adding up the costs and benefits. For a country such as Portugal, the empire may well have provided an excuse not to modernize and to remain less developed. By the mid-twentieth century the costs appeared excessive for many citizens of Britain and France.

As for the colonial state—that is, the regime put into place to govern the large territory and diverse populations taken over—it rested on particular sets of institutions and processes. To seek one model is misleading, because the administrations used in the regions of sub-Saharan Africa, for instance, where wealth derived from mining and the authorities ruled over many different "tribes," differed from those in settler colonies with significant European populations and in the post-1919 states carved out of Ottoman regions. Nonetheless, some commonalities existed, and the admittedly overabstracted colonial state remained a dominant force over vast areas of the world in a period of increasing stateness and governmentality. Africa retained only four sovereign countries by 1895: the ancient kingdom of Ethiopia, Liberia, the white Boer Republics of South Africa, and Morocco. The Boers would have to accept inclusion in the British Union of South Africa and the Moroccans would become a French colony by 1912. Complex confederations had contested Africa since earlier eras but fell to European rule: the Asante kingdom in Ghana, the Buganda kingdom, Shaka's Zulu state, and Samouri Touré's Wassoulu empire in Mali as late as the 1880s. Less extensive tribal communities had negotiated their trading and their security for centuries with the European settlers of the coast and river valleys. A poor and weak Korea, once the source of so much Japanese culture and nominally in a tributary relationship with China, was taken over by the Japanese between 1905 and 1910. The mini-kingdoms of Oceania would also be annexed, as would the Caribbean states. In Central Asia, Iran and Afghanistan evaded annexation if not great political pressure.

The colonial state was run by administrators or proconsuls who had vast amounts of discretionary power. They were expected, however, to cover their costs of administration, if not, as in India, to send a stream of payments back home; and most of their meager budgets went to police and measures designed for security. They could not simply govern without reference to the indigenous peoples whose labor they needed and respect they demanded, so generally they administered through favored intermediaries. Mahmood Mamdani stresses that in Africa the state became bifurcated: into rural areas where the British ruled through chiefs, and urban areas where they had to confront a more complex social scale.[36] The rural chain of command amounted to a new form of despotism; colonial rule elsewhere had to become more subtle and, in effect, a series of transactions made by co-opting native intermediaries. There was a major distinction between tribal societies where political forms were not readily recognizable to the European conquerors, on the one hand, and the subordinate sultanates of the Dutch East Indies or the extraterritorial enclaves in China, on the other. The term *colonial state* takes us only so far in understanding the structure of the British Raj—that huge possession of the crown (including today's Pakistan and Bangladesh)—where London administered a major portion through Calcutta, the Madras and Bombay presidencies, and almost five hundred rulers as successor to the Mughals whose hold on the north of the subcontinent had evaporated as the British moved west from Bengal and added to the disintegrative momentum.[37] Still, a colonial regime it was: by 1900 the Indian Civil

Service comprised about a thousand administrators, of which about forty were Indian, no surprise since the entrance exams were given in Britain. Of the related administrative corps, about half of the approximately ten thousand were Indian or Anglo-Indian, but in the lower-paying ranks. The local courts and counsels were opening to Indians—although the British resisted trial under Indian judges.[38] Sovereignty, foreign policy, command of the army, and the monetary system remained in British hands. Europeans confronted the Indians, the Chinese whom they controlled, and the Southeast Asians with both contempt for their subordination and fascination with their culture and artifacts. Europeans tended to divide between those who believed the natives were children and potentially rebels, and those who for humanitarian, religious, cultural, or other reasons respected their civilization. This led to clashes among policy makers and administrators. The tough-minded who counseled sternness (often the military but not always) had contempt for the naive liberal native sympathizers who would undermine colonial rule by "the series of ineffectual compromises . . . the lamentable vacillations in facing open sedition or veiled rebellion."[39]

Africa was a study literally in black and white, although even there colonial rulers drew distinctions and lines, just as the technocrats of immigration did in America. The British encountered noble warriors (Masai), tall and attractive, versus bulkier West Africans; likewise they separated martial races in the Punjab (Sikhs) from the darker-skinned Tamils; the Belgians ascribed differences to the Hutu and Tutsi, which would lead to catastrophe many decades after their colonial rule collapsed in Rwanda. To be sure, what was taking place in the colonies ran in parallel with the reinforcement of racism in the colonizing societies, as Jim Crow legislation was imposed in the United States from the 1890s on, as old-stock Americans reacted to the new Japanese and Chinese labor and even to the Eastern European (Catholic and Jewish) migrants. For many in Europe the emerging proletariat

In charge of empire: George Nathaniel, Lord Curzon, in his regalia as viceroy of India (1898–1905). Curzon was a staunch defender of the British presence in India, with all its ceremonial grandeur, and was convinced that Britain and Russia were destined for a contest of empires—"the great game"—in Persia and Central Asia. His aristocratic demeanor probably precluded a later nod as Conservative prime minister, but he served as foreign secretary from 1919 to 1924. (Library of Congress)

represented the same dark threat as did natives: after the Paris Commune of 1870, the mass execution of the Communards was followed by the exile of many to New Caledonia, where another dangerous class existed.[40]

The colonies devalued life on the basis of race, but the racial separation was an aspect of the general classificatory mania and search for new hierarchies to replace old that characterized the late nineteenth century. So the modern state developed out of that dialectical thrust—inevitable democratization and wider communication, but reconfigured pyramids of status and authority. The brilliant Polish writer of the late twentieth century, Stanisław Lem (d. 2006) has a delicious short story about a German SS officer who after the collapse of the Third Reich seeks refuge in a remote corner of Argentina, where he organizes a miniature state among his fellow fugitives. But entranced with absolute authority, he disdains reproducing the National Socialist regime as too vulgar and populist and aspires to recreate the court of Louis XVI, insisting that his fellow mass murderers all pretend to speak French and conduct elaborate court rituals in a desolate geographic milieu that mocks the effort and finally leads to the downfall of the experiment.[41] It is doubtful that Lem was thinking of the colonial state when he wrote his fantasy, but it captures something about many of the states throughout the world in the late nineteenth and early twentieth centuries. They were theaters of ceremony—Edward VII's coronation as emperor in Delhi in 1903 claimed about 0.5 percent of the public revenue (imagine a $20 billion inauguration ceremony in today's Washington), and other grandiose state visits followed.[42] Lem's parody fails us, though, in that his obsessed leaders establish no relationship with the indigenous elite; they are self-absorbed, whereas the key to colonial rule was the selection of native chiefs or sheiks in a process of "indirect rule," most famously outlined by the British proconsul in Nigeria, Frederick Lugard, and France's Marshal Hubert Lyautey.[43]

And although not founded by mass murderers, the conditions under which colonies were established could encourage mass murder, as some advocates accepted without qualms. "Again, another conclusion from our proposition in reference to the mission of the Teutonic nations," wrote a contemporary legal theorist,

> must be that they are called to carry the political civilization of the modern world into those parts of the world inhabited by unpolitical and barbaric races, *i.e.* they must have a colonial policy . . . the larger part of the surface of the globe is inhabited by populations which have not succeeded in establishing civilized states, which have in fact no capacity to accomplish such a work, and which must, therefore, remain in a state of barbarism or semibarbarism, unless the political nations undertake the work of state organization for them. . . . There is no human right to the status of barbarism. . . . The civilized state may righteously go still further than the exercise of force in imposing organization. If the barbaric populations resist the same, *à la outrance,* the civilized state may clear the territory of their presence and make it the abode of civilized man. . . . It violates thereby no rights of these populations which are not petty and trifling in comparison with its transcendent right and duty to establish political and legal order elsewhere.

John William Burgess, the self-described Teuton who buried this license for genocide in his major treatise on the state, was in fact no German, but the leading Columbia University professor of constitutional law.[44]

The German general Lothar von Trotha put down the Herero uprising in German Southwest Africa by driving the insurgents and their families into the desert, where it was obvious they must perish. The Americans who took over the Philippines pursued the insurrectionary forces of General Aguinaldo with a war against the population. The Italians ferociously suppressed the Libyan tribes whose territory they took from the distant Turks in 1911; General Reginald Dyer famously emptied his machine guns against assembled Indians in Amritsar in

Resistance to empire: Hendrik Witbooi, ca. 1900. Witbooi, a well-educated and effective guerrilla leader, was born and educated in the northern Cape Colony in 1830 to a family of Nama tribal leaders. Migrating north to southwest Africa, he concluded a peace with the traditionally rival Herero to oppose the ambitious German colonial effort. From the 1890s until his death in combat in 1905, he led the combined Nama-Herero revolt, which was finally crushed by the genocidal tactics of the hard-line German commander. (Getty Images)

1919; the British made air attacks on Bedouin tribesmen a successful tactic of border control in their new possessions in the Middle East in the early 1920s, while the French bombarded Damascus a few years later; the Italians used poison gas against the Ethiopians whose land Mussolini coveted; and in 1945, as the war was ending in Europe, French troops killed perhaps 6,000 Algerians in wanton reprisals, perhaps many more, in inland Sétif after Muslim protests turned violent and took 100 European lives. But the casualties were far away; the peoples were dark and fanatic; each incident was an unfortunate exception in a narrative of progress; dominion could not be dismantled—even the tenderhearted agreed—without a catastrophe for civilization.

For many of the administrators and settlers, the natives were children; they had to be taught lessons. Baron Ferdinand von Richthofen, rector of the University of Berlin and China explorer (although his initial encounters with Chinese may have come during his years in California), referred to the relationship between a master and his dog; the colonial administrator must punish all challenges to authority immediately.[45] General Edmund Barrow, who headed the British expedition to suppress residual Boxer presence, explained his decision to blow up the white porcelain pagoda of the Beijing Bada temple complex: if Christians did not destroy the landmark, the Chinese would consider their gods more powerful. As German general Alfred von Waldersee noted, retributive beheadings of Qing officials (not Boxers themselves) by enlisted Chinese executioners were an exercise in "moral influence of far-reaching importance."[46] It is customary to balance these episodes against the hospitals or railroads and occasional schools that the European attempted. The colonial state could become a developmental state if it made sense to its masters. The Japanese built a vigorous, though often brutal, colonial empire from 1895 to 1945, and in Manchuria in particular nurtured economic and industrial development, whether coal mines or soy farming.[47] Still there was something essential to the enterprise in the relationship of arbitrary and, if need be, unfettered power far from the daily supervision of the state at home. Distancing was crucial to the exercise of power and to its ultimate legitimation, resting as it did on the racial or ethnic distance that separated the colonizer and the colonized, and making the colonial state a potential zone of day-to-day violence. Joseph Conrad has left us one essential allegory: *Heart of Darkness*—once again the fusion of violence, empire, and coming of age. Almost sixty years later the Nigerian writer Chinua Achebe left another tale, *Things Fall Apart,* from the viewpoint of the disoriented subject. Not all these stories were allegories in which violence had to follow from absolute power. E. M Forster's *Passage to India* is fraught instead with the inability to achieve personal friendship across the divide of the colonizer and the colonized; and there are many other stories of prejudice and encounter where the two sides wish for the unmediated relationship of equals but cannot achieve it given the insuperable differences of authority.

It would be tempting to conclude that the colonial state was the arena in which all the prerogatives of power earlier inherent in Western statehood could be exercised once they were no longer permissible at home—that is, that it allowed all the surviving impulses of domination to find an outlet at a time when they had to yield to democratic forms and public opinion within the colonizing state. The colonial state permitted the ceremonial staging of sovereignty and unchallenged rule. It allowed the articulation of fantasies of racial differentiation that Europeans sometimes felt with respect to their own urban masses or even peasants, and that many Americans felt toward their former black slaves and new contracted labor. In an era when the concept of equal citizenship was inscribed as the norm for the Western state or those regimes that aspired to be modern, the colonial state represented the exceptionalism permitted for global governance. It established enclaves of untrammeled power but it also allowed men of science and sensibility to see the commonalities of culture that they attempted to convey at home by studies in anthropology. This is all true, although it necessarily simplifies the myriad encounters of colonial farmers, businessmen, and soldiers with the people they were assigned to rule. In fact, the colonial state—insofar as we can speak usefully about this generalization—was an immensely complex and contradiction-ridden enterprise. Wherever whites confronted the "other," they confronted "themselves." *The "other"* became the fashionable historically discursive term during the 1960s, but the colonial subject was never simply just the other. And while the colonial state was different from the state at home, it was still a domain where its possibilities for sovereignty, authority, legislation, and violence might be tested. Ultimately what happened in the colonies in the way of violence and domination and exploitation did not just stay in the colonies. And it would never have happened in the colonies had it not been dreamed of at home.

CHAPTER FOUR

States of Exception, Exceptional States

"Sovereign is he who decides on the state of exception." Forget the nice descriptions of the legal order, so German political theorist Carl Schmitt was arguing in 1921: sovereignty belonged to whoever had the authority to set aside the law.[1] Schmitt, however, did not mean just de facto power: sovereignty was a metalegal status that evaded the constraints of the constitution. Schmitt, who would live almost a century, into the 1980s, was never free of a desire to transgress bourgeois norms; and he aspired to be the poster boy for counterrevolutionary legal and political theory in the decade after World War I and then the court theorist for the Nazis. His formula became all too relevant for so many states in the twentieth century, as they coped with civil strife, revolution, depression, and war. The state of exception or emergency arose when the legal or even constitutional order, with all its protections for citizens' rights, could not provide for confronting a threat to the nation and had to be suspended. It was the moment when the ruler had to act according to what since Machiavelli was called *raison d'état* or just the moment that President George W. Bush appealed to when he called himself, doubtless without benefit of reading Schmitt, "the decider."[2]

Twentieth-century history was marked by states of exception; and the states created in those states of exception could prove exceptional in their claims and their brutality. For Schmitt, however, they were not exceptional as such, for ultimately every state had to be exceptional and politics always took place in the interstices where law failed to reach—in a democracy above all. For democracy—as he would emphasize in his writings that we return to below—was not about human rights, not about resolving policy alternatives through discussion (which liberalism celebrated), but about a people defining and protecting its identity, about who constituted "us" and who "them." In that sense Schmitt's heirs are still around, shorn usually of totalitarian temptations but tending to see public life as constituted by irreducible ethnic antagonisms usually in the form of immigration from Asia, Africa, and (in the US case) Latin America. Between the world wars they talked about the bourgeoisie and the proletariat, kulaks and collectives, Jews and Germans. And of course, they didn't just talk. Threatened, as they saw it, by fundamental internal adversaries, they moved to eliminate them.

Schmitt's formula alerts us that the twentieth-century state (and many specific states in particular) might follow two agendas, conceptually separate but often entangled: one that might be labeled "soft," the other "hard." The soft agenda involved expanding the policies associated with Foucault's idea of governmentality and the modernization of society. Expansion of activity along these lines would lead to the contemporary welfare state as gradually elaborated from the occupational safety legislation, pension provisions, and early social insurance begun in Europe during the nineteenth century and significantly enlarged during the post–World War II era. In this role states acted to shape society as they provided for education, investment in infrastructure, and regulation of the economy. As they competed internationally during the Cold War, states also took on commitments to modernization and development. Soft agendas did not renounce large social goals, and critics from Friedrich Hayek to James Scott have argued that the soft agenda could be as quietly coercive as the more brutal hard agenda. Still, facing a tax for future pension payments or being subject to compulsory medical insurance hardly seems comparable to interrogation by the Gestapo. The "hard" agenda was precisely the one that invoked "exception" and emergency—political activity as a response to war, revolution, and unrest. States were not at leisure to just pursue the development of their societies: issues of sovereignty, identity, and violence intruded into history with renewed urgency once again as preeminent concerns in the first half of the twentieth century. They had been such in the seventeenth century, but had been gradually displaced by the Enlightenment's focus on civil society. As Schmitt realized, Hobbes was back.

Even for nations normally liberal at home, the hard agenda, the regime of "exception," intruded in two key sets of activities. One, as we have seen, was colonial administration; the other was the state at war. Colonial administrators and their restive subjects understood that sovereignty was or must become the underlying stake in the imperial world—sovereignty over acquired subjects, sovereignty vis-à-vis potential rival colonizers. Maintaining sovereignty, however, involved what French colonial advocates termed "valorization" of their "possessions," that is, modernizing and developing their economic potential whether in terms of commodities or manpower. But so too, colonial intellectuals and civil servants believed that modernization, pursuing wealth and power, was a prerequisite for standing up to the European powers. In the Pacific region, Japan's experience taught important lessons for both sides: The Meiji reformers had consciously and successfully chosen modernization to resist possible quasi colonization. But they were reconstructing nationhood precisely in an era when most successful statesmen believed that civilizations were divided into the vigorous and the feeble. They entered a world of states "red in tooth and claw," and believed their own teeth and claws needed to be as sharp as any other, and thus went on within the same generation to quickly create their own Asian empire. After Japan's victory over China in 1895, which the European powers moved to limit and then exploit for their own aims, the subsequent rivalry with Russia for preeminence in Korea led to the Russo-Japanese War of 1904–1905 and the first major modern military setback dealt to a European empire by an Asian power. Japan destroyed the Russian fleet, but the ground war bogged down in the sieges around Port Arthur and Dalian (Dairen), finally to be mediated by President Theodore Roosevelt in remote Portsmouth, New Hampshire. Japan won Russia's rights over Manchurian ports, South Sakhalin and other islands, and enough of a free hand to be able to annex Korea in 1910. Tokyo's new empire rested on both the harsh exercise of power and an agenda for development of Manchurian and to a lesser extent Taiwanese and Korean resources. Chinese reformers and revolutionaries seeking asylum in Tokyo were to learn a lot from Japan in the decade after their defeat at its hands. Given the vortex of imperial conflict that opened up where Korean and Manchu weakness sucked in Russia, Japan, and indirectly the Western powers, there is a case to be made for dating twentieth-century international history from the conflict of 1895.[3]

Consider the impact of the wars (including the Cold War) that would stretch through most of the twentieth century more generally. The fiscal exigencies of war in the seventeenth and eighteenth centuries had helped create Leviathan 1.0: that is, the dynastic territorial state, insistent on sovereignty, determined if possible to override local privileges, intent on developing its economic resources and infrastructure. The wars of the mid-nineteenth century, we have seen, were instrumental for the territorial and governmental consolidation of Leviathan 2.0. So too the great wars of the twentieth century played a fundamental role. Even as they originated in large measure from the expansionist role that the reinvented nineteenth-century nation-state found so compelling, so the world wars further impelled these states to mobilize their economies and societies to unprecedented degrees. War justified the accretion of power at home, and it beckoned the more ruthless leaders of the new century as a paradigm for seizing and exercising it. Readers of this book will have spent their lives in states whose claims on individual lives and ambitions to regulate their welfare, often their abodes, and sometimes even their demographic continuity and permissible utterances, were fundamentally enhanced by the world wars and Cold War struggles.

The experience of the two world wars in fact conflated the agendas of development and sovereignty. The states engaged in those long conflicts had to mobilize mass armies, coordinate their industries, their transports, and their medical and social services, and negotiate with their labor organizations to an unprecedented degree. Market mechanisms to allocate scarce manpower or raw materials had chaotic and inflationary results and were largely set aside for allocation by committees of the sectors involved. New ministries of munitions compelled industrialists who had resisted unions to accept trilateral bargaining among state bureaucrats and sometimes generals, unions, and employer confederations. Women emerged into the sphere of nondomestic work to an unprecedented degree. The warfare state became a proto-welfare state, but equipped with degrees of compulsion that were truly exceptional. The British Defense of the Realm Act (DORA) passed in August 1914 essentially turned over to the government the power to do what it thought necessary to prosecute the war. Powerful unspoken expectations of decent and liberal behavior persisted in Britain, and it was taken for granted that such a delegation of authority would not be used to prosecute political speech unless it challenged the war effort. The need to administer pensions and medical benefits prolonged the expansion of many of these services into the postwar eras. Although the interference with price and market mechanisms was generally rolled back after World War I, the Great Depression and the Second World War made some of the innovations into permanent features. If power in every state was defined by what happened during the exception, states of exception were no longer so exceptional.[4]

Finally the two agendas manifested themselves in the extraordinary role that military rule continued to play throughout the world, certainly until the 1980s. Outside the colonial world, the governing institution that had seemed conspicuously to triumph in the course of the

The rise of the warfare state: Canadian women workers operating machine tools in a munitions factory, September 1916. Canada and the Dominions entered the war alongside "the mother country" in 1914, and as in other belligerent nations where men were called to combat service, women took up traditionally male occupations. (Getty Images)

nineteenth century—arriving finally in Japan in 1890, in Russia in 1905, in China in 1910—was the legislative assembly or parliament. But parliaments, as conservative critics such as Schmitt or earlier Gaetano Mosca pointed out, found it hard to act decisively in their role as assemblies, and, for what decisions they could reach, relied either on a committee system or on the party leaders who organized their majorities. As of 1900, competing parties were still more clublike than cohesive, although first in the United States and then Britain, where electoral campaigns focused periodically on choosing the chief executive as well as parliamentary delegates, the parties became permanent regime fixtures with professional staffs and affiliated newspapers. But where these procedures were weak or very recent, or even nonexistent, twentieth-century development brought instead the paramount role of the single encompassing party or rule by the military.

Military rule and single-party dictatorship seemed to confirm Carl Schmitt's tough lesson that real authority emerges only outside the constitution. The sovereign was the army or the authoritarian party. Or was this true only in the short run? Military rule could guarantee neither national unity nor, certainly, internal pacification. In those large countries in which weak national regimes were breaking down under the pressure of imperialist encroachment or economic stagnation, territorial fragmentation or warlordism was a recurrent danger. Even when a unified military controlled the whole national territory, it found prolonged rule by bayonet frustrating. Increasingly it had to meet the needs of civil society—the realm of rivalries between capital and labor, free-trade and protectionist sectors, the restless voices of religious organizations, the media, and culture—and thus to enter the world of policy debate and pluralism. Some military rulers sought to do so by continued force, others by sponsoring authoritarian national parties. Decades later the generals and the dictators would find they were incompetent to deal with complex societies. They would not really know how to manage religious yearnings, consumer aspirations, and the technology of the computer age. They offered authoritarian solutions that were hard to prolong when the era of iron and steel was augmented by silicon and software. But their dismantling is the story of our own age, not the segment of time considered here.

Crises of Representation

Only in the sheltered bourgeois enclaves of Vienna or Paris or the discreet banks and clubs of London did it take the First World War to shatter the *douceur de vie* of the nineteenth century. From the mid-1890s on, the world of states—already reorganized in the second third

A synthesis of culture, wealth, and power: The inauguration of the Paris Opera season at the Palais Garnier, ca. 1890–1900. The sumptuous Paris Opera House, designed by Charles Garnier and constructed in the 1860s in the opulent Beaux-Arts style of the Second Empire, served, like its counterparts elsewhere, as a public showplace for the wealthy bourgeoisie, who came to play a major political role in the late nineteenth century throughout Europe and the Americas. (Library of Congress)

of the nineteenth century, then freighted with ambitious agendas of development at home and expansion abroad—entered stormy waters and generated new, eventually terrifying experiments. Episodes of upheaval came thick and fast. Review some of them as they would have made the gray columns of the metropolitan newspapers: famine in India and a revival of anti-British violence from the late 1880s; global depression in 1893 and a mobilization of protest movements in Italy and the United States and major strikes throughout Europe. Cascading wars again—between China and Japan in 1895, between Greece and Turkey in 1896–1897, between the United States and Spain in 1898, between Britain and the Boers in 1900–1902, between Russia and Japan in 1904–1905, between Italy and the Ottomans in 1911, between the Balkan states and the Ottomans in 1912, and then among the Balkans in 1913—wars that brought the growing tendency to massacre civilians: Armenians in the Ottoman Empire in 1897, Herero and Nama in the German colonies, 1905–1907, Bosnians and Albanians in the Balkans in 1911–1912. Although the wars themselves still took place "far away" from Western Europe and North America, the powers at the center extended their network of fateful alliances or commitments: between French and Russians after 1894, British and Japanese in 1902, British and French in 1904, British and Russians in 1907.

Starting with the Russo-Japanese confrontation, Niall Ferguson has chronicled what he aptly calls the twentieth century's "war of the world," which he finds fundamentally a product of racial or ethnic conflict.[5] Certainly distinctions of race were held to justify imperialism and, often, license atrocities. But war did not always arise from these distinctions, and certainly not the most destructive wars between the European powers. Crucial, I believe, were the political deficiencies of empire and the continuing sense of vulnerability they inculcated among those who championed them most ardently. Conflicts arose from imperial elites on the defensive (Ottoman, Habsburg, Chinese, and British) and those more assertive (Japanese and German).

Empires were praised as bringing peace within their far-flung frontiers and remote territories. But although they might defer internal violence and even war with each other, they could never do so indefinitely. The bills came due after 1900.

As in all revolutionary eras, legitimacy was at stake, and actually was wearing thin in many places by the 1890s. Legitimacy implies that authority does not rely on power alone; it rests on a moral basis that commands respect and obedience without continued coercion. By the end of the nineteenth century, legitimate states had to be representative to some degree; they had to act on behalf of the expressed or imputed interests of what the Victorians termed "public opinion." In the United States and Western Europe that had long meant deferring to a parliament and respecting individual rights. In the American democracy, President Lincoln put the idea most expansively: "government of the people, by the people, and for the people." By the turn of the twentieth century, representing "society" as a complex aggregation of identities and interests became the basis for legitimacy. But it was becoming harder and harder for states to represent the often conflicting interests within society.

This was true not only for autocratic states, but for countries that prided themselves on their civilized attainments, including the role played by an enlightened public opinion. The campaigns for enlarged suffrage were the most visible effort to encompass an enlarged sense of society. The European states managed slowly to concede broader manhood suffrage in the later nineteenth and earlier twentieth centuries. Sometimes conservative parties wagered that by enfranchising the broader middle class they might strengthen their domestic position (as did the British Tories in 1867); sometimes conservatives and reformers both calculated that reform would stabilize the society as a whole and their respective positions (as in Italy in 1912). Sometimes bureaucratic rulers calculated they could use broader suffrage to limit the influence of powerful elites, as when the Habsburg ministers pressed a major general suffrage on the two halves of Austria-Hungary. Sometimes political leaders conceded to massive demonstrations, as in Belgium in 1913. Often, though, there was resistance. Prussian conservatives and the monarch resisted demands to transform the franchise in the Prussian legislature from one skewed toward the wealthy to a more general one-man, one-vote system until they felt the need to enhance working-class support during the latter phases of the First World War. In Russia a mass suffrage conceded during the year of revolution in 1905 was progressively clawed back until the fall of the monarchy in 1917. And both Left and Right might resist the claims of new groups (as with women's suffrage or African-American suffrage in the US South). Suffrage alone, moreover, did not determine the strength or absence of democratic institutions and culture. Different parliaments had different degrees of power vis-à-vis their heads of state or military and bureaucracy. National political institutions could be located along axes that ran from democratic participation (as in Third Republic France) through various admixtures of elite influence reserved for ancient families and bureaucrats, ranging from the more liberal to the less, such as Britain and Germany or Japan. (Local and regional authority might be ranged along a similar continuum, but might also fall at a different point.)

However, a single aggregate scale for ranking democracy (such as Freedom House tries to calculate for today's governments) would have made little sense. Some states remained what might be labeled *constitutionally segmented,* no matter what their written charters provided for. They were effectively divided into one sector of the adult population that was admitted to political participation and one or more that remained excluded. With respect to gender most polities were segmented until later in the twentieth century, but even disregarding the disadvantaging of women, other politics were segmented by regional "backwardness" and ethnic or racial exclusion. The Italian state was governed by a liberal parliamentary class that indulged in electoral competition north of Rome but depended on patronage, clientelism, and landowners' strength in the south as a sort of ballast to limit the destabilizing impact of these rivalries in the north. American politics remained segmented by race. The US Republican Party ended its brief effort to enforce ex-slaves' newly enacted political rights by the late 1870s as part of a deal to keep control of the presidency. The dualist electoral settlement that allowed manhood suffrage in the North even for recent immigrants while enforcing racial exclusion from the vote in the South permitted the country to achieve sectional "reconciliation" at the cost of acquiescing in Jim Crow segregationist legislation and local repression by unofficial lynch law. In the atmosphere that prevailed, white Americans in the North as well as the South wearily accepted the view that African-Americans were not yet "ready" for equal citizenship—it was the equivalent of European colonial attitudes toward their Asian and African subjects, and in effect the pool of black labor provided the human resources of a nonterritorial colony. The reunited United States also enjoyed the great geographical resource of western lands as a stabilizing outlet for national energy. Then, too, the massive influx of European migrants tended to focus their efforts at ethnic representation though state and city political machines rather than insist on prominence at the national level. Neither did they pose "radical" demands: northern or Eastern European workers recreated the emerging social democratic parties of Europe in a few locations, but largely streamed into the US alternatives already available, whether the Democratic Party organizations in northern cities, or the more radical Populist currents in the West. Even so, middle-class urban reformers, largely of northern European ethnic stock, sought to stabilize their hold in cities by taking governance out of the hand of electoral machines and turning them over to professional urban managers. The settlement underlying US politics in the late nineteenth century consisted of a balance whereby the Republican Party usually captured a weak national government that sustained a protectionist tariff while allowing the Democratic Party to exploit the politics of the industrial cities and the reservoir of Southern white voters. Farmers in the South and West challenged the compromise in the 1890s but failed to dislodge it.

Racial segmentation also prevailed in the new Union of South Africa, where the whites who ruled constituted only a minority of the population. In effect the South African War ("Boer War"), which pitted the ambitious forces of white South African mining interests, backed by more than a hundred thousand British troops (and a strategy of forced removals and confinement of the Afrikaans-speaking rural families), against the agrarian Boer Republics, ended with an implicit compromise worked out between 1902 and 1910. The Afrikaans-speaking republics were forced to accept inclusion in a British Union of South Africa and an active policy of British administrative penetration under Alfred Milner. However, the British left the Boer republics a great deal of home rule and made no effort to challenge the segregationist political and social system they had constructed. In the Cape Colony, the white population of under a quarter of the whole constituted 85 percent of the electorate; in Natal, where the whites constituted 8 percent of a once Zulu-dominated region, they would make up 99 percent of the electorate. A mistaken belief that the Boers believed in a rugged democracy as well as the importance of South Africa for the British war effort against German colonial armies after 1914 (and the personal role that Boer leader Jan Smuts achieved) made it hard for London to contest the South Africans' racial state, especially because so many English shared the underlying premises of African racial inferiority.[6]

Segmented regimes formed one type of implicit constitution. Other implicit constitutional settlements opened up states to extensive foreign influence—military, economic, or pedagogic and cultural. The term *semicolonialism* has been used to describe the reserve power that European powers possessed in China, but authority could be less formally enshrined.[7] In Latin America's large republics, the ritualized party competition among elites separated those oriented toward commercial and financial ties with foreign lenders, notably Great Britain, from those claiming the traditionalist power of military, church, and landed property. Expansion of export commodities—coffee in Brazil, beef and wheat in Argentina, minerals from the Andes—strengthened the liberals and allowed a relatively cozy sharing of power and influence after civil war and violence. Brazil's new republic (and with it the compensated ending of slavery by 1889) benefited from the coffee boom and agreement on a highly decentralized federal system. Only in the interwar period, as the prices of commodities fell and new political leaders sought to broaden the political base to include manual workers or indigenous peoples, did these equilibria irrevocably break down and populist strongmen, often drawn from the military, emerge.

Once white male suffrage became generalized, regulation of the economy became more urgent. Trade unions and working-class associations had faced political restrictions in the 1870s and 1880s on the European continent, the United States, and Mexico. The First International Workingman's Association had disintegrated after the Paris Commune; Bismarck had outlawed the German Social Democratic Party (SPD) in 1878; the US Knights of Labor disintegrated after the Haymarket bombing and trial in 1886; striking workers had to face soldiers and judges in many countries. But a Second International emerged in 1889; the SPD was relegalized in 1890, and the organizing of workers increased in scope and intensity. Strike activity increased in all the industrializing countries, and after 1905 the strikes were often for greater political influence, and not merely higher wages. Russia's 1905 revolution helped to galvanize activism in Germany and France. Some of the labor movements' spokesmen envisaged that workplace organizations could displace elected legislatures and even socialist parties to become the basis for a new democratic politics. At the time of the 1905 revolution, Bolshevik leaders would describe workers "councils" (or *soviets* in Russian) as the avant-garde of a proletarian order. Such anarcho-syndicalism seemed even to infect British trade unions, formerly the most oriented on narrower demands for safety legislation or wage increases. Visions of a social war exhilarated some on the left—see Jack London's lurid description of the battle for Chicago in *The Iron Heel* (1908). Conversely, the prospect obviously frightened conservatives, many of whom expected a bloody upheaval akin to their folk memories of the Paris siege and Commune. But even more ominously, the coming Armageddon gave some writers a jolt of adrenalin, as they believed it would reinvigorate a tired and decadent social order. Georges Sorel, the engineer in Paris, and Vilfredo Pareto, the Italian economist teaching in Lausanne (as well as the young Italian student Benito Mussolini, who audited some of his lecturers), anticipated the coming clashes with gusto, just as the contemporary artistic movement of Italian Futurists looked forward to a cleansing hygienic war. Privileged French university students allegedly believed that a new war would be preferable to "perpetual waiting." Liberalism was hostage to ennui as well as social cleavages.[8]

Even harder to reconcile than proletarian class demands or the literati's impatience with political compromise were the demands for national representation within multiethnic units. The Irish, who in the early nineteenth century had been given seats in the British parliament at a time when only Protestants (largely landowners) might serve, wanted "home rule" or national autonomy with an Irish parliament, but Protestant loyalists resisted and compelled the Conservative Party and the British parliament to delay. Both sides were on the verge of resorting to armed force by the early twentieth century. Although a third home-rule bill was finally passed on the eve of World War I, it was shelved until the issue of the Protestant counties (Ulster) might be resolved. This did not happen until a period of Irish national insurgency and police suppression (the Black and Tan war) followed in the early 1920s and a segment of the nationalist Sinn Fein rebels were willing to settle for an "Irish Free State" without the northern counties comprising Ulster. Austria-Hungary and the Ottomans faced far wider ethnic rebellions than did the British. National groups progressively hived off the Ottomans in the early nineteenth century (Greece, Serbia, Romania), then the 1870s (Bulgaria), or were taken over by other imperial contenders, as in North Africa. As for the world's largest colony, British India remained under sufficient control to tamp down calls for greater national representation. India, of course, was ruled as an empire, by a government sent from London. It had no mass white population, but the legacy of multiple pre-British state structures and the failure in 1857 of rebellion (which was never fully articulated as a national upheaval) kept the national challenge relatively weak until after the world war. The Indian National Congress was a group that had a long-term vision but practiced short-term accommodation and gradualist inclusion in local organs, especially the judicial system. It was an irony of the British Empire that the coronation of a new monarch could be celebrated with the greatest pomp in New Delhi in 1910, even as Irish factions were moving toward violence almost next door to London.

Representation, furthermore, was a complex activity in its own right, no matter how much of a society it encompassed. The spatial metaphor that envisaged a state above trying to react to society below was misleadingly simple. Political demands did not simply flow "upward" from society to the state. Ambitious reformers pondered how states that had themselves been transformed in the nineteenth century should transform society in turn—that is, regulate it, develop it, improve and remake it. The states that emerged in the nineteenth century had a special relationship with technological modernity; they needed breech-loading and rapid-firing guns, heavier cannon; they needed velocity, railroads, and rapid communication, the telegraph, the undersea cable, eventually the radio. Beyond their requirements for material infrastructure, states had to educate citizens and to improve their health and vigor, even perhaps through the new concept of "eugenics," or restricted breeding.

Thus the late nineteenth-century state was not, could not be, an institution built for static equilibrium. It had to ensure the development of its civilian economy, not just its military. In Britain and later in the United States, governments might rely more on the inherent vigor of civil society than direction by the state. Americans viewed their economic enterprises and their multiple associations as both the beneficiaries and the sources of modernization. The protective tariff and the distribution of national lands to railroads and homesteaders (who would be clients of the railroads) meant significant state promotion of economic development. Canada was not so different in this respect. The French and later the German, Japanese, and Russian states felt they had to intervene to a greater degree, but began at different moments, the French before their great revolution, the Germans and Japanese during the mid-nineteenth century, the Russians at the end— more rapidly and impressively than other states. Russia, still an autocracy until 1905, and guided by Sergei Witte from 1893, embarked on the trans-Siberian railroad, a program whose costs aroused aristocratic opposition and the impatience of the faction anxious to keep Korea out of Japanese influence. The monarch yielded to the pressure and eased Witte into a more ceremonial role, only to recall him in 1905 to cope with the aftermath of the war with Japan and the revolutionary agitation that had followed his removal. Failure to modernize could cost territory and erode sovereignty, even if outright colonization was avoided, as was vividly demonstrated in the case of China, which had to grant extraterritorial enclaves where the Western powers retained local legal rights, and the Ottoman Empire, which was compelled to cede "capitularies," or legal immunities, to foreigners.

Modernization, however, provoked resistance from traditionalists at home and sometimes preemptive intervention from the Western powers. When Chinese administrators began an effort to reform within the permitted parameters of Confucian values in the 1860s after a second war, now with France as well as Britain, they faced disabling court intrigues, as did the "hundred-day" reform interlude of 1898, stymied by the empress dowager, and the attempts to institute local, then national, elections after 1905. Japanese reformers fared better. Alerted by the concessions and territory extracted by Britain from the Chinese in 1842 and warned by their own experience of having to open five "treaty ports" to the Americans in 1858, reform-oriented samurai began a nationalist mobilization against the perceived weakness of the Tokugawa shogunate. Conservatives were less successful in blocking reforms in Japan than in China. The court was not in the same position to play personal politics; rather, the emperor stood to gain in influence from reform. In Japan, moreover, the central state did not penetrate the autonomous domains *(han)* of the reform-minded *daimyō* and their samurai officials, who could in effect run laboratories of rationalization. No state examination system elevated Confucian and Neo-Confucian hierarchical concepts into a portal for public service; the Japanese military traditions were conservative but allowed for emulation of modern science and technology.

Other authoritarian rulers could also save their countries from being carved up or absorbed if they were skillful and willing to modernize institutions and infrastructure. Chulalongkorn of Thailand (ruling as King Rama V, 1868–1910, almost the same span as the Meiji emperor) managed to play off the British in Burma against the more threatening French in Indochina, formed a functionally organized cabinet, reformed the military, fiscal system, and national education system, and extended rail and telegraph lines throughout the kingdom. Emperor Menelik II of Ethiopia (1889–1909/1913) ruled a poorer do-

Modernization for national survival: King Chulalongkorn of Thailand posing with the crown prince and presumably some of his seventy-seven children, ca. 1900. A contemporary of the reforming Meiji emperor in Japan, Chulalongkorn abolished slavery, modernized the Thai government, military, and judicial and educational systems, and preserved the country's independence vis-à-vis the British in Burma to the west and the French in Indochina to the east. (© Hulton-Deutsch Collection / Corbis)

main, but inflicted stunning defeats on Italian forces and established a ministerial system.[9]

Global Revolution

Norman Angell had the courage to suggest in his 1910 study of international capitalism, *The Great Illusion,* that what historians today call the first globalization—the dense and rapidly thickening web of economic and financial ties among nations in the early twentieth century—should preclude major war. He overestimated the strength of interests and underestimated the force of alliances. Globalization did not compel peace.

Without needing to predict the future in 1916, Vladimir Lenin could write that the first globalization (which he interpreted as imperialism) had had to bring about a great war. We can't say he was wrong—but we can't confirm that he was right either.

The proposition that can be defended is that globalization helped produce revolution as regimes collapsed across Mexico, Eurasia, and China. This meant that revolution came not to the industrial societies of Western Europe and North America (except when military defeat discredited their rulers) but to the large, vulnerable states that were attracting the attention of imperialist rivals and the capital they brought with them. Skip over the machinations of American sugar interests in the Caribbean and Hawai'i and even the Cuban uprising against Spanish rule in Cuba at the outset of the period in the 1890s. But pay attention to the Boxer uprising in China in 1900 and the collapse of Manchu rule in 1911, to Russia's months of tumult during 1905 and then the regime changes of 1917, to Iran's constitutional revolution of 1906–1909, the Young Turks' uprising in 1908 and the fragmentation of the Ottoman state a decade later; and then to the layered rebellions in Mexico, unfolding over a decade from 1910 to 1920.

Widely separated geographically, these revolutions all had their own sources and history, but they also were products directly or indirectly of encroaching strategic rivalries and foreign investors seeking profits from local resources or investments and favorably supervised by their regimes at home. With some exception made for imperial Russia, the regimes under attack seemed to have become subservient to foreign power and foreign capital. To be sure, the foreigners' economic activity (and accompanying schools and churches, engineering and financial expertise) brought significant economic growth. Rail lines expanded by multiples; oil wells came into production, new banks channeled capital into a flurry of overseas companies; investors in London, Paris, Berlin, Vienna, and New York created local wealth even as they siphoned off significant shares for their bondholders. Socially, they nurtured in the process both a class of enriched local mediators, and countervailing forces of intellectuals, journalists, religious leaders, and military officers, who beheld a sellout of authentic national or imperial traditions. Thus, radical ferment grew apace, sometimes organized in clandestine societies, sometimes in barracks and clubs, among circles of intellectuals and newspaper editors, and professional military officers and cadets.

These developments produced the inconsistencies of early twentieth-century revolution: Resentments and frustration were intensely nationalist because they reacted to the progress of global and international capital. Revolutionaries called for modernization along Western lines but often drew on the primitive strength of religious traditionalism. Uprisings originated less among deprived workers and peasants than among nativist elites outraged by military defeat and by authorities who seemed complicit in national dependency and even humiliation.[10] But the elites that were prompted to organize and assert new programs—in Mexico by disputed elections, in the Ottoman Empire by the growth of Balkan nationalisms, in China by Qing humiliations—ended up triggering massive upheavals and civil strife. Nationalist in aspiration, they produced ten to twenty years of regional armies and territorial fragmentation. At the end of the eighteenth century, revolutions had begun as contests inside particular states, which then triggered international intervention from larger powers. Those conflicts had been articulated in the emerging language of rights and entitlements bequeathed to Americans today in their founding charters. At the end of the nineteenth century, however, the revolutionary situations developed in response to perceived transnational abuses of power arising when foreign governments and investors allied with local elites seemingly to exploit local labor or extract local wealth. Out of these transnational alignments emerged the language of imperialism and underdevelopment.

From another perspective, the amazing global spectacle of failed parliamentarism, military intervention and warlordism, coup and countercoup, and the penetration of sprawling but penetrated societies by rival capitalists and would-be colonizers, formed a delayed and defective version of the successful national reconstitutions of the mid-nineteenth century. Determined elites and strong states had emerged out of the mid-nineteenth century furnace. Partial projects of modernization, conflicting ideologies and decomposing sovereignties seemed to afflict those half a century later who had not made the earlier transition as they hurtled toward protracted revolution and civil wars. Ironically enough, these belated decomposing states would help drag the successful national constructions of half a century earlier into the great war that overtook them all: strong and viable states and crumbling empires together.

⟿

Of course, to go from a situation fraught with antagonism to actual uprisings involved the interplay of contingency and personality. In particular, the political classes of each population were growing impatient with long-term rulers or family that seemed unwilling to listen to calls for reform. In Russia the tsarina and in China the empress dowager seemed to manipulate the feckless males who held the nominal imperial title. In Mexico and the Ottoman Empire, the aging patriarchs, both arriving in power in 1876, had promoted economic development, but became increasingly domineering and autocratic. Sultan Abdülhamid II, increasingly viewed as an aging despot relying on police spies, would be ousted after thirty years in 1908, in a coup that only made his empire more prey to territorial dismemberment. Porfirio Díaz would have to stand down in 1910.

Yet these autocrats had decisively pressed in particular for major expansion of their nations' railroads—as had the Russian bureaucrats in the same period. Railroads in effect provided the sinews and axons of globalization: they enhanced the idea of a unified territory; they allowed the development of interior markets, or the transport of distant soldiers; they required the standardization of timekeeping. Early railroads in the 1840s and 1850s had helped increase revolutionary and national pressures, whether in Prussia, where a parliament was to be summoned for their financing, or in Illinois, where they opened up the plains for wheat growing and destabilized the precarious compromises on slavery. Now railroads brought the transformative pressures of global finance and investment and the development of long-distance markets into the perimeters of the developed world. Railroads were the complement of frontiers: defending frontiers was the precondition of state sovereignty since the seventeenth century—the frontier had been the prerequisite for Leviathan 1.0. The railroad promised to make the interior space of the national state a unit, economically and socially as well as politically. It was, in effect, the principal symbol of Leviathan 2.0. But it exacted a price, often a fiscal one that bore heavily on a population and required new levels of taxation as in Russia, or new degrees of foreign investment as in Mexico and the Ottoman realms. And it exposed the mechanisms of the semideveloped states into which it penetrated as insufficient to realize the promises of progress it tantalizingly held out. Finally, it created new coalitions of the privileged, composed of new and old investors, and new coalitions of protesters who felt they were being exploited by those who controlled monopoly access to privilege and power.

Ironically, however, national revolutions that erupted in reaction to global pressures often remained regionally fragmented. National parliamentary politics was quickly eclipsed. The arenas of revolution were often local, and integrated national movements emerged only after protracted and brutal military conflict. Power gravitated to rival military commanders, sometimes seeking to contest the country as a whole, sometimes just establishing their own territory. The existence of rival armies and local military rule or warlordism, often supported by dominant foreign patrons, remained a logical outcome, at least for a long intervening period of conflict. Such regional fighting often proved particularly brutal as feelings of betrayal and counterbetrayal ran high. Combat shaded into long-term feuding. Regional commanders did not always take prisoners—what should they do with them?—even if they accepted turncoats. The laws of war, weak in most circumstances, did not often temper internal combat. The leaders who seized local power might be generous, but they could also be impulsive and vengeful. Alternatively, new and ruthless parties might claim that they alone could channel the true revolutionary forces. These confrontations were often beset by internal contradiction: they mobilized working classes who were internationalist in their outlooks and middle-class or elite reformers who spoke the language of nationalism. But they were also revolts in predominantly rural countries where landlords continued to dominate the countryside, while their tenants wanted control of the land either for their households or, in parts of Russia and Mexico, for their village communes. Belated revolution, many on the left believed, meant peasant revolution—heroic and apocalyptic as in one of Diego Rivera's or Orozco's murals. In fact, countryside forces could not push through revolutionary settlements without linking up to townspeople, whether middle-class or working-class. Intellectuals and journalists, merchants and financial intermediaries, remained critical, just as religious leaders in Iran remained crucial urban-based participants. Cities and countryside forces had to reach some sort of accommodation for success.

∼

The Russian revolution of 1905 was in effect the last of the great European revolutions since 1789, though it was provoked by the fiscal and social strains brought on by the conflict with Japan over East Asian expansion. As in the aftermath of the Crimean War, when the authorities eliminated serfdom, Russia had to make accommodations when it was overstretched. In this case the demonstrations of February 1905 and the gunfire of Bloody Sunday opened a continuing wave of protest and strikes and party formation that finally led to the tsar's agreement in October to summon a parliament or Duma. This was hardly surprising: Russia was an anomaly in the world of developed states, clinging to theoretical autocracy, which meant in effect rule by an aristocratic bureaucracy. German liberal observers, who had complacently viewed their own country as far more progressive than tsarist "despotism," were astonished to see that the Russians had acquired at a stroke a national assembly unhampered by the reactionary reserve powers that the unequal Prussian electoral system allowed. This achievement, however, was hardly to be maintained; the suffrage would be rolled back; the Dumas successively prorogued, even as social conflict increased and the financial strains of preparing for possible European conflict grew. Still, 1905 outlined the spectrum of parties—Bolsheviks, social democratic Mensheviks, agrarian "Social Revolutionary" populists oriented toward the peasants, middle-class liberals (so-called Kadets, eloquent but limited to the professional classes), and conservative "Octobrists"—that would fill the Russian political space until all were silenced after the Bolsheviks seized power at the end of 1917. The year 1905 also stimulated a decade of cultural innovation, fervent political and social debate, and continuing industrial advance.

⌒

Iran's "constitutional revolution" of 1905–1909 took place in the shadow of the revolutionary unrest that undermined neighboring Russia and the Ottoman Empire and the larger international balance of power. Iran, the stagnant remnant of a long-lived and once brilliant empire, was ruled by the Qajar dynasty, clinging to decisive power in a country that was perhaps a third or more "tribal" and in which religious authorities played a significant political role. Shiʻa clerics, dominant in Iran, traditionally stayed more distant from secular authority than did Sunni, and they increasingly denounced Qajar family tyranny, even as they remained hostile to the secularism of emerging intellectuals. Neighboring Russia tended to take its own predominant influence for granted, especially because it helped train the shah's military units. Great Britain, long concerned about Russian expansion and its supposed threat to India, had long sought commercial advantages in Iran, but was increasingly preoccupied since 1890 with Germany's rise to global power. The dynasty was torn between concessions to the British for the sake of economic development and reliance on the Russians for military stability. Following an abortive grant of extensive privileges in 1872 for railroad building, the shah allowed the British to found a bank of issue in the 1880s, and granted a national tobacco monopoly to British subjects in the early 1890s—all concessions, of course, that enriched those close to the court. Tobacco, however, was a broadly based economic activity, and the concession led to "the first successful mass protest in modern Iran, combining ʿulamaʾ, modernists, merchants, and townspeople in a coordinated movement against government policy."[11] The shah was assassinated in 1896, and the new shah, Muzaffar al-Din, found himself compelled to replace his conservative minister in 1903. The Russian revolutionary agitation during 1905 also spilled over to Iran: the Azeri region of Azerbaijan on the west of the Caspian that was divided between Russia and Iran proved a ready conduit for social democratic and Islamic organizational efforts, and protests roiled Tehran.

British and Russian interests were converging on a moderate solution for Iranian unrest. The Russian authorities were seeking to contain agitation at home, and like the British perceived a rising German threat, especially as Berlin seemed to be gaining military and economic influence in the Ottoman Empire. Both the British and the Russians sought to become patrons of the Islamic opposition and its call for a *majlis* or parliament. The 1905 standoff of protesters and the shah led the clerics to flee to Qum and the merchants to shut their markets. By August 1906, almost a year after the tsar had conceded a Duma, the shah agreed to convoke a legislature. The assembly was soon transformed from the role that conservative clerics envisaged for it, as a Muslim congress, to a national parliament in which minority religions would also be represented, even if the elections left it safely in the hands of clerics and wealthy merchants. Election of the *majlis,* however, meant that the struggle for constitutional government was only half over; the question of its future role was still open. A reluctant shah signed the fundamental laws in December 1906, but died shortly after, and divided *majlis* members prepared a contest for the all-important "supplement," which was to determine the power of the prime minister and the official role of religion. Advocates of freedom of conscience, journalists, and Western-oriented aristocrats spoke on behalf of parliamentary rights while the new shah, Muhammad Ali, and conservative clerics, who wanted to retain a large role for religious law, resisted. After a temporizing prime minister was assassinated in August 1907, the shah gave way and the constitutional supplement was passed in October, providing for a balance of executive and parliamentary power but with a council of religious notables to ensure that civil legislation conformed to Muslim law, or shari'a.

As long as the Russian authorities, cautioned by their own revolution although progressively limiting liberal gains, and the British worked together, they could secure the triumph of the moderate constitutionalists in Tehran and the consolidation of their respective interests. Thus motivated, the two great powers reached a crucial accord in 1907 that effectively suspended London's long-standing wariness of Russian imperial ambitions. The Anglo-Russian Convention provided for the nominal preservation of Iranian territorial integrity while recognizing a predominantly Russian sphere in the north and a British sphere in the south, where British exploration for oil was successful a year later. Iranian public opinion understandably beheld it as de facto partition, signed on their own soil. The agreement also forestalled rivalry over the northwest frontier of India and either side's takeover of Afghanistan. Thus the two powers adjourned their potential conflicts in Central Asia, facilitating in turn the emergence of the Triple Entente with their mutual partner, France, and potentially confronting together the Austro-German alliance in Europe and the colonial world. But having been guaranteed that Russia would not partition Iran and would not threaten Britain's frontier zone in India, London seemed to withdraw from active policy in Iran, while the Russian ambassador now urged a hard line on the shah, who deployed Cossack-led troops to shut down the parliament in 1908 after continued street agitation.

Counterrevolution was not the last word, however, and European politics impacted again. Pro-German Young Turks staged a revolution in Constantinople; Berlin in 1909 compelled a humiliating Russian confirmation of Austria's annexation of Bosnia; and Russia decided it needed British cooperation, given the threatening international situation. Again working together in Iran, the two powers could urge a compromise constitutional settlement, which restored the *majlis*. Clerical conservatives recovered the theoretical right of religious review of legislation, but the provision was never implemented. The victory of secular liberalism remained provisional and precarious, however. When the Iranians brought in an American financial expert, William Morgan Schuster, to establish a modern revenue service, the Russians demanded his dismissal, on the grounds that the Anglo-Russian Convention gave the powers the final say over such an appointment, and marched on Tehran when the *majlis* resisted. The cabinet gave way, dismissed Schuster, and dissolved the *majlis* in December 1911. The constitution remained but no new elections followed until 1914. Russian forces and the Azerbaijani revolutionary movements after 1917 dominated the northern half of the country, until the new Bolsheviks decided British trade was more important than insisting on heavy-handed control in Iran. They agreed to withdraw their troops. The British may have sponsored the coup d'état of 1921 led by the imposing military commander Reza Khan, who seized supreme power as shah in late 1925 and inaugurated the Pahlavi rule that lasted until the Islamic revolution of 1979.[12]

⁓

Iran was a poor and backward region compared with the Ottoman Empire, although Iranian intellectuals remembered when their empires had fought each other on a level of parity. Seeking to weather the international opprobrium that the attempted repression of the Balkan rebellions of 1875 had aroused, the new Sultan Abdülhamid II (1876–1908) first summoned a new parliament in 1876, then prorogued it and suspended the new constitution within little more than a year as Russia intervened militarily to support the hard-pressed Bulgarian uprising. Over the next three decades the sultan tightened a repressive political regime even as he sought to modernize economic and military institutions and develop the sleepy southern provinces of the empire. Istanbul's reform from above, however, led to incompatible ideological programs for sustaining a multinational empire: an effort, on the one hand, to woo Arabic Muslim elites, and, on the other, to advance a Turkic national movement, the Committee on Union and Progress (CUP), or Young Turks, particularly concerned about the influence of Greeks and Armenians. With the reduction of his European domains (formal cession of Romania, Serbia, Bosnia, Bulgaria, and Macedonia in 1856 and 1878), the new sultan began to stress an ideology of Pan-Islamism. Finances were the weak point: attempts to collect taxes in a decade of world economic downturn had helped to provoke the 1875 Bulgarian rebellion and the disastrous war with Russia. Part of the Berlin settlement involved establishing an international public debt oversight (Public Debt Administration) in 1881.

The sultan's efforts to consolidate his position by development in the Arab provinces and emphasis of his Muslim role, however, were destined to create vulnerability in the remaining European regions of the empire, long a site of its more capable administrators and soldiers. Rebellion and assassination seethed in ethnically and religiously mixed Macedonia, where the neighboring Balkan states and European interests all saw their opportunities. Tax revolts were erupting in Anatolia. The British and Russian monarchs, whose countries had recently negotiated their division of interests in Iran, met at Reval in June 1908, to discuss, so it was believed, intervention in Macedonia. Istanbul's humiliating feebleness provoked a nationalist reaction among so-called Young Turk officers stationed in Salonika, who formally constituted a Committee on Union and Progress, and mutinied to compel Abdülhamid to reinstate constitutional rights and parliament in summer 1908, and then ousted him a year later.[13] The sultan who succeeded him remained a powerless monarch, appointing the ministers that the parties and military who had led the last uprising or coup d'état imposed in the final acts of Ottoman constitutionalism until mid-1913.

CUP adherents had diverse aims: Ottomanism or a restoration of imperial control, including the compulsory teaching of Turkish, may have been dominant; some members advocated decentralization and perhaps dismantling into ethnic units; others were attracted to the idea of Turkic national leadership. Some were secularists and Westernizers; others advocated reasserting the commitment to Islam. All wanted a vigorous restoration of direction and an end to the temporizing, corruption, and clientelism they were convinced was rotting the legacy of a once great power. What they achieved, however, was an interval of coup and countercoup.

Open elections based on territory seated a parliament that was half non-Turkish. There was a CUP majority but a strong liberal opposition; and resentment grew against CUP domination. After the assassination of an opposition newspaper editor, there followed a counterrevolutionary mutiny and the potential debacle of the CUP in mid-April 1909, only to be reversed when Salonica military units of the Committee marched on the capital and forced reinstatement of the Young Turk government. The renewed CUP regime quickly lost power to military commanders and a reunited liberal opposition after it had been discredited by the Italian seizure of Libya and an uprising of Albanian Muslims. Still, CUP strength in the provinces allowed it to dissolve the parliament and win a resounding victory in 1912, only to be ousted by a military coalition, the "Saviour Officers," later in the year. The military saviors did not save European Turkish territory from the Balkan League of Serbs, Bulgarians, Montenegrins, and Greeks, who exploited Ottoman disarray to attack in October. Only their mutual jealousies let Constantinople recover the small strip of European coast that Turkey controls today. But the overall military humiliations of the Balkan wars gave the CUP a chance to reseize power and defend it from a counterputsch in the spring of 1913. Assassination of their vizier provided a pretext to impose authoritarian control and hammer the liberal opposition through arrests, show trials, and harsh sentences. Young Turk foreign policy was an opportunistic search for an ally: the British rejected the overture, while William II accepted it—fantasizing that the Caliphate might encourage Britain's Muslim subjects to revolt. CUP generals took over the ministry of war and the navy, brought the empire into the European war in late 1914, and made the infamous decision to massacre the Armenian minority a year later. The cadets and intellectuals who a decade earlier had organized to renew the empire ended up with a triumvirate that would ultimately destroy it.

The military option seemed initially to stabilize Turkish politics. Remarkably, the army that had so thoroughly disintegrated in the Balkan War of 1912—because of long neglect by Abdülhamid, according to German observers—was made into a relatively efficient force by 1914–1915 under German military advisers. But the pressures of a long war on four fronts (the Dardanelles, the Caucasus, Mesopotamia, and the Palestinian coast) took its toll. The empire was left as a rump state after the end of the world war: with ruinous

From empire to nation: Mustafa Kemal Atatürk in 1923. Kemal appears here as the successful Turkish military leader who has forced the end of the Ottoman Sultanate and negotiated with France and Great Britain the revised Treaty of Lausanne, which stabilized his country in its present borders. He is not yet wearing a business suit and homburg. The relentless authoritarian modernizer and secularizer of his country accepted the title *Atatürk* (Father of the Turks) in 1934. (Private Collection / Roger-Viollet, Paris / The Bridgeman Art Library)

inflation and debts, the last feeble sultan holed up in Constantinople with Greeks and British on the Ionian coast, and Italians seeking their own slice of territory. The Arab-speaking territories were carved up into British and French provinces, an Armenian state, and autonomous Kurdistan, created in eastern Anatolia, with international control of the Dardanelles and of Ottoman finances. Confronted with the humiliation of the Treaty of Sèvres, a nationalist parliament rallied in Ankara as the Grand National Assembly of

Turkey, while the vigorous military commander Mustafa Kemal, who had assumed ever greater organizational and command responsibilities in the war, emerged as the leader of a resurgent resistance. Over the next three years the nationalists secured Soviet recognition, reconquered Armenian territory, and eliminated serious rivals in the West to Kemal's authority. The French came to terms over the Syrian-Turkish border, and in 1922 Kemal smashed the Greek-British forces and compelled a new treaty of Lausanne by 1923, remembered today preeminently for the massive exchange of Greek and Turkish populations it stipulated. The Sultanate and Caliphate were separated; the sultan was declared to have vacated his post and the office was abolished. The Caliphate did not survive long, nor did religious schools. The Assembly officially declared Turkey a republic and elected Kemal as president. The Law for the Unification of Education established the secular state, although it recognized Islam as its official religion. In April 1923 Kemal founded the People's Party, which, to preempt an emerging opposition, reorganized as the Republican People's Party (RPP); by the early 1930s, after a brief interval of allowing a tolerated opposition, he began a concerted drive to make the ruling party into the exclusive instrument for changing society and state. Conservatives and traditionalists remained resistant to the reforms, which included changes in dress and the status of women. By 1934 Kemal took the title Atatürk, or father of the Turks, and the RPP was theoretically fused with state offices in the following year. Atatürk, though, resisted following the totalitarian model as it was gaining strength around him and preserved scope for private capitalists, but his death in 1938 and the approach of the war left Turkey with an uneasy balance between a semitolerated opposition and a powerful military-supported statist party.[14]

⌒

Consider finally the two revolutions at geographic extremes from the heartlands of Eurasia: in Mexico and China—the one the product of a state repeatedly contested by Europeans and North Americans; the other a sprawling empire that seemed, in the fears of its reformers, ready to be sliced apart like a watermelon. Developing states remained vulnerable because economic growth and modernization accentuated rather than overcame failures of representation. As president, Porfirio Díaz (1876–1910) progressively tightened an authoritarian regime after the long era of civil war and foreign intervention in Mexico, favoring a privileged circle of beneficiaries, including regional party bosses, industrialists, and large land and ranch owners. The ruling group became known collectively as the *científicos* because of the economic growth they supervised as they opened up the country to European and American investment in industry, mining, and railroads. But outsize rewards flowed to the favored elite. The first decade of the new century produced a host of dissatisfied claimants to a voice in government: the liberal middle classes, who had benefited from economic advance, a growing urban working class in the northern industries, spokesmen for Indian communal rights that had been eroded since the liberal victories of the 1850s, and rival generals. Díaz cracked down harshly on the labor unions; middle-class entrepreneurs resented the foreign-owned firms that remained closed to them; powerful regional families took offense at the clients Díaz favored. The increase in foreign investment (with inflationary price rises and a sharp drop in real wages in the North) gave way to an economic downturn in the wake of the US panic of 1907. The oligarchy managed to win its rigged congressional elections with implausible unanimity in 1910. Still, revolution seemed excluded by most observers—as it usually does on the eve of great uprisings, from 1789 to Eastern Europe in 1989 and Egypt in 2011—until a local uprising broke out in Chihuahua at the end of 1910. The leader of the opposition, Francisco Madero, a wealthy rancher who had denounced the regime, threw in his lot with the rebels, then accepted an agreement that provided for a now-deserted Díaz to resign before the presidential election of October 1911. Madero was triumphant, but political and territorial decomposition followed—it was not a coherent social revolution, but, so John Womack argues, "a struggle for power, in which different revolutionary factions contended not only against the old regime and foreign concerns, but also, often more so, against each other, over matters as deep as class and as shallow as envy." Looking at the results, "the victorious faction managed to dominate peasant movements and labour unions for the promotion of selected American and native businesses."[15]

This does not mean that different groups had no conflicting interests; they were as staunchly defended as anywhere else in this turbulent decade. But they remained unaggregated, concentrated on one or more of the regionally based armies (and often fragmented at even more local levels) that coalesced around the successive leaders seeking power. Victoriano Huerta removed Madero (murdered after stepping down) on behalf of conservative forces, including the Church, but resigned in mid-July 1915 before the threatened advance of forces led by Venustiano Carranza and Pancho Villa—the gifted military commander in Chihuahua who in late 1913 initiated a program of land redistribution. Carranza's and Villa's delegates met at the October 1914 convention at Aguascalientes, and Villa persuaded Emiliano Zapata to commit his southern army in return for further land reform, outlined in Zapata's Plan of Ayala, the most extensive agrarian program of the revolution. Zapata and Villa met as revolutionary heroes in Mexico City in late November 1914, but the strategically crucial Carranza-Villa agreement soon dissolved in acrimony. Aguascalientes had called on both leaders to stand down their military forces and renounce their own candidacy for the vacant presidency. Each imputed bad faith to the other; by 1915 their armies were involved in the fiercest fighting of the revolutionary decade.

Were there issues as well as ambitions that divided Carranza and Villa? According to Villa's biographer, a long-term historian of the revolution, they divided over the contrasting attitudes that had separated centralists and federalists in the preceding century: Carranza spoke for disciplined authority and control emanating from the capital, Villa for an improvised regionalism.[16] As of 1915, Villa was more willing to deal with President Wilson's efforts to control Mexican outcomes and ensure continuing oil supplies. But fortunes and alignments could change rapidly. Villa's friendly relations with the American representatives in Mexico and his military fortunes turned sour in late 1915. Although Carranza had been a staunch nationalistic opponent of Wilson's expedition to Veracruz in 1914, once Villa attempted his raids on US soil and the United States entered the war with Germany, the White House endorsed Carranza's presidency. Zapata's alliance with Villa also frayed, and he was killed shortly after the brief, exuberant triumph in Mexico City. Carranza was elected president and inaugurated a constitution in 1917; and by late 1920 his military ally, Álvaro Obregón from Sonora succeeded him and began the work of reconsolidating the greatly indebted Mexican economy—providing an interval of stabilization at a moment, too, when bourgeois normalization was returning to Europe and its colonies after the global upheavals of 1917–1921. Obregón did continue the distribution of hacienda lands to smaller proprietors or communal *ejidos,* although rather selectively where this program had helped to ignite revolution, as in Zapata's home state of Morelos. He also sponsored the energetic educational reforms of José Vasconcelos, the *spiritus rector* of the revolutionary state, who helped create the mythic history of Indian-Hispanic cultural fusion through school expansion, murals, and mobilization of the populist intellectuals. Obregón's successor, Plutarco Elías Calles, supervised a major anticlerical campaign worthy of the struggles a century earlier and provoked a tenacious pro-clerical Cristero uprising by rural Church adherents. Then his four-year term as president ended in 1928, and the election again of Obregón (to be assassinated a day later) threatened a shift to the left, Calles as unofficial godfather of the emerging regime managed to organize the major vehicle for stabilization, the Partido Nacional Revolucionario (PNR), the predecessor to the Partido Revolucionario Institucional (PRI) that would govern until the 1990s.[17]

⟋

Halfway around the world, in China, the regime finally fell only in 1911 after seventy years of defeats to foreigners, exhausting rebellion, and continued infringements of sovereignty, all of which culminated in a wave of setbacks in the 1890s and paralyzing court politics. The defeat by Japan in 1895 and the renewed Western scramble for further territorial concessions finally jolted a widespread but contested intellectual opening—forcibly stifled, however, by the empress dowager's countercoup against the young emperor and his radical advisers—only to throw her support to the nationalist organizations known as Boxers who attacked the Beijing legations and provoked a united foreign intervention. Still, the years from 1898 to the final Qing abdication were an epoch of extraordinary reformist effort, which could not be kept under conservative gentry control nor ultimately held in check by the Europeans. The ancient examination system that had structured elite access to rule was removed in 1905; meanwhile reformers were asking for inauguration of a hierarchy of local assemblies as well as a national parliament.[18] The Confucian ideologies appealed to in earlier reform efforts were superseded by images of modernization and of Darwinist national competition, already seen by many Chinese as successful in Japan. Impatient exiles (such as Sun Yat-sen) and military leaders converged to launch what, from the vantage of the centennial of the 1911 revolution, can be interpreted as a long trajectory that would lead, via the Republic (1911–1949), then devastating war and civil war and the vast costs of Mao's revolution, to Deng Xiaoping's emulation of capitalism.[19]

In China, the parliament established in Beijing fell under the influence of Yuan Shikai, the talented military (and police) leader, who was tempted to claim the imperial throne but died by 1916. His death led to a dozen years of rival claims and the emergence of powerful war-lords who imposed de facto territorial governments, collected or extorted "tax" revenues, raised peasant armies, and joined shifting "cliques" or alliances, holding out longest in the Manchurian area around the Liaodong Peninsula, where the Japanese held the key ports and railroads since their wars with China (1894–1995) and Russia (1904–1905). The Japanese could help finance the leading northern warlord, Zhang Zuolin, in return for his deference to their own position, but he was ousted in 1928 after a failed effort to reorganize central-state politics in Beijing. The revolutionary forces in the south under the ambitious Chiang Kai-shek set up their own rival base, entrusting subordinate power to the graduates of the new Whampoa military academy. Chiang was more than a general: he inherited Sun Yat-sen's Guomindang (GMD, or National People's Party) and drew on Russian Bolshevik aid and counsel to create an authoritarian party. Bolshevik leaders in Moscow sharply divided on the issue of whether to instruct the Chinese Communist Party (CCP) to work with Chiang or challenge him. Stalin, seeking in the mid-1920s to establish his own succession at home against Trotsky and other possible rivals who urged autonomy for the CCP, insisted on subordinating the CCP to the GMD. The policy led to catastrophe in 1926–1927, for as his power increased Chiang turned on his former Communist allies and destroyed part of the party, murdering thousands first in Shanghai, then in Wuhan and Nanjing—leaving the remnants to retreat from Shanghai, and ultimately in the 1930s to trek thousands of miles to establish their mountain sanctuary under Mao Zedong in Yan'an in Shaanxi Province.

Despite the fragmentation, violence, and confusing succession of the revolutionary decade in China, the turbulence involved more than just the final denouement of a massive state structure hammered by foreigners and increasingly unable to overcome an ossified ideology, vast population increase, and ecological catastrophes and impoverishment. It also allowed a belated but energetic effort to merge traditional cultural resources with models of development frenetically taken from abroad. Warlords continued to contend for power around Beijing and in Japanese-occupied Manchuria, but by the end of the 1920s Chiang's army, and party—now drawing on German rather than Russian advisers—seemed poised to take Beijing (a development, as explained below, that would lead the ambitious Japanese military government of the region to establish the "puppet state" of Manchukuo under the nominal rule of the last deposed Qing emperor, "Henry" Pu Yi). Ultimately neither Chinese army leaders nor the revolutionary parties could impose a clear success without some fusing of effort, reflected still today in the strong role that the People's Liberation Army plays in the Communist state.[20]

Generally economic growth and development have been viewed as an asset in the path to political liberalism. During the Cold War most American social scientists did not doubt that they went together. Perhaps this was true in eras when development had homegrown roots, but the remarkable economic and financial advances of the era from 1895 to 1914, as they unfolded in the context of global inequality that marked the age of high imperialism, could not ensure liberal outcomes. The epochal revolutions in Russia, China, Mexico, Iran, and Turkey certainly mobilized masses of rural families and workers as well as urban dwellers across all classes. They awoke new currents of nationalism and encouraged cultural awakening: intellectuals envisaged awakening nations, but were also stimulated by the very awakenings they sought to advance and shape. But the mass forces, and the breadth of the social and religious movements whose volunteers descended from their homes into the city squares across half the world, were not easily contained by constitutional and parliamentary debates. As these raw and vigorous, sometimes violent, ideological transformations worked themselves out, usually over a span of at least two or three decades, it was the determined cadres of committed parties and military corps that disciplined their sometimes generous but often intolerant forces. The twentieth-century world that emerged from the wave of global revolution was a more participatory one, but not necessarily a freer one. Or more precisely, the bonds of private subjection—to landlords, local bosses, mine and factory owners—were exchanged often, not for liberal values (which seemed to reinforce private bonds of subjection for so many), but for the bonds of public discipline. Ironically enough, it was the very countries that were exponents of liberalism at home, but also convinced of the civic virtues of economic expansion, that helped plunge the huge countries outside Europe (and its offshoots) into the turbulence of foreign-controlled development, revolutionary protest, and military and one-party solutions. Sixty or seventy years later these experiments—their own disfunctionality having been repeatedly demonstrated in the years after consolidation in the 1920s—might finally be yielding to the sort of world that their early exponents envisaged.

Politics as War

No one can say what would have been the upshot of this widespread turbulence had war not broken out in Europe in 1914 and then developed into a protracted and unprecedented conflict. Where economic and voting issues were at stake, gradual compromise might have had a chance: suffrage reform and welfare legislation were all emerging before 1914. An unruly Russian republic might have settled down as of 1920. Racial minorities in the United States and South Africa might have had to wait a long time to secure voting and civil rights—as they did in fact. Nationalist aspirations might not have waited so long, and it is hard to envisage their solution without local violence—precisely the situation, however, that did ignite general war in summer 1914. The Habsburgs could not easily make their territories into a confederation of nationalities. The Germans within the Austrian half might have allowed it, but Hungarians would have resisted, and whether the Romanians and South Slavs outside the empire would have accepted such a compromise for their own irredenta within is doubtful. Would a restored and sovereign Polish nation have emerged without war? To review the alternatives is to realize that at best local clashes were hard to avoid even if better crisis management might have avoided the fatal great-power involvement that made a new Balkan crisis into World War I. Would the Ottoman state—led since 1908 by a party that feared subversion from all the non-Turkic peoples it attempted to control— have avoided continued war and decomposition? The British government's imperial compromise in South Asia with upper-class Hindus and Muslims would have gradually come undone, as it did from the 1930s on.

Historians conventionally describe decolonization as a sequel to the Second World War, an epochal transformation, compelled in part by their European rulers' interim defeat and financial exhaustion. In fact, the points of inflection came earlier. By the end of the 1920s a new generation of young nationalists came to the fore, impatient with their elders' clientelistic bargains with European rules. The economic crisis of the 1930s then brought its misery not only to Europe and North America but to the colonial economies as well. It added widespread labor unrest, in cities and on plantations, to nationalist sentiments as a potent challenge to the colonial state. By the mid-1930s, the alternatives were escalating violence or reform efforts that must ultimately lead to far more self-government than reformers wished to admit.[21] Of course, the interwar economic crisis itself might not have assumed such proportions without the disruptions of international finance and trade that the war of 1914–1918 left behind. Historical causation is always cumulative and sequential.

Stability and representation without multiparty democracy might have served many states. Single-party rule, such as emerged in Mexico and later in many postcolonial states, might have provided transitional stability for divided polities. Not all single parties must be repressive structures; some allow outside groups to dissent and can serve—at least for a generation or two—to represent different social currents and ideas. World War I did not preclude such outcomes. Nonetheless, even before the war, more radical party claims suggested a different outcome for some of the states in difficulty. The Russian Social-Democrat V. I. Lenin argued in his 1902 tract, *What Is to Be Done?* (echoing the title of a Russian radical's celebrated appeal forty years earlier), that revolution required a centralized political party demanding unswerving discipline. The single party allegedly spoke for the proletariat, endowed the working class with revolutionary consciousness, and was thus summoned to impose revolutionary dictatorship in their name.[22] Later Lenin seemed briefly to entertain the idea that a Bolshevik utopia might ultimately lead to the end of the traditional state, but the hard politics outlined in his 1902 essay remained the agenda for the foreseeable future. The Bolshevik Party would guide the authoritarian dictatorship that governed Russia (and its reorganized empire) from the civil war of 1917 to 1921 through the death of Lenin's successor, Joseph Stalin, in March 1953—and, with a softer mix of surveillance and punishment, for another thirty-some years until the late 1980s.

French Jacobins had outlined a concept of revolutionary terror and the ruthless elimination of enemies under Robespierre, but the Jacobins had improvised dictatorship and a theory of republican virtue to rationalize the harsh measures they were imposing. On the basis of Marx's historical dramaturgy of class conflict, Lenin transformed the ad hoc Jacobin rationalizations of 1792–1794 into a doctrine of long-term revolution long before he could impose power. Even more disturbing than his own authoritarian claims was the assent that this theory of party dictatorship could win from many Western intellectuals. After the Revolution, sympathizers abroad claimed that the Soviet homeland after 1917 was isolated and beleaguered and the only site where the socialist revolution existed in practice. Any questioning of

The promise of the proletariat: A poster from 1920 depicting Russian leader Vladimir Lenin addressing workers against an industrial backdrop at a moment when the Bolsheviks still felt that their revolution might spread to the West. The caption, which reads, "A specter is roaming across Europe, the specter of communism," echoes the famous opening lines of Karl Marx and Friedrich Engels's *Communist Manifesto* of 1848. (Museum of the Revolution, Moscow / The Bridgeman Art Library)

its policies must be subordinated to the cause of its survival, as defined by the leaders in Moscow.

No one can understand the history of twentieth-century political debate and experience without working through the problem of Communist obedience. Did the Communist intellectuals and the nonparty sympathizers ("fellow travelers," to use the later term) somehow crave self-abasement, as critics such as the Polish exile Czesław Miłosz later suggested with his fable of the magic pills that made them happily yield to the charms of totalitarian power?[23] Was it the merciless logic imposed, as they believed, by the unyielding laws of history? Good communists took pride in their commitment to a disciplined body that demanded obedience even as it reassured members that they alone understood and were advancing the inexorable processes of history. In his 1922 essay *History and Class Consciousness,* the Communist philosopher Georg Lukács—who after a subsequent generation of Stalinist repression would actually strive to moderate dictatorship in 1956 Hungary—set out the dialectical logic of a party dictatorship already emerging in Russia as the Bolsheviks shut down alternative parties, established their Cheka or secret police, and used military force to suppress the Kronstadt fortress mutiny: "The forms of freedom in bourgeois organizations are nothing but a 'false consciousness' of an actual unfreedom. . . . Only when this is understood can our earlier paradox be resolved: . . . the unconditional absorption of the total personality in the praxis of the movement, was the only possible way of bringing about an authentic freedom." Praxis meant discipline and subservience, but to policies that in the long run had to be objectively correct (although errors might be made from day to day). "The question of discipline is then, on the one hand, an elementary practical problem for the party, an indispensable precondition for its effective functioning. . . . The Communist Party must exist as an independent organization so that the proletariat may be able to see its own class consciousness given historical shape. . . . [T]he fact that it is a fighting party presupposes its possession of a correct theory, for otherwise the consequences of a false theory would soon destroy it."[24] Such reasoning and commitment could justify the visceral hatred of "bourgeois" privilege, the vituperative attacks on social democratic critics and rivals, the Nazi-Soviet pact of 1939, and the show trials and executions of the 1930s and the 1950s. Nonetheless, it is not enough to recite a record of intellectual and sometimes moral debasement; the historian has to account for how the communist vocation could appear so compelling to so many adherents. They attributed their choices to the disasters they felt capitalism was accumulating, whether the carnage of the First World

War or the mass unemployment and misery before which bourgeois statesmen seemed so hopeless. For them communism alone offered a viable alternative to the fascist violence that no other parties effectively opposed, to the colonial rule that the Western countries seemed determined to perpetuate, and, in the United States, to the deep-seated racism that neither mainstream political party would challenge.

Admittedly, too, the lives actually constructed in the Russian society that the Party aspired to transform were far more diverse and disorderly, negotiated during an era of vast economic and social transformation, crowded, communal, and demanding, accompanied by bewildering policy shifts—and not to be simply understood as a neat working-out of dialectics. Still, at the time Lukács was claiming this higher freedom, he was well aware that the Leninist party ruling the Soviet Union had purged—that is, at this time, expelled—tens of thousands of its early members and shut down all other party organizations as a conclusion drawn from its supposedly privileged insights into historical necessity. By the time Stalin consolidated his personal power, the term *purge* would also entail the waves of mass arrests, long sentences to the forced-labor camps of the gulag with mortality rates estimated at up to 25 percent annually, or execution in obscurity—one reasoned estimate suggests that over seven hundred thousand did not return. Historians have debated whether the impulse to purify the party and the organizations of culture, administration, the military and economic life came from Stalin's own continual distrust of the revolutionary movement or responded to enthusiasms and impatience from the rank and file. In any case these convulsive waves of lives blighted or destroyed came to be seen as the characteristic phenomenon of the regime.[25]

The Soviet Party would create the Soviet Union in 1922 and would impose allied parties in Eastern Europe from 1945 until the end of the 1980s, although there would be differing degrees of compliance. (Yugoslavia became a communist dictatorship, although it broke with the Soviet bloc in 1948.) Party structures that demanded the same discipline would govern China, North Korea, Vietnam, and Cambodia for parts of the second half of the twentieth century and seek to take power in many other states. Even where that possibility was remote, as in Britain and the United States, Soviet party emissaries would often ask local members to engage in clandestine espionage on behalf of Moscow. Even the fascist parties, and the National Socialist Party, who ran a system just as cruel, did not make party membership as such so central a component of exacting total commitment. And although by the outbreak of World War II, in 1939, the rulers of Germany were running a chain of perhaps eight hundred concentration camps, most of them small labor dependencies of the notorious large *Lager,* such as Dachau, Sachsenhausen, Buchenwald, Belsen, and Mauthausen, they filled them with close to a million opponents and not usually their own membership. There were two waves of the collective arrests and punishments we term "purges": the liquidation of the Sturmabteilung (SA) leadership (and other potential opponents) initiated on June 30, 1934, and the roundup, arrest, and execution of the army, civil service, and remaining democratic elements implicated in the assassination attempt of July 20, 1944. Each wave was on the order of a thousand; executions were far fewer. This is not to suggest a gentle state: tens of thousands passed through interrogation and detention, further tens of thousands of "handicapped"—so-called life unworthy of life—were murdered in state hospitals, tens of thousands of German soldiers would be executed by their own army during the war, and, all told, millions of Jews, non-Jewish Poles, Roma and Sinti, Russian prisoners of war, and captured Soviet party officials and others were liquidated in occupied Europe.[26]

For the Bolsheviks, class war remained a vivid doctrine; but the term usually referred to a rather impersonal process taking place through collectivization of agriculture from the late 1920s and of industrial production during the 1930s. When national groups resisted, as in Ukraine, then class war took on dimensions of genocidal starvation, as in the early 1920s and again with even greater force at the end of the decade and into the thirties. Warfare in the sense of military combat became central to the Soviet experience in the civil and Polish wars from 1918 to 1921 and after the German invasion of 1941; Marx and Engels had been keen observers of the mid-nineteenth-century wars of national reconstruction. But warfare as a dimension of human experience did not play a central ideological role in European Marxism-Leninism. This would change with the anticolonial struggles in Asia and Africa after 1945, as Communist leaders such as Ho Chi Minh, Vo Nguyen Giap, and Mao Zedong affirmed that peasant struggles and guerrilla warfare were central to the historical process of workers' emancipation.

However, another ideological constellation emerging from the First World War did place the experience of combat front and center in personal and political life. Fascists affirmed not only that war was an experience important for manhood (that belief had long had advocates), but that politics at its most basic must be akin to war, was in fact a form of war itself. War called forth the essentials demanded by manhood: loyalty and comradeship, command and obedience, and courage. Soldiers sacrificed themselves for their nation and for their fellow comrades. Liberal politicians in World War I had stayed at home, immune from danger, chatting away in their feckless parliaments while the youth of their societies were consumed in distant battlefields. War, the Prussian general Carl von Clausewitz had written, should be thought of as politics—as the pursuit of rational policy, by other means. Wasn't it true, though, to think of politics as war by other means? Insofar as there was a common content to the doctrines we think of as fascist (and here I am including National Socialism), it lay in this belief. Political life must be waged as a struggle, a search to dominate, not just legislate. It was adversarial and hard, it demanded obedience to a party and leader just as military organization did, and often its leaders and cadres donned quasi-military uniforms for party gatherings.

Several variants of this stance developed, diverse in key respects but elaborated around this common belief. Fascists and Nazis often claimed to despise abstract ideas, but intellectuals competed to elaborate their doctrines, and some were serious thinkers. Fascism originally claimed to be revolutionary and highly nationalist: from Mussolini's organization of the Fascio di Combattimento in March 1919, to Hitler's call for a National Revolution, to French fascists' belief that they needed a revolution against bourgeois morality. Fascists and National Socialists alike knew what they were against: certainly the organized parties and labor unions affiliated with Social Democracy, and the liberal democratic parties inherited from the nineteenth century. Toward organized political Catholicism they remained more open, disdainful in Germany but willing to compromise, and ultimately courting the church in Italy with concessions on education and marriage that abandoned the claims of the earlier liberal state.

⁓

Fascism and communism cannot be appreciated just as fixed doctrines. They claimed to be revolutionary movements before they seized power. Generally the fascists considered Bolshevism as their most fundamental ideological adversary, but occasionally the two groups cooperated opportunistically, as during the crisis of the German Republic in the early 1930s. They both rejected the premises of political liberalism as developed since the late eighteenth century. Both claimed to leave bourgeois sentiment behind—the communists in favor of a new proletarian collectivism, the fascists on behalf of a contradictory mix of values rooted in the ancestral soil but also in the modern claims of technological innovation. Georges Sorel, the French theorist of revolutionary violence and a self-professed despiser of the bourgeois humanism he traced to the Enlightenment, outlined a regime of "syndicates," or unions of producers cutting across capital and labor, before the First World War. Only political combat, not necessarily sanguinary, based

Collapse of the German military machine: An improvised trench filled with German dead after the hard fighting of late July 1918 as French and Americans retook the Soissons region in the Second Battle of the Marne. The French would lose 1.3 million, the Germans 1.8 million, in a war that made military discipline, mass suffering, injury, economic devastation, and death an unexpected denouement of nineteenth-century European "civilization." (Private Collection / Ken Welsh / The Bridgeman Art Library)

on "myth" or grand abstractions of Armageddon, could renew society.[27] Sorel would welcome Lenin in his postwar editions; the Italian syndicalists (some of whom spent time organizing workers as "Wobblies" in the American West before World War I) and antidemocratic Right would read Sorel. But this common prewar source could invigorate political movements: constructing a state on their basis, as we shall see, required further ideas and more repressive decrees. Both fascism and Bolshevism would emphasize the single party, with its mass youth organizations and suborned cultural associations, as the instrument for seizing and exercising power. Once safely in power, however, their leaders would discipline their parties so that they took on more and more personal authority, even if they exercised it inconsistently. Both parties in power would seek to shape civil society and actually claim to remake "man." They would alternate periods of "normal" authority and the proud achievement of "consensus" with convulsive efforts to revivify their original dynamism, whether through party purges in the Soviet Union or preparations for national expansion and war in Italy and Germany. Both systems exalted the grand enterprise or project, some of which were merely hollow theatricality (the March on Rome itself) and others really transformative—the clearing of malarial lands around Rome, the German autobahns, or the industrialization of the Donets Basin, Magnitogorsk, the huge hydroelectric stations, and ultimately the rearmament programs in Germany and Russia.[28] The "project" admittedly was a fixation wider than the fascist and communist states—they shared it with many regimes before and after and certainly in the 1930s, including the New Deal.

Fascist and communist movements emerged at a common historical moment—as between 1917 and 1923 political momentum arced in a trajectory from Left to Right. The Bolshevik seizure of power reinforced a worldwide explosion of radical claims—whether by industrial workers and the left in Europe or fledgling anticolonial movements in Asia. Protests against a peace settlement that seemed to backtrack from

Wilsonian rhetoric sent students and intellectuals into the streets of Beijing on May 4, 1919. In India, workers were striking in Punjabi cotton mills and protesting the British refusal to relax wartime martial law. Radicalized labor unions struck throughout Western Europe. Self-declared communists seized power briefly in Bavaria and in Hungary. But while the Bolsheviks held on in Russia, the worldwide moment of the left passed. In the United States there was a crackdown on radical publications and recent socialist immigrants. Communist uprisings in 1921 and 1923 Germany proved fiascos—the right came back, not only in authoritarian form in Hungary, Italy, and Spain, but as a reorganized bourgeois order in which industry and state authorities stabilized Western Europe, and the colonial powers reasserted their authority from the Middle East to South Asia.[29]

Mussolini's small movement had no success in its original effort to win parliamentary seats in the November 1919 elections. But extralegal action became a more promising way to win adherents in the turbulent political and labor conditions of postwar northern Italy. Public-service strikes were frequent; workers staged sit-down stoppages in the industries of Milan and Turin; socialists organized agricultural laborers and imposed new labor contracts on resentful landowners, while militant Catholic priests encouraged small peasant proprietors to unionize. For the proprietors and lawyers and industrialists of northern Italy, it seemed that revolution was gathering momentum from the ground up. At the same time, returning veterans felt that their recent military service was devalued. The nationalist poet Gabriele D'Annunzio organized a group of nationalist soldiers and seized the former Habsburg port of Fiume on the Adriatic, which they feared would be awarded by the Allies to the new Yugoslav state. The government in Rome did not approve but feared the repercussions of ejecting him. Mussolini and his early adherents could observe that grassroots nationalist activism, resentment at local labor militancy, and the weakness of Rome's policing power in the provinces gave him an opportunity to implant fascism on the basis of local "squads" that would shatter the local unions and socialist party administrations. The emerging fascist movement thus won key support from the agrarian elites of the agriculturally rich Po Valley during 1920–1922, as their local black-shirted "squads" drove into towns to beat up local labor organizers and devastate the union or party headquarters. The militias went from trashing union halls to invading city halls, compelling the cabinets in Rome—divided on whether to exploit fascist violence against the Left or to attempt to reimpose law and order—to suspend socialist town councils and appoint commissioners. By 1921 Mussolini had created enough of a force to reorganize his movement as the National Fascist Party and claim a place alongside the amorphous liberal groups in the electoral coalition of 1921, winning thirty-five seats in the new Chamber of Deputies (the lower and decision-making house of the parliament ever since 1848). By the autumn of 1922 he seemed the indispensable partner for the more conservative groupings of the loose coalition that still described itself as "liberal," and he was threatening to extend to the south of Italy the same quasi-insurrectionary movement his lieutenants had installed in the north.

Mussolini and his sympathizers exploited a final liberal coalition crisis by preparations for a march on Rome by his black-shirted columns when the king called him to be prime minister at the end of October 1922. For two years he governed supposedly as a legal prime minister, and held elections in April 1924 under a revised voting law that guaranteed his supporters almost two-thirds of the Chamber. But the habits of revolutionary violence among his youthful troops were not easily disciplined, and the younger radicals in his ranks feared he might become just another party leader. Despite the coalition's majority, the old parties and parliamentary deputies that had supported him threatened to desert after close lieutenants were implicated in the kidnapping and beating to death of an opposition socialist leader, Giacomo Matteotti, who had denounced campaign violence. As the liberal politicians and journalists chided him, while his young radical supporters urged a "second revolution," Mussolini decided that he would have to choose between his party base and political defeat. In early 1925 he imposed emergency legislation to control the press and arrest opposition leaders. The twilight liberalism of 1922 to 1924 was ended.

Over the next few years the regime leaders installed the institutions of a fascist state: a political tribunal, extensive secret police spying and eventually arrest of the opposition, and a Grand Council of Fascism that combined Fascist Party officials and cabinet ministers in a supposed fusion of the state with the single party. The new institutions reflected the contribution of Alfredo Rocco, who had come from the far-right Nationalist Party that had emphasized turn-of-the-century functional legal theory, and would in the mid-1920s design the political tribunal and press for an unchallenged state.

What observers often identified as the distinctive contribution of the Fascist state (aside from its alleged fusion with a single party) was the replacement of parliamentary by functional or occupational representation. This took place by stages from the mid-1920s to the mid-thirties. Although socialist and Catholic trade unions were marginalized, there was a tradition of fascist unions (called syndicates, as unions were in French, too), who did occasionally stand up to employers. Their leaders had emerged from the prewar syndicalist movement and had been active in organizing Italian dockworkers, and had sometimes even migrated to the American West as labor organizers, before returning with the war and becoming enthusiasts of Mussolini. A major strike of northern steelworkers in the spring of 1925 proved their last quasi-independent labor action under the Fascist regime. The strike was ended; the labor representatives were centralized into a single official Fascist union federation whose official status was to be recognized by the employers grouped in the Italian Confederation of Industry—now reorganized themselves as the Fascist Confederation of Industry.

When the new Fascist labor federation appeared to claim too much influence, it was split again three years later into various occupational groups. Meanwhile, representatives of the different industrial sectors and the service, medical, hospitality, agricultural, and other divisions of the economy were organized into official syndicates to be grouped by the 1930s into a network of corporations.

But in many ways the Fascist state represented continuity with the older liberal institutions. Mussolini's title remained "Head of Government" (prime minister), even though unofficially he became known as "Il Duce," or the leader. The king remained the head of state and finally exercised his prerogative to dismiss Mussolini as the wager on joining Hitler in the second war threatened disastrous invasion by the Allies in the summer of 1943. To enhance his own domestic position at the end of the 1920s, Mussolini actually retreated from the secular claims of the Italian liberal state and signed the 1929 Lateran Pact with the Vatican, which restored Church control over marriage, installed crucifixes in schoolrooms, and recognized the sovereign ministate of the Vatican. By the 1930s, Mussolini could take pride in having achieved a certain "consensus" at home. Political adversaries went into exile or, if arrested at home, were punished largely by being sent into forced residence in remote southern villages *(confino)*. There were only a handful of executions, largely imposed for assassination efforts. Most of the violence—beatings, some fatal, castor oil, the devastation of Socialist and trade-union offices—took place in unofficial clashes on the road to power. Franco's military dictatorship after seizing power, later the Argentine generals and General Pinochet in Chile, would accumulate far more corpses, with arrests and illegal torture and murder in the tens of thousands.

But those were presented as emergency interventions. Fascists claimed that their mission was not just to defeat communists, but to rule as the stewards for an entire historical epoch: the Nazis talked of a thousand-year Reich. Fascism would somehow fulfill man in a way the program of liberal individualism and party pluralism never could. Fascism, so Rocco agued, was rectifying the terrible wrong turn that history had taken in 1789 when the French Revolution had enshrined the rights of man and the citizen. But it did not claim to reject democracy in the name just of tradition and monarchy, as, for instance, such rightist authoritarian groups as Action Française did in France. It was not merely reactionary: it was designed to institute a new historical stage that Mussolini—borrowing a term from his detractors of the early 1920s—made into a particular merit: it aspired to be "totalitarian." Fascist doctrine had evolved significantly since Mussolini's demand for revolutionary renewal in 1919: now fascism was presented as a regime that reestablished a state that transcended individual or even group interests. How does the fascist state differ from the liberal state, Rocco asked rhetorically: "The fascist state is the state that realizes to the maximum the power and cohesion of the juridical organization of society. And society, according to the fascist concept, is not just a sum of individuals but an organism that has its own life and ends that transcend those of the individuals and its own spiritual and historical value. The state too . . . is an organism distinct from the citizens who compose it at any moment: it has its own life and its own ends superior to those of individuals and to which ends must be subordinated." As Mussolini put it in his contribution to the authoritative Treccani Encyclopedia in 1932: "for the fascist everything is in the state and nothing human or spiritual exists—even less so, can have value—outside the state."[30] Men and women fulfilled their potential, not as individuals with inalienable rights, but as members of a nation and subjects of a state with obligations and duties, among which was military virtue. Politics was a form of war, but designed to prepare for war: better a day as a lion than a year as a jackal. Mussolini thought periodically to posture as a man of peace, but the ideology was connected with military virtues. He resorted to force over the Dodecanese Islands with Greece, and in 1935–1936 provoked a war with Abyssinia, using air power and poison gas. He muscled in on Albania in 1937 and after casting his lot in with Hitler declared war on France in 1940, occupying Nice.

In practice the state was far from totalitarian in the sense of unremitting control through terror that later critics suggested was essential. The Church continued as a sanctioned presence although the Party sought to undermine its youth organization, Catholic Action. The family was glorified and the Party encouraged child bearing for the Duce, but the family was also a node of resistance to state claims. Later apologists ridiculed the pretenses of the leader and his regime, in effect presenting the experience as a form of *opera buffa,* distasteful but hardly to be taken seriously. Such a view, however, underestimates its novelty, its brutality on the path to power, its determination to silence those who did not agree. Like the glorious baroque edifices of Rome, façade was crucial to fascist politics—but like them, too, there was an authenticity to its grandiose style.[31]

The Italian model was influential and would be imitated. In 1923 the Spanish monarch installed General Miguel Primo de Rivera as a dictator, calling him "my Mussolini," but this was in the tradition of nineteenth-century strongmen—there was no ideological ambition. In Argentina the military took over in 1930, and its army strongman, General José Félix Uriburu, came close to asserting the fascist claims of transcendent leadership and encouraging a nationalist and authoritarian movement.[32] More durably, the Brazilian civilian political leader Getúlio Vargas seized power in the same year in Brazil, created a "New State" with authoritarian corporatist institutions, until ousted in 1945 as fascism seemed to crumble the world over, but was then elected president in 1950, governed as a nationalist dictator until 1954, when, faced with impending overthrow, he took his own life. António de Oliveira Salazar became prime minister in the Portuguese military dictatorship that had seized power from the republic in 1926 and instituted his "New State" from 1933 until 1968, administering a Catholic authoritarian corporatism, tenaciously holding Portugal's colonies, and becoming a NATO ally.

The variant of fascism that came to power in Germany was different in key respects. Hitler understood the sort of power Mussolini was striving for, and like him adopted the paramilitary uniform—the boots, the colored shirts—and the paramilitary organization. He learned from his unsuccessful "Beer Hall Putsch" in 1923 that no matter how divided the Weimar Republic might be, if the army stood behind the enforcement of the law, he could not seize power by force. During the years of economic and political stabilization from 1924 through 1929, his movement seemed destined to wither away, but the economic difficulties of the Protestant countryside (and the demagogic campaign at the end of the 1920s against a revised reparations plan) started raising his local voting totals even before the world depression struck in 1929 and 1930. Like Mussolini he railed against the system, pouring scorn on the divisions among parties that led to unwieldy policy compromises over welfare or foreign and military policy. Proportional representation meant that the postwar Italian Chamber and the Weimar Republic's Reichstag were afflicted with party fragments that found it hard to coalesce into stable majorities and oppositions. When the world depression began to take its toll on employment after 1930 and no majority could be found to finance unemployment insurance, the president and chancellor had to resort to constitutionally sanctioned decree provisions (under the fateful Article 48 of the Weimar Constitution) for passing the budget. Under such conditions Communists on the left and Hitler's National Socialists on the right (though that term hardly conveyed their radicalism) could rail against "the system." They could always denounce the reparations payments imposed after the Versailles Treaty, and even the mitigation of obligations embodied in the Dawes Plan of 1924 and the Young Plan of 1930. They could claim that the postwar Eastern borders (and the Polish Corridor that separated

East Prussia from the rest of Germany) had to be rectified. And differing fundamentally from the Italian Fascists (until 1938), Nazis could excoriate the Jews as a racial minority responsible for these evils and fundamentally hostile to German interests. Although some Nazi adherents and propagandists found enough to attack without specific reference to Germany's Jewish misfortune, anti-Semitism remained a core element of the movement just as it had infected much of the other parties' discourse as well—it was the political lingua franca of the right in Central and Eastern Europe. Jews supposedly controlled banks and journalism, infiltrated the university and theater, exploited the peasantry, and ultimately defiled the blood of the gentile women they took to bed.

After two years of parliamentary paralysis and elections in 1930, July 1932, and November 1932, which saw the Nazi parliamentary delegation rise to almost 40 percent of the Reichstag (and brought them to coalitions in some key state governments), the political system of the Weimar Republic fell apart. Rival chancellor candidates torpedoed each other and called in army generals to claim that the country might become indefensible. The paramilitary party militias fought in weekend city brawls, suggesting that civil war might threaten at home. The coterie around the aging president Field Marshal von Hindenburg suggested that only Hitler's appointment might provide stability and that in power he would be controlled by traditional conservative circles from the economy and the military. They underestimated his skill and dynamic populism. Hitler moved far quicker than Mussolini had, although he benefited from the fascist model. Appointed as chancellor of a right-wing coalition on January 30, 1933, he dissolved the Reichstag and called new elections, which would yield the National Socialists 43 percent (but not a majority) of the votes after a month of charged political events. The party used the successful arson attack against the Reichstag building in late February (blamed on the Communists by the Nazis, then attributed to a Nazi provocation by the left outside Germany, but probably the work of a Dutch anarchist) as a pretext to arrest the Communist deputies and clamp down on the press. What Hitler sought was a constitution-amending majority of two-thirds of the parliament for a grant of decree power, tempered only by the proviso that the Reichstag would in theory remain free to reassert its role. Formally the Weimar Constitution remained in place; but this new Enabling Act served in effect as a charter for expanding domination. Having removed the Communist delegation, he came to an agreement with the Catholic Center and the Vatican. In return for a Concordat with Berlin, guaranteeing the Church's religious presence, the Center Party abstained on the decisive vote, leaving only the Social Democrats in opposition and securing the needed two-thirds majority.

In the same crowded weeks the regime set up its first two concentration camps outside Munich and Berlin—Dachau and Sachsenhausen-Oranienburg—to hold political prisoners (not yet Jews as such) without formal trial. Storm troopers led a boycott of Jewish stores. Over the next months the government would announce control over the press, "reform" the civil service by removing Jews from government employment and teaching positions, press the political parties to dissolve themselves—the SPD executive went into exile—replace elected state legislatures with appointed commissioners, and announce the so-called fusion of party and state. This achieved, Hitler, like Mussolini in the late 1920s, actually tended to subordinate Party autonomy. The hopes of Nazi radicals to push through a second revolution based on the SA—an aspiration the professional army viewed with contempt and alarm—was cut short on June 30, 1934, when the SA leadership, a few Nazi dissidents, and several earlier political leaders were summarily executed. The army returned the favor in August when Federal president Hindenburg died and Hitler won army approval to combine the offices of head of state and head of government with the titles *Führer* and *Reichskanzler,* an accumulation of powers that Mussolini never achieved. Soldiers henceforth were to swear an oath of personal loyalty to Adolf Hitler.[33]

The process of consolidating hitherto unheard-of power against a background of racial demagogy punctuated by violence and the abrogation of civil liberties apparently made the regime more and more popular. Hitler walked out of the stalled disarmament talks in Geneva in late 1933 and held a plebiscite to approve his decision and overall course, and won the first of his staggering votes of approval—of over 90 percent. Unemployment dropped and businessmen invested again, knowing that they faced no real opposition from the official German Labor Front. In 1935 the Saarland voted to rejoin Germany after fifteen years of enforced separation; in the same year Hitler abrogated the military clauses of the Versailles Treaty, announced the resumption of conscription and a German air force, and in March 1936 moved troops into the demilitarized zones bordering and west of the Rhine River, all moves that destroyed the clauses of the 1919 peace treaty designed to provide Germany's neighbors with military security. In 1938 he could triumphantly annex his native Austria after its precarious republic, as we shall see, had eliminated its own democratic institutions. By legislation announced at the Nuremberg rally in 1935, Jews had been defined as a separate group within the Reich—subjects still of a German state that humiliated and harassed them, but not citizens of the German Reich. Persecution was intensified in 1938 with the pogroms and confiscations of Reich Crystal Night, as Nazi policies radicalized in general. After annexing Austria, then convincing the British and French governments to browbeat Czechoslovakia to cede its German-populated Sudetenland rim, awarded at the Munich conference in October 1938, thereafter annexing the western Czech lands of Bohemia and Moravia in March 1939, and finally securing the neutrality of the Soviet Union in August, Hitler invaded Poland on September 1, 1939. By this time even Neville Chamberlain's government decided that he must be opposed and together with France responded with a declaration of war. Not, however, before Hitler had ominously announced at the beginning of 1939 that if war came, it would be the fault of the Jews and must lead to their destruction. Britain and France, however, had no effective concept for mounting an offensive against the Germans in Eastern or Western Europe and instead met disastrous defeat when German forces struck in Scandinavia, the Low Countries, and France by mid-1940.

Hitler's government was recognizably fascist with its uniformed Party supposedly fused with state offices, the paramilitary paraphernalia, the even more ruthless and rapid silencing of any legal opposition, the abolition of formally independent labor organizations—although, as in Italy, the government unions occasionally tried to stand up against employers. Organizationally it was a confusing regime; Hitler did not like clear lines of authority, and different organizations competed for his favor. The long-standing cabinet ministries continued and pursued the activities of the German bureaucracy. However, police functions that normally were tucked into the state governments were soon accumulated with confusing overlapping jurisdiction into the Prussian secret political police (Geheime Staatspolizei, or Gestapo) headed by Hermann Goering in his capacity as head of the Prussian government, then folded into the Chief Office for National Security (Reichssicherheitshauptamt), which became the commanding agency for the new Security Services, or SS, that came under the command of Heinrich Himmler, seconded by Reinhard Heydrich. In turn the SS would eventually dissolve into three divisions—the secret police, the military units that fought in the field during the war, and the units that ran greater Germany's concentration camps and the new extermination centers sited in formerly Polish territory (Chełmno, the first, constructed in late 1941, then Bełżec, Treblinka, Sobibór, Majdanek, and Auschwitz, enlarged from an IG Farben labor camp by an extermination facility at adjacent Birkenau). Several million Soviet prisoners of war, opponents from the European resistance movements, Roma and Sinti, homosexuals, and millions of Jews who were systematically rounded up from Western Europe, the Mediterranean lands,

Dictatorship and adulation: Adolf Hitler thronged by admirers at a 1938 rally. At this moment, when the National Socialist leader was probably at the zenith of his charismatic popularity, Germans were enjoying a rearmament boom, had remilitarized the Rhineland, had annexed Austria, and were about to wrest the Sudetenland from Czechoslovakia. Adulation went with absolute power: tens of thousands of those who expressed their opposition were already in brutal concentration camps; German Jews were being systematically degraded and expropriated. (Private Collection / Peter Newark Military Pictures / The Bridgeman Art Library)

occupied Poland, and Hungary, would be expropriated, abused, and murdered.

Hitler removed the long-term career diplomat Konstantin von Neurath as foreign minister to replace him with a compliant Nazi, Joachim von Ribbentrop, in 1938, and the once elitist agency effectively enlisted in the service of Nazi objectives, whether preparing to liquidate the states of Central Europe or later to facilitate the deportation of Jews. Hitler removed the top army officers under the pretext of a trumped-up homosexual scandal, installed a far more compliant commander in chief, and made himself the effective minister of defense. In 1936 he overruled the economics minister, Hjalmar Schacht, who insisted on the financial limits to rearmament, and appointed a Four-Year Plan office to rearm the country within four years. Hermann Goering became commissioner for the Four-Year Plan, adding it to his functions as minister for the new Luftwaffe. As part of the armament effort, he established a special agency called simply Organization Todt after its director, Fritz Todt, which took on increasingly more power in the war and, after Todt died in a plane crash, was taken over by the ambitious architect Albert Speer, who effectively became economic tsar after 1942. The war also meant the growth of a huge directorate for the six to eight million foreign workers, either recruited or forcibly moved to work in German factories. And throughout, the Ministry of Public Enlightenment, or propaganda, headed by Joseph Goebbels, extended its influence over the organization of the media and the world of art and music.

Of course, these offices, headed by ambitious men who had no compunctions about the conscription of millions of foreigners and the despoliation and eventual murder of Jews, were bound to clash. Goebbels and Goering, and later Goering, Goebbels, Party head Martin Bormann, and Speer, eyed each other's authority warily. Hitler tried to avoid coming down definitively on one side or another; he left few unambiguous directives; he knew that the zealous satraps would

Major concentration and extermination camps in Germany and German-occupied territory during World War II. The principal death camps appear in italics.

anticipate his general intentions. Ultimate power was compatible with quasi-anarchic administrative practice. This paradox has led some historians to judge him as a "weak dictator"; but the term doesn't do justice to what was stake. The dictatorship could be unsystematic; it allowed vast amounts of personal influence to accumulate under officials and it also allowed interstices where intellectual and religious and artistic life could continue somewhat undisturbed unless opponents felt compelled to make a public fuss. Given, for instance, the long-standing German cultural achievements in the musical sphere, control of musical programs and commentary was naturally a potentially important arena for patronage and generating ideology; but after a while the government essentially gave up higher ambitions and focused on providing "entertainment" music. Goebbels condemned jazz as "Nigger Mu-

A last stand for fascism: Anti-aircraft tracer shells illuminating the night sky above Algiers during a German air raid in the winter of 1943. Algeria as a possession of Vichy France had fallen to Anglo-American and Free French troops in the first major Allied landing against the Axis in November 1942; German and Italian troops remained in waning control of Libya and Tunisia to the east until the spring of 1943. (National Archives, photo no. 111-SC-182285)

sic," but underground bars continued to play it and semi-alienated youth danced to swing.[34]

〜

The paradox of strong overriding goals and administrative sloppiness was not confined to Germany or to fascist dictatorships. The American New Deal revealed a similar rivalry of powerful figures ensconced in different and often rival agencies: some created early on as the National Recovery Administration (NRA), the Works Progress Administration (WPA), the Public Works Administration (PWA), and so on, known collectively as "Alphabet Soup." Faced with powerfully defended policy alternatives, Franklin Roosevelt, like Hitler, preferred to put off clear decisions in favor of trying to compromise administrative decision. The point is that the Great Depression and then the world war (including the rearmament efforts that led up it), which presented large and powerful states with immense new challenges, met with ad hoc policy responses. Franklin Roosevelt, the outstanding democratic world leader of this challenging era, usually buoyant and generous in spirit, and Adolf Hitler, with his warped agenda of conquest and elimination, were motivated by totally different spirits, but their administrative responses to difficult government agendas had some similarities.

German state officials and those in the private sector seeking influence had to become Nazi Party members, as in Italy they had to join the Fascist Party. But alongside the various state agencies were those of the Nazi Party—its powerful Secretariat and its regional administrative officers of Gauleiter. In both Germany and Italy the Party waxed and waned in influence. The fusion of party and state was a slogan for both regimes, but Mussolini and Hitler soon sought to deprive the respective parties of real influence and make them instead into effective transmission belts of the authority they established. Neither leader was prepared to tolerate a "second revolution" that would have displaced the army for the party militia. Still, there were many parallel offices, and when Germany got deeper into a war whose demands it had not totally calculated, the government relied more on the Party Gauleiter and officials to organize welfare and civil defense functions. As Secretary of the Party, Bormann thus became an influential figure. Preparation for war and wartime itself only increased the welter of organizations.

Although the Nazis learned from the Italians, and deep into the war Hitler retained a certain respect for Mussolini as a sort of ideological godfather, significant differences, too, separated the two fascisms—and not only the central anti-Jewish fixation in the German regime. In contrast to Italian fascist ideology, which exalted the state's absolute authority and an implacable legal order, Hitler's lawyers stressed the personal arbitrary power of the Führer as the expression of the *Volksgemeinschaft* or national, even racial, community and attributed to so-called Führer decrees, even casual ones, supreme legal authority. Let us call it a theory of legal "vitalism," an effort to attribute the most arbitrary authority to a living leader who personified the will of the national community, not to be fixed within the boundaries of any independent legal framework.

The most notable German thinker whose ideas helped prepare for such a theory (although he never would have formally elaborated it) was Carl Schmitt, mentioned earlier in discussion of the nature of sovereign decision. Schmitt (alas) was a powerful legal mind. He had made his reputation in the controversies over the nature of law, parliamentarism, and democracy early in the Weimar Republic, arguing among other points that what constituted the realm of politics, including democratic politics, was the existential opposition of an enemy. Schmitt was sophisticated, persuasive, steeped in the classics and in the tradition of the fierce Catholic authoritarians of the nineteenth century—Joseph de Maistre, Louis de Bonald, and Juan Donoso Cortés, who believed that the revolution of 1789 was fallen mankind's recapitulation of Satan's rebellion against God. He was hopeful of being taken up by the Nazis as their official thinker, but ultimately was too intellectually arrogant to make headway in their crude infighting. The political unit he believed fundamental was not the state, which so many German conservatives and Italian fascists emphasized, but the political community—once the polis, now the nation—that coalesced in opposition to its adversaries. Politics thus was about us versus them, friends versus foes. True democracy was not the same as the endless discussion that parliamentary liberalism praised, but the regime that followed from the fundamental identity of a people. In fact, he argued, parliaments no longer served even as arenas for free and rational discussion, as earlier British liberalism had postulated, but only for the representation of concrete interests already determined before discussion began.[35] Weimar constitutionalism was a defective mixture of liberal and democratic elements, a diagnosis he believed was confirmed by the paralysis of the Weimar parliament in the early 1930s, when he called for a democratic dictator.

Such views of course set Schmitt against the liberal theorists who believed that the essence of law had to lie in its general applicability, its underlying rationality and values. But Schmitt also rejected the German school of legal positivism, which said that the power to impose a law replaced any discussion of inherent normative legitimacy. He implied further that those ideas of international law based on universal values and treaties were utopian. As it was becoming clear under Allied bombs that the Third Reich was doomed and his ideas would be discredited, he turned to argue in his astringent way that international law was a doctrine Europeans had devised to keep themselves from quarreling as they appropriated the territories of the non-European world. This sort of international doctrine, he claimed, was realistic; it presumed a geopolitics of large but finite territorial empires and thus justified Nazi *Grossraumpolitik*. At the same time, however, it likewise ruled out America's Wilsonian claims of supposedly universal values as well as the former British commitment to market liberalism, both claims to global ambitions that he felt were far more nakedly imperialist in scope than Germany's claims in Europe.[36]

〜

It was dismaying but hardly remarkable that fascism seemed to have a privileged insight into the future as the Great Depression became longer and more devastating, and as the framework of the Versailles Treaty was abandoned piece by piece. Above all in Central and East Central Europe, where the French and the British no longer seemed set on helping the smaller countries, themselves sometimes obsessed with nationalist issues, to remain independent of their large authoritarian neighbors.[37] Austria, the German-speaking remnant of the Habsburg empire (leaving aside the Germans of the Bohemian Sudetenland), was ideologically divided between the Socialists, largely entrenched in Vienna and industrial upper Austria, and the deeply Catholic and conservative rural population organized by the Christian-Social Party. By the end of the 1920s, a quasi-fascist "Fatherland Front" emerged as a political contender, and contending party militias clashed in the streets. In response to the Fatherland Front, the older Christian Socials sought to retain hegemony on the right by transforming the parliament into a fascist-like chamber of corporations. The Socialists feared that the Austrian Right was prepared to liquidate the remnants of liberalism and unadvisedly began their own revolt in February 1934, only to be forcibly suppressed and jailed if they did not scurry into exile in Prague. For the next four years, the Christian Socials sought to run an authoritarian state that Mussolini could patronize. Impatient Austrian Nazi admirers of Hitler attempted to seize power in a coup in July 1934 and assassinated the chancellor. They failed in their effort—in part because Mussolini made it clear that he was not ready to countenance an enlarged Germany on his Alpine border. Over the next four years, however, semi-independent and semifascist Austria lost his protection. In 1936, angered by the West's opposition to his invasion of Ethiopia, the Italian dictator decided to become a German partner in the so-called Axis, a move that let Hitler gradually put more and more pressure on Vienna until outright annexation or Anschluss in March 1938.

Meanwhile, the Polish military transformed their republic into a military regime step by step; dictators took power in the Baltic States. Hungary, which had been governed as an authoritarian state but with continuing parliament and some degree of open debate since the counterrevolution of 1919, vacillated between the fans of England or France, who hoped to keep a semi-open government of discussion (so long as

the establishment was not seriously threatened) and the outright admirers of Hitler's Germany. The king of Greece placed dictatorial
power in the hands of General Ioannis Metaxas in 1936. Czechoslovakia remained a parliamentary regime under the venerated Tomáš
Masaryk, but after his death the internal stresses made its crises difficult, and the three million Germans in the Sudeten mountain rim-
land increasingly fell under the demagogic leadership of a pro-Nazi
politician who presented their conditions as supposedly intolerable.
By 1938 Hitler was determined to destroy the Czech republic, and the
crisis he and the Sudeten Germans inflamed persuaded the English
Tories, as mentioned above, that the only solution was to cede the geographic region to Germany.

The Spanish Republic that had been instituted on the wave of an-
timonarchical municipal elections of 1931 became increasingly polar-
ized. Its conservative forces who governed from 1934 to 1936 sought to
roll back the measures for secularizing education and regional autonomy that the left had enacted from 1931 to 1933. An ill-conceived socialist uprising (a strategic miscalculation parallel to the 1934 uprising
in Vienna a half year earlier) brought right-wing suppression, which in
turn prompted the organization of a Popular Front, which now included Communist alongside Socialist and left-liberal parliamentary
candidates, in both France and Spain. Blessed by Moscow, but against
a backdrop of growing street clashes, the Popular Front won elections
in Spain and then France (and in Chile in 1938) on a broad platform of
opposition to fascism and advocacy of pro-labor reforms. Spain in particular descended into a period of conflict and what seemed to conservatives and Church authorities to be intolerable violence, and a military
uprising, coordinated for July 1936, managed to seize the garrisons in
about half the country. The resulting full-scale civil war became the
emblematic ideological clash of the decade, drawing in Soviet-
supported International Brigades and major Italian and German military aid on the Republican and insurgent Nationalist sides, respectively.

After two and a half years of fighting, the authoritarian coalition of monarchists, military, and fascists, organized by General Franco's Falange, prevailed. Tens of thousands of the left went into exile; and even more faced prison and firing squads. To be sure, democracy was maintained in Britain, France, Scandinavia, and the Low Countries. But increasingly it looked as if the vital political forces of the epoch were those that spoke for disciplined collectives, that praised or practiced war, and that had no compunction about locking up or even murdering dissenters.

⌒

The fact that on the other side of the globe Japanese armed forces had delivered the first major blow to the League-supervised order of collective security in September 1931 made the rise of nationalist authoritarianism all the more menacing. For the Japanese military, their bases on the Liaodong Peninsula in Guangdong Province seemed the key to controlling Manchuria, which in turn seemed essential to safeguard their Korean colony and keep Soviet Russia at bay and China deferential. All the more urgency, they reasoned, for their local army units to expand their beachhead on the Manchurian mainland, especially with Chiang's growing assertion of control in the north of historic China. Careful planning led to a staged bomb attack on the South Manchurian Railway the Japanese administered and a decisive response: the military occupation of southern Manchuria. The Manchurian "incident," quickly endorsed by the minister of war in Tokyo, was equally an attack on the forces of moderation in Japan, and the cabinet accepted the fait accompli. Those parties and leaders who had been willing to build a cooperative international order in the twenties, including moderate ministers drawn from the military, lost influence and occasionally their lives to impatient military radicals. Over the course of 1932, a cowed Tokyo cabinet decided to reorganize Manchuria as the supposedly sovereign state of Manchukuo and install the last Manchu emperor, Pu Yi, as its "puppet" sovereign. League condemnation led Tokyo to withdraw from the organization in March 1933, about nine months before Berlin followed suit, allegedly over dissatisfaction with Franco-British refusal at the League's Disarmament Conference to reduce their armed forces to parity with the German military.

Whether Japan in the 1930s became a fascist regime or not has been repeatedly debated. Perhaps it was not, in a formal canonic sense, if the criteria require a fascist party that will take over and transform a state, but its rulers gradually imposed a very coercive militarized regime that glorified emperor and state and conquest. At home in Japan, military influence tightened over the government: the brief interlude where parliamentary politics remained active, known as Taishō Democracy (named after the reign of the Taishō emperor from 1912 to 1926) withered with the onset of the world depression. Younger officers, drawn from rural areas that were suffering agricultural poverty, and hard-line expansionists criticized decadent bourgeois liberalism and the lively urban culture and political debate of the twenties, much as did the Nazis in Germany. The nationalists aspired to a "Shōwa restoration," where power and property would be taken from the politicians and corrupt capitalists and would supposedly be restored to the new young Shōwa emperor, Hirohito. Attempted coups d'état by radical nationalist officers (known by their dates: 5-15 in 1932, and 2-26 in 1936), marked by the assassination of politicians, pushed divided cabinets ever further toward nationalist and authoritarian policies. Even though putschists (and the inspirational ideologue Kita Ikki) were executed, moderates were cowed into silence or imprisoned. The main political parties were dissolved while the rulers organized a supportive national movement, if not a formal party; the Imperial Rule Assistance Association trained youth in the military virtues (which came to include merciless treatment of enemies), elevated the state Shintō national religion that glorified the emperor, and claimed an Asian racial superiority. The new governments seemed divided by the 1930s between those suave nationalists, preeminently Prince Konoe Fumimaro, who felt it prudent to expand into Asia gradually so as not to arouse the British and Americans, and those military leaders who were convinced that a larger war with the Westerners and with the resurgent Chinese Republic was just a matter of time. Among the latter, General Ishiwara Kanji, instrumental in planning the Manchurian incident, envisioned wider and wider warfare, while Tōjō Hideki would emerge as a political leader and serve as the premier who would preside over Japan's fateful enlargement of East Asian hostilities against Britain and the United States in December 1941.[38]

That step, however, culminated the self-fulfilling logic of continued aggression to safeguard the expansion already undertaken: war necessitated by war. Concerned with Chiang's efforts to modernize a Chinese republic that drew on some similar national convictions, the Japanese launched an invasion of the historic Chinese provinces in 1937. By 1940, deeply engaged in China, Tokyo announced adhesion to the Rome–Berlin Axis and later to the German–Italian Pact of Steel, and awaited the outcome of the war in Europe to resolve whether, as some military planners wished, to march north from Manchuria against the Soviet Union or, as the ultimately prevailing strategy envisioned, to strike south at the European colonial dominions of Southeast Asia. Moscow's free hand obtained by its Nonaggression Pact with Hitler, as well as the evident strength of Soviet armed forces demonstrated by some major border skirmishes with Japan, and the weakness of the resource-rich Dutch and French colonial possessions (whose governments had been decisively defeated in Europe in spring 1940), made the "southern way" all the more beckoning. American insistence that Japan pull back, not only from the bases pried from the French in Vietnam but from China itself, seemed to compel a fundamental choice between humiliation or readiness for wider war. The fact that the Dutch East Indies promised the oil required by its military once the United States effectively embargoed American exports to Japan

Flawed bravado? Chiang Kai-shek addressing a rally in Hankou in 1938. The genera-lissimo, heir to Sun Yat-sen's nationalist party, the Guomindang (GMD), used radio, the decisive medium for political leaders of the 1930s, an era of mass politics. China's authoritarian Nationalist government tried to wage a desperate war against the full-scale Japanese invasion that had escalated the year before. (Getty Images)

made the option of widening the war again seem compelling. Unfor-tunately for Tokyo, expansion south entailed preemptive strikes against British and American bases—once again war necessitated by war. From the vantage of the early 1940s, China presented Japanese leaders with a dilemma similar to that which the Soviet Union posed for Hitler, even though China lacked Russia's tremendous offensive capacity. Still, it was a vast society whose domination the Japanese believed the prerequisite for continental leadership, but whose resil-ience drew them into far more costly efforts than foreseen and ultimately drew in an overseas adversary with far greater resources than their own.

As of the mid-1930s, trends were already sufficiently ominous to make either defeat at the hands of fascism or resistance alongside the communists the terrible choice for many intellectuals. American democracy seemed too remote, unconcerned with the wider world, and was itself suffering from mass unemployment. Fortunately the mass of Western public opinion resisted such apocalyptic thinking, clinging perhaps too long to hopes of muddling through, indulging in what the poet W. H. Auden would call the hopes of a "low, dishonest decade," but committed understandably enough to states that resisted the total politicization of private life and sometimes even dared to experiment with progressive social legislation. The Soviet Union claimed to be on the opposing side of the spectrum from fascism but developed a control of society that was fully as pervasive and repressive, and was probably the most thoroughly penetrating of all the dictatorships. The novelist André Gide, a left sympathizer, went to Russia in 1936 and wrote that nowhere else in the world was thought and liberty more controlled—not even in Nazi Germany. George Orwell came to understand the Stalinist pervasive concern for ruthless control of the left in the Spanish Civil War.[39] Nonetheless, Western communists and their supporters could still argue (as would Jean-Paul Sartre after the war) that the Soviet Union embodied the hopes and aspirations of the world proletariat and had to be supported. The Soviet Union was also a declared dictatorship (which supposedly, according to its 1936 constitution, was a perfect democracy).

Even more completely than in Italy and Germany, the agencies of the Russian state were subjected to the party acting frankly as a dictatorship of (or at least on behalf of) the proletariat. Until the reforms of Mikhail Gorbachev in the 1980s, the Russian leader served as first secretary of the Communist Party of the Soviet Union (CPSU). As was the case in Italy and Germany, the dictator himself accumulated

World War II in Asia: Japanese tanks, still light and primitive, advancing rapidly as Japan invades southward from its Manchurian colony into China proper during 1937 and 1938. World War II began in Asia; by the time it started in Europe, Japan controlled a broad coastal strip of China, while the Chinese Nationalists settled down in Chongqing in the upper Yangzi Valley and the Communist forces in their stronghold in northwest Yan'an. The populations trapped between the two armies increasingly suffered famine, inflation, and disease. (© SZ Photo / The Bridgeman Art Library)

tremendous personal authority, but Stalin would never have dared to delegate party leadership to another comrade, whereas Mussolini and Hitler both did. The German and Italian state apparatuses retained some autonomy and tradition; after the civil war and the 1920s, when the Party still recruited older officials willing to serve the Bolshevik regime, this was harder in Russia. Party officials would serve alongside commanding officers in the army during World War II, sometimes resented and subject to execution if captured. The potential rivals to the First Secretary were also party positions—for a while in the 1920s the leadership of the Communist International, which rivaled the People's Commissariat for Foreign Affairs, and increasingly the leadership of the successive political police agencies. The presidency of the Soviet Union was more of a ceremonial position. No state parliamentary organ as such remained; in theory the constituent assembly and Duma had belonged to a bourgeois state that had been displaced. The Party Congress, the smaller Central Committee, and the ruling Politburo remained the legislative organs. The Party Congress, supposedly the supreme organ although really designed to acclaim the decisions of Politburo and Central Committee, was chosen by election among Party members. It seems paradoxical, but communist states always devoted great attention to noncompetitive elections; for they served not to choose among alternative personalities or policies, but to mobilize and reinvigorate the faithful.

Historians used to separate the Leninist period (1917–1923) and the subsequent years of changing rival "triumvirates" (1924–1929) from the arbitrary and terroristic rule under Stalin, who managed to secure his own undivided control by 1930–1931. But although Stalin's mind was filled with dark conspiracies and the apparatus of state terror did reach unprecedented heights in the mid- to late 1930s, the authoritarian potential of the state manifested itself early on. Nonetheless, the early period of the regime existed under conditions of civil war and the hostility of Britain, France, and the United States. Sympathetic observers could interpret Lenin's regime as the state of "exception" that the theorist Carl Schmitt had defined as the crucible of sovereignty. By the time Lenin died, after prolonged disabling by a stroke, the "white" or counterrevolutionary armies, supported by the Western states, had been defeated, and the government had backed away from the ruinous economic collectivism they imposed under conditions of civil war and had introduced the New Economic Policy or NEP (a partial restoration of market conditions and foreign investment). Briefly through the late 1920s, Moscow and Petrograd were home to experimental theater and futurist art, which attracted Western intellectuals, all the more so as the world economic crisis tightened its hold on the capitalist world as the thirties began.

But such an equilibrium, which might have left the Soviet Union, like Mexico, to stabilize its broad upheaval under a "big tent" one-party regime that held on to positions of power without operating a police dictatorship, did not come to pass. There were historical, personal, and societal reasons. The rivalry bequeathed by a disabled Lenin meant that venomous rivalries developed above all between Trotsky and Stalin. Trotsky was of Jewish background, traveled, a theorist of revolution. Stalin was indigenous, a gifted in-fighter with intellectual ambitions, who saw his comrades as rivals and potential conspirators. From the end of the 1920s he accumulated power that transcended even the institutional supremacy that leadership of the party (and thereby also the state) should have bestowed. He was feared and adored. All the totalitarian leaders exercised a strong component of personalist rule—Hitler and Mussolini felt it necessary to communicate directly; Stalin less so—he was remote but watchful like some vigilant patriarchal deity.

There were differences rooted in institutions as well. Of all the authoritarian states—not counting the Chinese Republican regime—Russia had had the shortest experience with representative institutions. Italy had had a parliamentary government since 1860 and Germany since 1870. The Russian Duma had sat only from 1905 until 1917 and its suffrage had been increasingly constricted. Local self-government had been vigorous in Germany and northern Italy. In addition, the Soviet Union inherited a social structure that frustrated the Bolsheviks from the outset—a massive peasantry that they regarded as a hostile and backward force. As one of their programmatic slogans during the interim republic from March to November 1917, the Bolsheviks had promised peasants the right to take over the land they cultivated as their own property. But individualized landholdings were not the ultimate form of property they envisaged, nor did small peasant holdings promise to be very productive. The economic task, as they saw it, was to raise the productivity of the agrarian sector and move the labor power released to cities for industrial development. Peasant proprietors, moreover, would always confront the Bolsheviks as a massive and sullen opposition. Some Bolsheviks, preeminently Nikolai Bukharin, advocated at least a long period of letting the peasants sell their output on a private market and retain their holdings. Preoccupied with securing his domestic supremacy, Stalin turned on any gradualist policies at the end of the twenties. After attacking the internationalist Left in 1928, he turned on the so-called rightist leadership and declared that no cooperation was possible with Social Democrats in Europe, a policy that had disastrous consequences for German democracy. And whether as a corollary or out of doctrinal conviction, Stalin also reversed the economic compromises of the earlier 1920s and introduced a policy of collectivization in the countryside. Peasant holdings were merged into collective farms that were to retain control of tractors and implements. For over a year, the Communists wrought a devastating revolution in the countryside before they had to ease up. In Ukraine in particular there was harsh opposition, and Stalin effectively blockaded the province for 1931–1932, using mass famine as a means to smash its inhabitants' resistance.[40] In the same period he embarked on the first Five-Year Plan, which nationalized industry and shut down the private economy, even as the government embarked on vast industrialization projects in the Donets Basin (Donbass). Workers were essentially conscripted in harsh conditions to build steel mills and hydroelectric installations. Youth were recruited as young communists to work on the Moscow metro, and at the most coercive end of the spectrum of labor mobilization, political prisoners would be sent to the Arctic for construction of the White Sea Canal.

Soviet industrial growth advanced rapidly during the first two Five-Year Plans of 1928–1937 during the gray era when the capitalist economies were mired in the Great Depression. It remained robust during the third Five-Year Plan, designed to run from 1937 until 1942, at a time the Soviets moved many industrial plants back from western Russia, where they were vulnerable to German attack, to the Urals. Economic planning by the end of the 1930s came to appeal to many on the non-Communist left in the West. Whether the quality of Soviet output kept pace with the quantitative indices has been debated; certainly the agricultural sector did not advance—it remained a vastly underproductive and probably hostile, if silenced, sector of the country. The standard of living was far lower than in Central Europe. But even more, the regime embarked on a vast upheaval of its own supporters—a purge of the large Communist Party (several million strong), dismissing thousands, sending tens or hundreds of thousands to prison camps under appalling conditions, and culminating in show trials, where the old comrades of Stalin, and about half of his general staff, would be forced into degrading and absurd confessions, and shot, or sentenced to long terms of forced labor. And yet this regime and this dictator, who so misread Hitler's intentions in 1941, was able to mobilize unfathomable national loyalties—to Russia if not to Communism—to withstand the massive German attack and survive vast losses of territory, to incur huge sacrifices of military and civilian lives, and defeat the German military apparatus. Without Soviet efforts the Nazis might well have ruled the European continent far longer than they did. Unless they used atomic weapons on Germany after 1945, Britain and the United States would have remained offshore antagonists for decades and democracy might have flickered even more precariously than it did. The inhabitants of Eastern Europe had to pay their own heavy price for that victory over the decades from 1945 into the 1980s, but by the late 1930s there were no good choices.

Estimates of Soviet victims vary—from about seven hundred thousand officially recorded as executed or deported to labor camps, in some of which mortality rates may have risen to one-third of their prisoners annually, to millions who perished as entire peoples were deprived of food or sent into forced migrations. Only the catastrophic German invasion and the war, with its additional twenty million or more casualties, may have abated the war Stalin conducted at home. Historians have debated whether he was responding to party enthusiasts who wanted some vast upheaval or whether he personally insisted on such a massive terror. (A similar debate arose over Hitler's extermination. Certainly, the dictators signaled that ruthless zeal was welcome.) After the war, as Boris Pasternak recorded in the conclusion of his novel *Doctor Zhivago,* some hoped for a more normal life amid the devastation that had to be repaired, and for a few years it appeared as the worst of the terror was over. But by 1947 and 1948, the same mechanism of denunciation and show trial descended on the countries of Eastern Europe, where the Russians had helped install communist governments. When Marshall Tito of Yugoslavia—certainly as "pure" a Marxist-Leninist as the Soviet leader—decided not to accept Cominform "discipline," that is, not to align himself with the new international communist bureau that the Soviet Union organized in 1947 to replace the Communist International it had dissolved during the war, he was denounced by the Soviets as a traitor. Titoism became as evil as Trotskyism, a deviation in league with American capitalism just as Trotsky had supposedly connived with German fascism. By 1952 Stalin's residual anti-Semitism seemed to be building up to a purge directed at the three million Jewish inhabitants of the Soviet Union, who had remained beyond the reach of Nazi killing squads; and he may have been planning to deport them all to a Soviet Jewish homeland. His Jewish physicians, it was alleged, had plotted to poison him. Only the dictator's death, supposedly by natural causes, averted this impending purge and possible forced resettlement. Gradually his successors—fearing each other, but combining to liquidate the head of the secret service, whom they all feared most—unwound the worst of the excesses, though hardly the party-state. Nikita Khrushchev's "Secret Speech" at the Twentieth Party Congress of the CPSU in 1956 finally dared to suggest that the great leader had yielded to paranoid fantasy and some woeful policy choices. Khrushchev, himself caught up like his fellow survivors as an accomplice in the ruthless policies of the 1930s, intended at least in part to exculpate the party that would continue to rule. Still, it was the first real tremor in a series of shocks that over the next thirty-five years would gradually reveal how flawed the regime had become.

Political Pathology

As Western political analysts and commentators confronted the human wreckage produced by the German and Soviet regimes, they sought to make intellectual sense of these orgies of civic destruction. Marxist theorists and historians sought to separate the two: the Germans and Italians operated terrorist and thuggish regimes that had basically left the capitalist order intact, whereas the Russians were creating socialism, and if they had committed excesses, this was because they had taken power in a backward country. According to the "vulgar" theories propagated by the Third International (that is, those Marxists who had rallied to the Soviet regime), fascism was just the most brutal strategy for "monopoly capital" to retain power. Dissident Marxists suggested with more subtlety that fascists were politically autonomous: as "Bonapartist" regimes they arose when the different sectors of the bourgeoisie were paralyzed by rivalries.[41] Still, fascists and Nazis were allegedly spurious revolutionaries because they left intact the basis of capitalist society. Later students of the fascist economy at war suggested that in fact the regime so limited the choices of entrepreneurs by controlling their investment possibilities that it represented a grave incursion into capitalism. Marxist critics in the 1930s and 1940s such as Franz Neumann and Herbert Marcuse sought to claim that the Third Reich was not in fact a state—that it was just the expression of the strongest naked interests inside Germany, whether industry, party bosses, or the military, and that the balance of power might evolve. This was not just a Marxist analysis. For a while Franklin Roosevelt and the New Deal shared such a view: at the end of the 1930s the administration argued that fascism amounted to unrestrained private monopoly power.[42] It was true that fascists rarely sought to nationalize industries unless to bail them out or develop new production. Nazi leaders did praise industrial capitalism, engineering, and innovation, although they were demeaning about finance, which they thought exploitative and often dominated by Jewish interests. But their regime was not just a puppet in the hands of monopoly capitalists. They certainly ran a state.

It also flouts ordinary language to insist that a German regime that quickly abolished parties, acquired dictatorial power, imposed legal restrictions against Jews not seen since the pre-Napoleonic era, locked its adversaries up in brutal facilities without trial, or often guillotined them after trial, was not revolutionary. Beyond the authorities who established hundreds of labor and concentration camps, many Germans thought in fact that they were reachieving a happy society of full employment, a warm communal feeling of the *Volksgemeinschaft* or ethnic community, marked, for instance, by the Christmas collection for the poor (the *Winterhilfe*) or the sharing of an occasional simple stew *(Eintopf)* or workers' cruises and other well-organized leisure activities

(*Kraft durch Freude* and the Italian *dopolavoro*) to demonstrate inter-
class solidarity. It was not the least achievement of the party to get
ordinary Germans to look away from the brutality of the regime, the
humiliation and then the disappearance of the opposition parties and
then of the Jews. Germany was awakening, casting off the supposed
shackles of Versailles; one legislative restriction or another was placed
on its willing or cautiously grumbling citizens, but did not the United
States also impose racial segregation and make it clear that resorts and
parks were reserved for whites? *Kristallnacht*—the organized burning and destruction of synagogues across Germany on November 9,
1938—caused some disquiet; it was clearly outright arson and violence
visible in cities and towns throughout their civilized country. By then
anti-Semitism had become a national ideological tenet: the Jew was
enemy to the German, and any isolated dissent to this policy might be
dangerous. With rare exceptions, even Christian pastors acquiesced.
The regime had gone on first to humiliate and despoil and force into
emigration as many German Jews as possible, then to seize the remain-
der of the Jews in all the lands they swept into, to transport them to
the extermination factories constructed in occupied Poland, and murder them, sometimes after exploiting their labor, sometimes without
any effort to do so. If for a while German policy makers did not think
beyond putting the western Polish Jews into ghettos where they could
manipulate mass malnutrition and let nature take its course, with the
conquests of 1941 they decided they must act more proactively, first by
mass machine-gunning, then by extermination camps.

This seemed different from the Soviet experience to many intellectuals. Certainly there was residual anti-Semitism in Russia and Poland,
but the Russians condemned anti-Semitism as a bourgeois nationalist
ideology. Even at its worst they had Jewish old communists; and many
of the communist leaders of Poland and Hungary and Czechoslovakia
who found asylum in Moscow or elsewhere were identified as Jews by
the countrymen who hated their role in clamping down communism

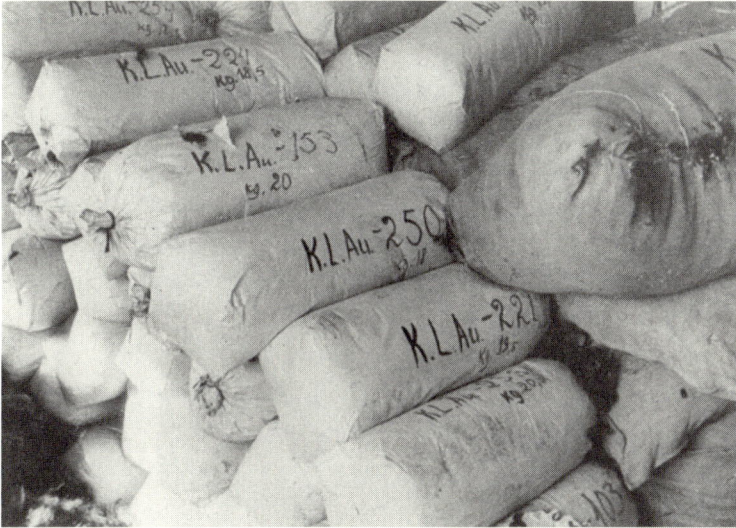

Leviathan's perversion: Bales of hair from female prisoners numbered for shipment to Germany, found by the Soviets at the liberation of the Auschwitz-Birkenau concentration camp, January 27, 1945. Hair was shorn from prisoners, sometimes at arrival; sometimes, as at Treblinka, before gassing; sometimes from corpses, to be used for cloth, rope, mattress stuffing, insulation for boots, and more. (United States Holocaust Memorial Museum, courtesy of National Archives and Records Administration, College Park / Belarusian State Archive of Documentary Film and Photography / Dokumentationsarchiv des Oesterreichischen Widerstandes)

in 1946–1947. Nazism had this central preoccupation with an almost atavistic ideology—which in fact had long been central to rightist forces, hostile to capitalism and socialism and liberalism, throughout Central and Eastern Europe. Communism as an ideology was also "internationalist"—it aspired to proletarian or Marxist revolutions throughout the world as conditions became ripe, but war on nationalist grounds it condemned. Nazism—and perhaps Italian fascism—was so tied up with the celebration of martial virtue that it wanted war for fulfillment, whereas there was no equivalent Soviet eschatology. (Which did not prevent Stalin from building a massive air force and a fine tank corps.)

But was ideology what counted? Perhaps intellectuals on the left might be excused for not understanding that the famine in the Ukraine, with its millions of victims, derived from Moscow's decision to cut off imports of food. The Italian and other consuls were not deceived, but their reports were buried in the Foreign Offices.[43] Certainly political thinkers would give particular concern to differences of dogma between the ideologies, just as once church leaders sniffed for heresy in disputes over the real presence in the Eucharist or the similitude versus equality of God and son. Still, the realization grew with the Stalinist years, and then with the opening of the Cold War, that what the regimes shared in practice united them as significantly as the ideological enmity divided them. Both fascism and communism were based on the claim of a single party to capture and then exercise power (more completely even in a postrevolutionary Russia than in Germany and Italy, where bureaucratic agencies remained relatively immune); their adherents shared the tendency to adulate the single leader, to attribute legal status to his pronouncements, and even to anticipate what further uniformity he might wish to impose even before he had articulated it himself.[44]

Of course, not only totalitarian states demonstrated the intolerance of opposition and the idea that it must be suppressed and silenced by censorship and punishment. There were and would be plenty of ordinary tyrannies and even murderous despotisms. Idi Amin ran a homicidal regime in Uganda in the 1970s; Reza Shah Pahlavi governed with a zealous political police; the Argentine military would murder many thousands of students and potential opponents. What distinguished the totalitarian state was its reliance supposedly on a collective instrument of transformation. The party-state supposedly entertained grandiose projects—in physical infrastructure, reeducation, and refashioning the nation as an ethnic unit (in Germany), as the heir of empire (as in Italy), or as the homeland of a historical process of inevitable change (as in the Soviet Union). Not only did the state claim that power vis-à-vis supposed individual rights (which it claimed to be really protected), but it did so by elevating the political police into a key component of rule. The Russians founded the Cheka early in the revolution as "sword and shield" of the revolution. It morphed into increasingly pervasive intelligence and police agencies continually reorganized into commissariats and ministries—the GPU, folded into the NKVD during the 1930s, divided into the MVD and KGB in the 1950s—huge enterprises that ran the vast "gulag archipelago" in Russia or the concentration camps in Germany with their hundreds of forced-labor subsidiaries, all established before the extermination centers were constructed on conquered Polish territory. Still, there was a difference in those selected. The German state tended to define known enemies—those who dissented, who spoke out or leafleted their opposition, and ultimately all who were Jewish. The "ordinary" citizen who kept his opinions to himself was relatively safe until wartime came. In the Soviet Union arrest often seemed arbitrary and random. As later in Mao's China and Pol Pot's Cambodia, the Soviet Union invented categories of guilt: prosperity as a peasant, family background and connections, political moderation, so that the spectators who escaped the suspect categories might be spurred into rituals of denunciation, complicity, and identification with the regime. Gazing at these nightmarish landscapes of terror, what an early postwar French writer called "l'univers concentrationnaire," the concentration-camp universe, the historian of the state must ask: Were they the perverted culmination of centuries-long claims of state sovereignty, or instead the dark cloaca of private brutality where ideas of public rationality, so long a supposed property of the modern state, never penetrated—or perhaps a coexistence of law and total arbitrariness that the German critic Ernst Fraenkel memorably termed the "dual state"?[45]

Public awareness in the West of what twentieth-century dictatorship entailed culminated in the Cold War before the death of Stalin. By the 1950s, analysts who emphasized the similarities between Nazism and Communism seemed more incisive than those who still tried to redeem the "idea" of Soviet socialism by emphasizing the theoretical differences. The defenders insisted that ultimately state socialism (the name I prefer to mere socialism) would transform itself and that the liberal states that were colonial powers had to take responsibility for the equally grievous sins of colonialism and racism. When pressed, they also contended that ultimately only the Soviet Union had enabled the defeat of Hitler's Germany. Those who argued by body count and not ideas argued that in fact the twentieth century had created a new paradigm of politics and the state—that of the totalitarian party-state with tremendous ambition and the willingness to sacrifice millions of individuals to its cause.

Some of the analysts excelled in describing the subjective experience of the dedicated Communist—easier to convey to Anglo-American or continental European readers because so many premises of the ideology seemed to spring from a common Enlightenment liberalism. Of the writers who sought to analyze the institutional experience, Hannah Arendt remains the most challenging and original. For all the particular comparisons or imputed origins the reader can quarrel with, Arendt understood the centrality of the imperialist experience to the ideologies of dehumanization, and likewise the importance of anti-Semitism to Central European doctrines. She identified the role of party and terror and attempted to analyze the totalitarian society as one of isolated atomization that destroyed solidarities outside the state. She probably credited the regimes with too much efficacy in reducing men and women to isolated beings—social networks remained to challenge all these regimes, which did not so much shatter and destroy associative life as penetrate it and subvert it.[46]

The label *totalitarian* has left a set of controversies. Were the states really so total? They did not succeed in changing human nature; after the decades of the harshest repression softened, Russians still craved the church; the Chinese still treasured family. A non-Jew could retain his irony and skepticism in Hitler's Germany if he didn't insist on publicly sporting it. When liberated from the harsh practices of dictatorship, people seemed anxious to dismantle the experiences; the number of neo-Nazis, outright fascists, and those willing to plunge Russia or China back into untrammeled violence was small. And yet the term—difficult and problematic as it was, and certainly when applied to the fatigued late socialist regimes of the 1970s and 1980s—was an effort to capture a basic state experience, that of the hyper-state, or, to use the term that followed from Schmitt's decisionism, the exceptional state. The totalitarian state—related to the wartime state and the revolutionary state, both of which were usually deemed finite in time—was the most extreme application of an instrumentality remobilized in the 1860s and 1870s to take advantage of new technologies to build cohesive national communities or overseas empires. It represented the desire to impose a powerful transformative agenda—to carry out positive projects with government and not just quietly administer. But it also sprang from the pervasive conviction that government and social change had to be mobilized in a world of enemies who wanted you powerless if not killed. Again, politics was war, had no choice but to be war.

The world wars—and then the long-term struggles in the colonial world, either to retain colonies or to shake off colonial powers—made these projects of magnifying power even more plausible. For wartime states took on many characteristics that in peacetime would be thought verging on tyranny: the commandeering of young men for dangerous labor, the imposing of restrictions on entrepreneurs so they produced what was needed for the national struggle, the fanning of public and patriotic loyalties, the persecution of dissent from policy, and even in liberal societies, a new recourse to mass detention. War-time states were dismantled when the justifications disappeared—but they were part of the twentieth century; for they made liberals and democrats believe too that states could legitimately claim an exalted power of decision. All this had been prefigured in earlier situations: the French revolutionaries' wars against the monarchs of 1792–1803 or their own enemies within the country; the Paraguayan total war of 1864–1870; the berserk kingdom of the Taipings; von Trotha's campaign against the Herero; the Turkish massacres of Greeks and Armenians. The repertories of military commitment lay at hand, so it was hardly surprising they could be seized on when wars were in abeyance. Were the states of exception, then, no more than wartime states erected on a permanent basis? Was their treatment of opposition as racially different, as colonies within their borders, no different from their treatment of colonial subjects?

In fact, they were more absolute. Colonial massacres and colonial genocide followed what local settlers and soldiers believed was resistance. They were an effort to rule a subjugated people by terror. Some of the labor practices in the colonies rested on a willingness to impose inhumane discipline; they bore some similarity to what Nazi Germany would impose on the "slave laborers" recruited or dragooned from other countries. But the hyper-regimes at home rested on the idea that this sort of mastery, absolute hegemony, suspension of the liberal rules, glorification of decisions and devaluation of discussion, accorded with the way men and women should live throughout their lives. They extended to one's own nation the notion of differentiated humanity that race and war made "natural" when confronting others. They demonstrated that the practices that arose in "natural" situations—confronting people of color, confronting invaders—were not just grounded in racial difference or the exceptionalism of wartime antagonism, but a lurking project of purification within.[47] With these projects history reached a state claim that was exceptional. Perhaps resorting to the metaphor of our title, it was no longer 2.0, but somewhere between 2.1 and 2.9. Our postscript will suggest what might constitute Leviathan 3.0. But first we must recall that not every twentieth-century state was a state of exception.

Although the conduct of the Second World War itself demonstrated that all major belligerents must become states of exception for the duration, the outcome of the war suggested more hopefully that the earlier states of exception might in retrospect come to seem exceptional states. Communist rule would be advanced by Soviet armies; colonial struggles would be intensified; but the war also revealed possibilities for democratic renewal. Franklin Roosevelt enunciated war aims, inscribed in the Four Freedoms and the Atlantic Charter proclaimed after his August 1941 shipboard meeting with Winston Churchill, which looked toward the restoration of democracy, human rights, and even a minimum of material well-being. The Resistance forces inside the occupied countries issued charters that echoed similar aspirations for political and economic democracy. Resistance groups also called for a regeneration of their nations as communities of emancipation in a language rarely heard since the days of Mazzini. Two of the major European leaders, who without the war would have seemed merely archaic nationalists, provided precisely the inspiration needed to stand up to Germany: Churchill as prime minister from 1940 to 1945, and Charles de Gaulle, resistance leader in British exile until France was liberated. Their respective defiant stances ensured that they found each other hard to bear, but together they (and Christian Democratic conservatives on the continent such as Konrad Adenauer and Alcide De Gasperi) suggested that a decent postwar conservatism might also reemerge. Neither Churchill nor de Gaulle was prepared to contemplate the renunciation of empire; nonetheless their anticolonial adversaries insisted that their countries were ready to fight for independence, and the European leaders had to yield—if only after prolonged conflicts in British Malaya and Kenya, and bitter wars for the French in Vietnam and Algeria. To be sure, pro-Soviet Communist leaders sought to instrumentalize the Resistance struggles on behalf of their postwar influence and to discredit opponents. (So did monarchist authoritarians, although with less success.) "People's Democracy" became Moscow's slogan for compliant postwar regimes. Nonetheless, new possibilities for political cooperation and discourse beckoned, to be achieved in Western Europe, including West Germany and Italy, and even Japan within a few years, and in Eastern Europe only after another half century.

A Glance Ahead: From the States of Exception to the Renormalized State

The fascist party-state ended with the war it had unsuccessfully launched. Its authoritarian militarist kin continued in Spain and Portugal, and it would reassert itself in Latin America, parts of Asia and Africa and the Middle East, and, briefly, in Greece during later decades. The Communist party-state in Russia and Eastern Europe would become less harsh but still aspire to undisputed control into the 1980s. By the 1960s, however, the dominant regime in Europe, North America, and Japan was the "welfare state"—not fundamentally different from the extension of the European liberal or even conservative regime of the late nineteenth and early twentieth centuries but with more extensive social insurance and often ownership of key infrastructural enterprises. Its antecedents could be traced to church and town provisions for taking charge of orphans and the old. In the nineteenth century, occupational safety measures were added as well as legislation designed to prevent the worst abuses of the early factories and to establish minimal ages for those entering them. The growth of industrial towns made misery more visible than it was in rural households. It also made socialist schemes for collective insurance more plausible and to Europe's conservatives more threatening, hence often prompted new welfarist responses. Bismarck is credited with legislating state provisions for old age and infirmity. Civil servants developed self-insurance schemes. Some states, such as the Prussian, had a more active role; others left assistance to families and churches and occupational benevolent associations. After the American Civil War and the First World War, the legacy of social needs of disabled veterans and widowed wives compelled national responses. By the new century, Europe's reformist Left had tried to set its own stamp on these schemes, as in the British Liberals' program of 1906–1914, the policies developed by the Swedish social democratic coalitions of the 1930s, and the national responses that were a centerpiece of the American New Deal.

From these patchworks it was an easy transition to envisage states that took a comprehensive role in ensuring minimal standards of income and insurance against the social risks of unemployment, old age, and (outside the United States at least) disease. This agenda marked the report commissioned by the British minister Arthur Greenwood from the social reformer William Beveridge during World War II, which outlined a notion of "cradle to grave" support that would overcome poverty and provide access to education and health. Out of these experiences would come the welfare state—the accepted mix of private economic ownership and social guarantees that tended to mark the policies once peace returned to Europe in 1945.

As it developed, the welfare state tended to converge with other remedies for economic distress and perhaps economic inequality that the Great Depression of the 1930s had made acute. It would supervise social compacts between labor unions and representatives of industry—an initiative that had taken shape during World War I, had been made compulsory by fascist and occupation regimes in World War II, and was now to be encouraged as a normal political activity. Ideas of national planning had become popular on the left in the 1930s and were instituted for wartime industries as a matter of course by the British, Americans, and Germans. After the war, the French instituted an agency for indicative planning headed by Jean Monnet. It did not own the constituent firms but could provide strategic incentives of capital for modernization. The state, so the democratic and social democratic left urged in Western Europe, should run key industries: certainly the banks of issue, probably the railroads (the French Popular Front had nationalized their rail network), and perhaps the mines. The Labour Party had inserted a commitment to public ownership of what became known at the commanding heights of the economy as Point IV of their Party Program in 1918; and when they came to power in 1945 they nationalized the steel industry, the rail system, road transport, and the coal mines, and by 1948 they established the National Health Service.

All these measures after the Second World War tended to be associated with the democratic and social democratic Left. Trade Unions and leftist parties, after all, had gained a decisive voice in politics by their moral and wartime contribution to the defeat of fascism. Conservative opponents were often in eclipse because of their role in collaborationist regimes. But conservatives often generated or inherited similar policies, and had often had a paternalist ideology of social protection. The leading French welfare initiative for family allowances had grown out of Catholic and employer concepts for regional or occupational *caisses*. The German Christian Democrats differentiated themselves from the National Socialists but championed concepts of ordo-liberalism, which stipulated embedding competitive industries and business in a broader social order that provided for extensive welfare provisions and an overall milieu of a very structured and highly organized social market economy, not so different from what postwar Japan was developing. The Italian Christian Democrats inherited a massive state holding company—the Institute for Industrial Reconstruction, or IRI—which the fascists had created as they bailed out and took over massive shares of Italian coal, steel, and chemical firms and the Italian petroleum industry. A new elite of government planners and technocrats developed to supervise the Italian economic "miracle" of the 1950s and 1960s.[48]

The welfare state and mixed economies seemed to provide political consensus for a generation, and then from the 1970s were the object of criticism and deregulation. That forms the subject of another history. Perhaps the most comprehensive single index for the role of the re-normalized state was the proportion of national spending (national income or, viewed from the production side, gross domestic product) that went through government hands, for investment in infrastructure, military expenses, and transfer payments or entitlement programs. It has been estimated that the French Ancien Régime of the late eighteenth century was spending perhaps up to 25 percent of national income on its armed forces, its roads and canals, the expenses of the Court, and the interest to bondholders. Welfare was left largely to Church institutions. But nineteenth-century government in Western Europe was largely cheap government. As World War I approached, Britain and Germany may have had public expenditures of about 12 to 18 percent divided among armaments, infrastructure and education, and national debt service. The First World War drove up state expenses drastically—up to perhaps 40 percent in France (although much was covered by foreign loans), perhaps 45 to 50 percent in Britain and Germany. This vast expansion of state claims could be covered only partially by taxation; most was taken in the form of loans, some directly from citizens, but mostly from the central bank—what today we call quantitative expansion—which raised prices and transferred purchasing power through inflation. State claims dropped off after the war, although never to the levels seen earlier, because many delayed claims of tending to disabled soldiers and soldiers' families remained. The Great Depression forced expansion of unemployment assistance, so that the Western states of the late 1930s were probably spending a quarter of their national output; with rearmament starting drastically in Germany in 1936, in Japan perhaps earlier, in France and Britain by

1938, and in the United States by 1940, the shares went up again. By the middle of the Second World War, the United States was probably spending 45 percent, the Russians and Germans well over 50 percent, and of those sums, the largest share was going to military and war-related expenses. Again, the state share retreated after the end of the war, although Britain spent large sums on fighting colonial wars. The United States helped finance the French struggles, but by the late 1960s and 1970s, the expansion of social programs, welfare states, and university systems was increasing the ratios for a third time, up to 50 percent, and slightly more in West Germany, the Netherlands, and Scandinavia, but now prevailingly for social welfare and transfer expenses, as military budgets had fallen to below 5 percent of most countries' budgets. Some retrenchment in the 1980s has led to profiles of normal state expenditure at perhaps the 40 to 50 percent level. The United States, with smaller public sectors, spends probably about a third of its national income at all levels of government. The renormalized welfare state thus remains an active constituent of citizens' lives.

But the welfare state in its North American, Western European, and British dominion model was only one of three prevalent types. As of the 1950s and 1960s, the "socialist world," which passed almost all the national product (local garden crops or handicrafts sometimes excepted) through state hands, furnished an alternative and apparently still viable model. State socialism relied less on terror, although dissidents were hardly tolerated. The socialist state became increasingly bureaucratized, and the economic energies they possessed went largely into military innovation. The Soviet Union had to spend perhaps twice the share of public expenditure (perhaps 40 percent of the budget and up to 20 percent of GDP), compared to the United States, to remain a feared nuclear-armed adversary. The crisis of this system is also a subsequent story. So-called Third World states, which pursued a developmental model, followed different strategies. India remained attracted by the model of state socialism (even as it continued to admire village self-sufficiency as praised by its early architect of resistance, Gandhi.) Other states borrowed models inconsistently, but in most of them until the 1970s, state-owned pilot industrial sectors remained attractive, as they did for petroleum in Mexico, Brazil, and the Middle East. Japan, on the other hand, followed two decades later by other East Asian states, wagered on immense work effort being harnessed to technologically advanced consumer products, including automobiles and later electronics. Family networks remained important as connective tissue among the most elaborate alliances of banks and manufacturers.

As for political apparatus, the third state model, growing alongside the Western renormalized welfare state and the seemingly stable single-party states of the socialist world, remained that of military rule. Government by military officers would remain a frequent recourse throughout Asia, Africa, and Latin America. Soldier-rulers were a prevalent form of regime since antiquity, with or without empire—justified always on the notion that emergency conditions required intervention. As we have seen, armies were often the logical winners of a revolutionary process if civilians could not arrive at unity. When civilian leaders were corrupt or paralyzed, then military leaders, perceiving themselves as the best and most dedicated core of the community, had to step in. Military organizations were by essence nondemocratic, structured for obedience, sometimes subject to civilian control, but often considering themselves more devoted to state and nation than the corrupt civilians they booted out (or locked up and occasionally hanged). Sometimes the generals or colonels returned power to civilians, but having once seized power, their renewed intervention usually threatened. The creation of the Pakistani state by partition in 1947 would collect the northwestern military castes of the Raj and give them their own domain from tribal highlands to teeming coastal and Indus River cities for repeated interventions.

Mustafa Kemal Atatürk had provided one of the most convincing models of such rule—creating a secular and modernizing republic in the 1920s and 1930s. And although after his death the Turkish army relinquished control, it intervened at several points into the 1960s when it feared the principles of his secular nationalist state (and their role in it) were precarious. Eastern Europe had seen the military take control of Poland, Greece, Romania, and the Baltic States in the 1930s. The Thai monarch threw in his lot with military saviors in 1932, and the Thai army remained a frequent presence in that country's governance thereafter. General Franco ruled Spain for almost forty years after his coup and civil war victory in the late 1930s. Independent Egypt fell under military control in 1952 and remained unable to provide a coherent democratic alternative six decades later.

The Argentine military cultivated its own state within a state, proud of its large territory, blessed by Catholic bishops, angry at the ultra-Europeanist cosmopolitanism of the capital. General Uriburu seized power in 1930; and the military's stalwart authoritarians remained distrustful even of their own gifted demagogue, Juan Perón, who knew how to solicit mass loyalties on behalf of their continued influence. After Perón no longer seemed to serve them, they would intervene more brutally than ever in the 1970s. Hardly lagging, the Brazilian military took power in the late 1960s, the Uruguayan military would impose its own terror against urban guerrillas, and the Chilean military would oust Salvador Allende in 1973. The Indonesian military moved preemptively against a feared Communist uprising in the mid-1960s and probably massacred several hundred thousand suspected opponents. Washington's perception of US national interest during the Cold War ensured American tolerance and perhaps encouragement of these authoritarian initiatives.

Generals remained attractive candidates for civilian posts in the United States, and three major commanders of the Second World War played key roles in the postwar period—Dwight Eisenhower, the European commander, served as an eminently civilian president in the 1950s, and General George C. Marshall, wartime chief of staff, as an eminently civilian secretary of defense and of state. The third, General Douglas MacArthur, on the other hand, raised the first major challenge to civilian supremacy by his public dissenting policies concerning the Korean War but was decisively removed by President Truman. In the late twentieth century military governments emerged in two milieus. In the postcolonial states they were significant in Nigeria, Indonesia, and Pakistan, and, as noted, seized power when a radical left seemed to threaten (Indonesia). They were not absent in Europe (Spain, Greece), but seemed slated for extinction there. Military regimes could be taken as relatively benign interventions when normal states had lost control and communities descended into civil war and cycles of revenge that could not be stanched. The "dirty wars" of the 1970s produced levels of internal brutality that rivaled more formal fascist regimes. And sometimes military tyrants revealed paranoid tendencies that outran even their ideologically motivated harshness (as, for instance, in Iraq, Uganda, Libya, and Sierra Leone).[49]

Still, it would be historically wrong to end with such deformations of statehood. By the 1990s states were becoming more responsive to claims of justice and human rights. Just as globalization had helped to bring revolution eighty years earlier, it also brought benchmarks of progress that could not be gainsaid by the 1990s. The idea of bringing tyrants to an international bar of justice advanced, as did the sense that states must examine their dark and repressive episodes through so-called truth commissions. So, too, did the conviction that to be modern was not to march in mass formations but to travel, discuss, and allow international scrutiny and to develop new structures for policy making across borders. Finally, the fact that there were some leaders of truly heroic willingness to work for reconciliation, such as

Nelson Mandela, meant hope and deserved celebration. Yet it also indicated that states were again in flux: statehood seemed almost universal by the end of the twentieth century, but states also claimed less exclusive power as regional associations were established, and nongovernmental actors took on functions of transnational governance. Still, there can be no endpoint for summing up; the long century of modern statehood merges into the continuing record of an ancient and persevering institution, sometimes oppressive, sometimes emancipatory, continually contested and transformed.

Postscript: Toward Leviathan 3.0?

In the 1980s and 1990s the Eastern European Communist regimes, South Africa's Apartheid state, and the military dictatorships in Latin America transformed themselves into recognizable democracies. Economic strains, restrained leadership, and mass protest all played a role in these remarkable nonviolent transitions. The Soviet Union at least started down that path. This great wave of liberalization forms part of a subsequent history. It was nurtured by prosperity and by the dawning realization of how much private fulfillment had been postponed or diverted by the public demands of the years from 1914 through the 1950s. Perhaps it was connected to the progressive advent of intimate communication technologies that replaced the mass publics of the cinema and the radio harangue from the 1930s and 1940s: first by the family audiences for television in the 1950s and 1960s, then by the transistor and integrated circuit and software innovations that would sweep young people and their music through the era of the Walkman, to cell phones and the Internet. By the 1980s, European and American elections registered a general reaction against, not just abusive and pathological states, but state authority in general. Conservatives argued that the state was inimical to liberty no matter how democratic. And it appeared as if one might be able to outsource its functions, devolve them on what would be called the sphere of civil society.

Was there to be a Leviathan 3.0, which might in fact not be Leviathan in any recognizable sense but a form of functional association, as envisaged by many thinkers in the nineteenth and twentieth century? Many analysts in the 1970s and 1980s, myself included, had believed that the direct state-supervised negotiations among interest groups such as unions and employers—what was called corporatism or neo-corporatism—was slated to play a large role in public regulation. But such a role, so theorists of corporatism believed, would allegedly serve to replace the free market more than the state. They were as surprised by the revival of the liberal market as a form of economic regulation under Reagan and Thatcher (and then continued under parties of the left) as by the collapse of state socialism, which was in fact a related phenomenon.

Since the 1990s, the idea of governance has shimmered as the possible alternative to the state. It suggests a different outcome from what corporatism was intended to achieve. *Governance* as a term aims to sublimate politics, not economics. And rather than arriving at public outcomes through negotiations among class or interest-group representatives, governance has tended to imply that consensus can be found among disinterested experts, that is, experts who are advocates not for their own interests, but for the public welfare of humanity (or sometimes animals). Governance implied that regulation would emerge from the recommendations of NGOs and communities of knowledge. This process was not democracy per se. Schmitt had a point: democracy rested on a perceived community—a group of people who claimed an identity (perhaps territorial, perhaps ethnic, linguistic, or religious). But Schmitt implied that such an identity could exist only when a boundary separated friend from foe, us from them, whether they were within a territory or outside. By the late twentieth century, however, contemporary politics often encountered peoples with a sense of self-identification and a sense of loyalty to more than one territory, communities we term diasporas. Nonetheless Schmitt would certainly have recognized the heightened security measures we all live with today as testimony to the underlying realism of his views. Democracies, he would have argued, needed the state because their citizens had to be preoccupied by the danger that all outsiders and not just terrorists represented. Surveillance agencies in the democratic nations often argued the same. Perhaps (as I, for one, hope) there are less security-oriented reasons-of-state and reasons for states.

⌒

We started this history of the modern state at the Little Bighorn in the 1870s with peoples who preserved a plastic sense of territory, of land that was theirs but with an ill-defined border; and we end by evoking communities that might be post-territorial. "Citizens beyond borders?" But how could one organize government for such transnational communities? Perhaps democracy might be dismantled into human rights plus experts. Information on the web, private providers such as the media or Google, might play a larger public role. Still the contemporary world had institutions that collectively covered the globe, held elections, maintained armies, entered alliances, and attempted to control trade or conditions of work. The term *governance,* which had become so popular by the end of the twentieth century and continued to fascinate social scientists and foundations, testified to the hope for government without "stateness"—as if policy making might no longer require aggregating preferences and finally wagering on one choice or another, but could take place by consensus and the force of rational discussion. Disaggregate state offices, such as courts and regulators, and enmesh them into "global government networks," argued a leading advocate, and the result would be actually to enhance state power. Foundations, university elites, social scientists, men and women of goodwill loved the idea of governance—which suggested transparent and self-justifying administration without partisanship and without tears.[1] Governance was the utopia of the Masters of Public Policy.

No historian can envisage the future, or futures. Contending nations and empires—now with the addition of the Asian powers among others—may yet reassert old patterns of rivalry that reinforce state structures. Regional associations such as the European Union may play a larger role. States currently seem to have a bad reputation.

Whether tyrants or compulsive bureaucrats, their managers see the need to classify, count, and control. But as Hobbes and Hannah Arendt had stressed in their different ways, being stateless was often a worse fate: States protected vulnerable individuals and communities. They provided the legal carapace for the soft-bodied creatures of humanity, lying exposed to the cruel and rapacious or even just the profit-seeking or zealous. Power and violence do not disappear when states are feeble; rather they are exercised without the restraint of law. Teens pressed into trafficking may fear the law but are ultimately victims of state absence, not presence. Being stateless in Gaza or, even worse, in Darfur in the first decade of the twenty-first century was not an enviable condition.

Between the mid-nineteenth and mid-twentieth centuries, states had recreated themselves in many ways: They had fought for territorial cohesion; enlisted the middle classes, consolidated territory, subjugated "nomadic" or tribal peoples, and turned on each other in unparalleled wars. They had experimented with revolutionary parties whose members were intoxicated by visions of transformation through violence and had virtually worshipped the most brutal of leaders. And finally they had sought normalcy and a precarious equilibrium with the ever more powerful forces of the economy. Of course, states were the inherited creations of individuals, communities, and parties infused by ideas, interests, and perhaps even instincts. They acted through policies and instrumentalities that they could not fully control. We can work to diminish their constraints or their tutelage. But the needs and ambitions that created them will remain in some hands or others, and certain questions will not disappear—not only Hobbes's question: What is life like without the state? But also Aristotle's question: Do we control the state by the one, the many, or the few? Or the question posed by the American founders: How do we run it for the welfare of us all? These issues abide.

Notes

INTRODUCTION

1 See, most recently, Nathaniel Philbrick, *The Last Stand: Custer, Sitting Bull, and the Battle of the Little Bighorn* (New York: Viking, 2010).

2 See Rudi Linder, "What Was a Nomadic Tribe?," *Comparative Studies in Society and History* 24 (1982): 689–711, at 691.

3 Reşat Kasaba, *A Moveable Empire: Ottoman Nomads, Migrants, and Refugees* (Seattle: University of Washington Press, 2009), 116. For the long history of native American struggles, resistance, and removals, see Daniel Richter, *Facing East from Indian Country: A Native History of Early America* (Cambridge, MA: Harvard University Press, 2001); Pekka Hämäläinen, *The Comanche Empire* (New Haven, CT: Yale University Press, 2008); and Hämäläinen, "The Rise and Fall of Plains Indian Horse Cultures," *Journal of American History* 90 (2003): 833–862. For the Zulu and other peoples of southern Africa, I have relied on the contributions by Monica Wilson and Leonard Thompson, editors of *The Oxford History of South Africa*, vol. 1, *South Africa to 1870* (New York: Oxford University Press, 1969); also Andrew Roberts, *A History of Zambia* (New York: Holmes and Meier, Africana Publishing Co., 1976).

4 James C. Scott, *The Art of Not Being Governed: An Anarchist History of Upland Southeast Asia* (New Haven, CT: Yale University Press, 2009). Scott writes, "The huge literature on state-making, contemporary and historic, pays virtually no attention to its obverse: the history of deliberate and reactive statelessness" (p. x). But of course we have long celebrated "those who got away"—at least from Robin Hood on. For Scott's critique of state regulatory projects, see his *Seeing Like a State: How Certain Schemes to Improve the Human Condition Have Failed* (New Haven, CT: Yale University Press, 2008).

5 As Max Weber defined it, the state is the human community that claims a monopoly of legitimate power in a given territory. "Legitimate" is a crucial adjective—the mafia doesn't count—and "territory," he declared, was a critical attribute. See Weber, "Politics as a Vocation," in *From Max Weber: Essays in Sociology,* ed. H. H. Gerth and C. Wright Mills (New York: Oxford University Press, 1958), 78; also in Max Weber, *Gesamtausgabe,* Abt. 1, Bd. 17, ed. Wolfgang J. Mommsen, Wolfgang Schluchter and Birgitt Morgenbrod (Tübingen: Mohr, 1992).

6   Quentin Skinner, *The Foundations of Modern Political Thought,* 2 vols. (Cambridge: Cambridge University Press, 1978), 2:348–358. A useful discussion of the early development of the concept of the state in comparative contexts is provided by Oleg Kharkordin, "What Is the State? The Russian Concept of *Gosudarstvo* in European Context," *History and Theory* 40, no. 2 (May 2001): 206–240. See also Charles S. Maier, "Nation and State," in *Encyclopedia of Transnational History,* ed. Akira Iriye and Pierre-Yves Saunier (New York: Macmillan, 2009)—a summary I would now rewrite to allow for non-Western categories.

7   For an encyclopedic treatment of the development of the early modern state in particular, see Wolfgang Reinhard, *Geschichte der Staatsgewalt: Eine vergleichende Verfassungsgeschichte Europas von den Anfängen bis zur Gegenwart* (Munich: Beck, 1999). There are many treatments of sovereignty: among recent ones, see Robert Jackson: *Sovereignty: Evolution of an Idea* (Cambridge: Polity Press, 2007); Stephen D. Krasner, *Sovereignty: Organized Hypocrisy* (Princeton, NJ: Princeton University Press, 1999); Daniel Philpott, *Revolutions in Sovereignty: How Ideas Shaped Modern International Relations* (Princeton, NJ: Princeton University Press, 2001). Andreas Osiander has contested the importance of Westphalia—see Osiander, "Sovereignty, International Relations, and the Westphalian Myth," *International Organization* 55, no. 2 (2001): 251–287—but it has become the common designation for modern statehood.

8   David C. Kang, *East Asia before the West: Five Centuries of Trade and Tribute* (New York: Columbia University Press, 2010).

9   I am indebted to the ongoing dissertation research of Macabe Kelliher at Harvard on the Board of Rites in late imperial China. See too Joseph Peter McDermott, ed., *State and Court Ritual in China* (Cambridge: Cambridge University Press, 1999), in particular the summary essay by James Laidlaw, "On Theatre and Theory: Reflections on Ritual in Imperial Chinese Politics," 399–416, which stresses how ritual inserts state power into cosmological concepts. For a discussion of state power, see also Michael Mann, "The Autonomous Power of the State," in *States in History,* ed. John A. Hall (New York: Basil Blackwell, 1986).

10   There is a large literature, from the 1970s and 1980s in particular. See J. G. A. Pocock, *The Machiavellian Moment* (Princeton, NJ: Princeton University Press, 1975); Isaac Kramnick, *Bolingbroke and His Circle: The Politics of Nostalgia in the Age of Walpole* (Cambridge, MA: Harvard University Press, 1968); Charles S. Maier, " 'Fictitious Bonds of Wealth and Law,' " in *Organizing Interests in Western Europe,* ed. Suzanne Berger (Cambridge: Cambridge University Press, 1981); Pierre Rosanvallon, *Le moment Guizot* (Paris: Gallimard, 1985).

1. THE WORLD IS WEARY OF THE PAST

1   Two recent and important treatments of global history choose the entire nineteenth century as their temporal unit of analysis: C. A. Bayly, *The Birth of the Modern World, 1780–1914* (Malden, MA: Blackwell, 2004); and Jürgen Osterhammel, *Die Verwandlung der Welt* (Munich: Beck, 2009).

2   Eric J. Hobsbawm popularized the idea of the short twentieth century, 1914–1989, and then used it as the subtitle of the 1994 edition of his *The Age of Extremes: The Short Twentieth Century, 1914–1991* (London: Michael Joseph, 1994). Taking account of the transformative changes of the late eighteenth century and its impact, the German historian Reinhart Koselleck termed the era a *Sattelzeit* or "saddle time"—a metaphor he derived from the German expression for a "mountain saddle" or pass between two peaks—that is, the transition from one age to another. For the idea of moral narratives (as contrasted with analysis of long-term processes), see Charles S. Maier, "Consigning the Twentieth Century to History: Alternative Narratives for the Modern Era: Forum Essay," *American Historical Review* 105, no. 3 (June 2000): 807–831. The underlying idea of simultaneous scales—the history of events, of eras, and environmentally determined "longue durée"—was presented in Fernand Braudel, *The Mediterranean and the Mediterranean World in the Age of Philip II,* trans. Siân Reynolds (London: Collins, 1972–1973). For historians' theories of crisis, especially as applied to the late eighteenth century, see Reinhard Koselleck, "Crisis," *Journal of the History of Ideas* 67, no. 2 (2006): 357–400; and James R. Martin, "The Theory of Storms: Jacob Burckhardt and the Concept of 'Historical Crisis,'" in *Journal of European Studies* 40, no. 4 (2010): 307–327.

3   Shelley, *Prometheus Unbound,* act 4, lines 572, 576–578.

4   Karen Barkey, *An Empire of Difference: The Ottomans in Comparative Perspective* (Cambridge: Cambridge University Press, 2008); Halil Inalcik, *Essays in Ottoman History* (Istanbul: Erin, 1998); Cemal Cafadar, *Between Two Worlds: The Construction of the Ottoman State* (Berkeley: University of California Press, 1995); M. Sükrü Hanioğlu, *A Brief History of the Late Ottoman Empire* (Princeton, NJ: Princeton University Press, 2008); Donald Quataert, *The Ottoman Empire, 1700–1922* (New York: Cambridge University Press, 2000); *The Cambridge History of Turkey,* vol. 3, *The Later Ottoman Empire, 1603–1839,* ed. Suraiya N. Faroqhi (Cambridge: Cambridge University Press, 2008).

5   Karl Polanyi described this process for England in *The Great Transformation* (1944; Boston: Beacon Press, 1958) but paradoxically argued that the resulting unrest was responsible not for liberalism, but ultimately for fascism. E. P.

Thompson emphasized the tenacious resistance to market trends in agriculture in "The Moral Economy of the English Crowd in the Eighteenth Century," *Past and Present,* no. 50 (February 1971): 76–131. For a discussion of peasant communalism in Southeast Asia, see James C. Scott, *Weapons of the Weak: Everyday Forms of Peasant Resistance* (New Haven, CT: Yale University Press, 1985).

6 Alfred W. Crosby Jr., *The Columbian Exchange: Biological and Cultural Consequences of 1492* (Westport, CT: Greenwood, 1972); for the impact of smallpox, measles and other diseases (comparable in the Americas to the Black Death in Europe two centuries earlier), see Sheldon Watts, *Epidemics and History: Disease, Power and Imperialism* (New Haven, CT: Yale University Press, 1997); and Suzanne Austin Alchon, *A Pest in the Land: New World Epidemics in a Global Perspective* (Albuquerque: University of New Mexico Press, 2003). For shadow acres, see Kenneth Pomeranz, *The Great Divergence: China, Europe, and the Making of the Modern World Economy* (Princeton, NJ: Princeton University Press, 2000); and the classic text by Sidney Mintz, *Sweetness and Power: The Place of Sugar in Modern History* (New York: Viking, 1985).

7 Rhoda Murphey, "Deforestation in Modern China," in *Global Deforestation and the Nineteenth-Century World Economy,* ed. Richard P. Tucker and John F. Richards (Durham, NC: Duke University Press, 1983), 111–128, quotation at 111.

8 Cited in Mark Elvin, *The Retreat of the Elephants: An Environmental History of China* (New Haven, CT: Yale University Press, 2004), 57. The stele recorded the resolution to reserve all the land on Mount Houlong as communal land that could be neither bought nor sold, and to care for the trees.

9 Warren Dean, *With Broadax and Firebrand: The Destruction of the Brazilian Atlantic Forest* (Berkeley: University of California Press, 1995), 190.

10 Domingo F. Sarmiento, *Facundo: Or Civilization and Barbarism,* trans. Mary Mann (New York: Penguin, 1998). For a modern portrait, see John Lynch, *Argentine Dictator: Jan Manuel de Rosas, 1829–1852* (Oxford: Oxford University Press, 1981).

11 See Jan de Vries, *The Industrious Revolution: Consumer Behavior and the Household Economy, 1650 to the Present* (Cambridge: Cambridge University Press, 2008).

12 See John H. Elliott, *Empires of the Atlantic World: Britain and Spain in America, 1492–1830* (New Haven, CT: Yale University Press, 2006).

13 Jeremy Adelman, *Sovereignty and Revolution in the Iberian Atlantic* (Princeton, NJ: Princeton University Press, 2006); Fred Anderson and Andrew Cayton, *The Dominion of War: Empire and Liberty in North America, 1500–2000* (New York: Viking, 2005).

14 See Peter Perdue, *China Marches West: The Qing Conquest of Central Eurasia* (Cambridge, MA: Harvard University Press, 2005) for the campaign against the Zunghars; and for a summary of the new interpretations of the Qing empire as a dynamic, Manchu-run imperial structure, see William T. Rowe, *China's Last Empire: The Great Qing* (Cambridge, MA: Harvard University Press, 2009).

15 Phyllis Deane and W. A. Cole, *British Economic Growth, 1688–1959: Trends and Structure,* 2nd ed. (Cambridge: Cambridge University Press, 1969), 62 for the British estimate. Firm statistics were available only from the 1850s. As of midcentury the French share was about 53 percent, Russia about 63 percent, Spain 70 percent. See B. R. Mitchell, *European Historical Statistics, 1750–1950* (London: Macmillan, 1978), table B1, pp. 51–64.

16 E. P. Thompson, *The Making of the English Working Class* (New York: Vintage, 1963).

17 William B. Taylor, "Banditry and Insurrection: Rural Unrest in Central Jalisco, 1790–1816," and John M. Hart, "The 1840s Southwestern Mexico Peasants' War: Conflict in a Transitional Society," both in *Riot, Rebellion, and Revolution: Rural Social Conflict in Mexico,* ed. Friedrich Katz (Princeton, NJ: Princeton University Press, 1988), 205–268.

18 Jerome Blum, *The End of the Old Order in Rural Europe* (Princeton, NJ: Princeton University Press, 1978); Geroid T. Robinson, *Rural Russia under the Old Régime: A History of the Landlord-Peasant World and a Prologue to the Peasant Revolution of 1917* (1932; New York: Macmillan, 1967); Boris N. Mironov, *The Social History of Imperial Russia, 1700–1917* (Boulder CO: Westview Press, 2000), 1:286–370.

19 William W. Hagen, *Ordinary Prussians: Brandenburg Junkers and Villagers, 1500–1840* (Cambridge: Cambridge University Press, 2002).

20 John Locke, *The Second Treatise of Government,* para. 41, in Locke, *Two Treatises of Government,* ed. Peter Laslett (Cambridge: Cambridge University Press, 1966), 296–297. For an extensive discussion of the doctrine of *terra nullius,* see Stuart Banner, "Why Terra Nullius? Anthropology and Property Law in Early Australia," *Law and History Review* (Spring 2005), http://www.historycooperative.org/journals/lhr/23.1/banner.html (5 Sep. 2011). On Mexico, see Emilio Kouri, *A Pueblo Divided: Business, Property, and Community in Papantla, Mexico* (Stanford, CA: Stanford University Press, 2004); the studies in *Liberals, the Church, and Indian Peasants: Corporate Lands and the Challenge of Reform in Nineteenth-Century Spanish America,* ed. Robert H. Jackson (Albuquerque: University of New Mexico Press, 1997); Raymond B. Craib, *Cartographic*

Mexico: A History of State Fixations and Fugitive Landscapes (Durham, NC: Duke University Press, 2004).

21 See the valuable case studies relating to the legal enforcement of land claims in *Contract and Property in Early Modern China,* ed. Madeleine Zelin, Jonathan K. Ocko, and Robert Cardella (Stanford, CA: Stanford University Press, 2004).

22 For insights into the reform program and its results, in addition to works cited in the notes above, see Richard Herr, *Rural Change and Royal Finances in Spain at the End of the Old Regime* (Berkeley: University of California Press, 1989); Franz A. J. Szabo, *Kaunitz and Enlightened Absolutism, 1753–1780* (Cambridge: Cambridge University Press, 1994); Emma Rothschild, *Economic Sentiments: Adam Smith, Condorcet, and the Enlightenment* (Cambridge, MA: Harvard University Press, 2001), 72–86; Luke S. Roberts, *Mercantilism in a Japanese Domain: The Merchant Origins of Economic Nationalism in 18th-Century Tosa* (Cambridge: Cambridge University Press, 1998); Ranajit Guha, *A Rule of Property for Bengal: An Essay on the Idea of Permanent Settlement* (Paris: Mouton, 1963); Sugata Bose, *Peasant Labour and Colonial Capital: Rural Bengal since 1770,* vol. 3, pt. 2, of *The Cambridge History of India* (Cambridge: Cambridge University Press, 1993).

23 For a good case study of the conquered Rhineland, annexed to France for twenty years, see Gabriele B. Clemens, *Immobilienhändler und Spekulanten: Die sozial- und wirtschaftsgeschichtliche Bedeutung der Grosskäufer bei den Nationalgüterversteigerungen in den rheinischen Departementen (1803–1813)* (Boppard am Rhein: H. Boldt, 1995).

24 Jan Bazant, *Alienation of Church Lands in Mexico: Social and Economic Aspects of the Liberal Revolution, 1856–1875* (Cambridge: Cambridge University Press, 1971), chap. 1 for the years after 1821; case studies in Jackson, *Liberals, the Church, and Indian Peasants;* Ethelia Ruiz Medrano, *Mexico's Indigenous Communities: Their Lands and Histories, 1500–2010,* trans. Russ Davidson (Boulder CO: University Press of Colorado, 2010); Robert J. Knowlton, *Church Property and the Mexican Reform, 1856–1910* (DeKalb: Northern Illinois University Press, 1976).

25 It has remained a major challenge for historians and historical sociologists to determine which communities remained loyal to the Church and which ones joined the revolutionary coalitions, turned on local priests, and participated in the reshuffling of landed assets. Proximity to towns and markets has been suggested as one variable: For France see, among other studies, Paul Bois, *Paysans de l'Ouest: Des structures économiques et sociales aux options politiques, depuis*

l'époque révolutionnaire, dans la Sarthe (Paris: Flammarion, 1978); also Charles Tilly, *The Vendée* (Cambridge, MA: Harvard University Press, 1976).

26 Hagen, *Ordinary Prussians,* 652–653.

27 See Carlos Marichal, "Las finanzas y la construcción de las nuevas naciones latinoamericanas," in *Historia General de America Latina* (Paris: UNESCO, 2003), 6:399–420.

28 See James J. Reid, *Crisis of the Ottoman Empire: Prelude to Collapse, 1839–1878* (Stuttgart: Franz Steiner Verlag, 2000), and, for a comparison of Mount Lebanon and northern Albania, Maurus Reinkowski, *Die Dinge der Ordnung: Eine vergleichende Untersuchung über die osmanische Reformpolitik im 19 Jahrhundert* (Munich: R. Oldenbourg Verlag, 2000)—both of which stress the fragmentation, violence, and yet military incapacity of the Ottoman state despite the reforms of the Tanzimat.

29 On the social and political background of these conflicts, see Bruce McGowan, "The Age of the *Ayans,* 1699–1812," in *An Economic and Social History of the Ottoman Empire, 1300–1914,* ed. Halil Inalcik with Donald Quataert (Cambridge: Cambridge University Press, 1994), pt. 3, 637–758.

30 *The Cambridge History of Egypt,* vol. 2: *Modern Egypt from 1517 to the End of the Twentieth Century,* ed. M. W. Daly (Cambridge: Cambridge University Press, 1998). I have drawn on chapters 6, 7, and 8 (pp. 139–216), by Khaled Fahmy, F. Robert Hunter, and Hassan Ahmed Ibrahim, respectively.

31 Halil Inalcik, "The Nature of Traditional Society: Turkey" [1964], in *The Ottoman Empire: Conquest, Organization and Economy* (London: Variorum Reprints, 1978). For the balance between Istanbul and the elites and the efforts at tax reform and control of land, see Donald Quataert, "The Age of Reforms," in Inalcik and Quataert, *History of the Ottoman Empire,* pt. 4, esp. 854–861.

32 Dwight H. Perkins et al., *Agricultural Development in China, 1368–1968* (Chicago: Aldine, 1969), chaps. 2–4.

33 For the crisis of the late Qianlong reign, see Philip A. Kuhn, *Origins of the Modern Chinese State* (Stanford, CA: Stanford University Press, 2002).

34 Adam Smith, *An Inquiry into the Nature and Causes of the Wealth of Nations* (Oxford: Oxford University Press, 1976), 1:89.

35 Cited by Kuhn, *Origins,* 32.

36 See Jack Gray, *Rebellions and Revolutions: China from the 1800s to the 1980s* (Oxford: Oxford University Press, 1990), 8–15.

37 For a pro-British account, see ibid.; but cf. Fred Wakeman Jr., "The Canton Trade and the Opium War," in *The Cambridge History of China,* vol. 10, *Late Ch'ing, 1800–1911,* pt. 1, 163–212.

38 Stephen Vlastos, *Peasant Protests and Uprisings in Tokugawa Japan* (Berkeley: University of California Press, 1986), 75–79.

39 David Dean Commins, *Islamic Reform: Politics and Social Change in Late Ottoman Syria* (New York: Oxford University Press, 1990).

40 Bayly, *Birth of the Modern World,* 333–357.

41 For an analysis of goals, composition, ideas, and resources see Philip A. Kuhn, *Rebellion and Its Enemies in Late Imperial China* (Cambridge, MA: Harvard University Press, 1970); also Kuhn, "The Taiping Rebellion," in *The Cambridge History of China,* vol. 10, pt. 1, pp. 264–317.

42 C. A. Bayly, *Indian Society and the Making of the British Empire,* vol. 2, pt. 1, of *The New Cambridge History of India* (Cambridge: Cambridge University Press, 1988), 172.

43 For the looting and symbolism of the British conquest in 1860, see James L. Hevia, *English Lessons: The Pedagogy of Imperialism in Nineteenth-Century China* (Durham, NC: Duke University Press, 2003), 68–118.

2. RECONSTRUCTION ON A WORLD SCALE

1 Cited by Federico Chabod, *Italian Foreign Policy: The Statecraft of the Founders,* William McCuaig, trans. (Princeton, NJ: Princeton University Press, 1996), 552.

2 Bonnie Smith, *Ladies of the Leisure Class: The Bourgeoises of Northern France in the Nineteenth Century* (Princeton NJ: Princeton University Press, 1981); also Smith, *Changing Lives: Women in European History since 1700* (Lexington, MA: D. C. Heath, 1989); for British middle-class women's history: Leonore Davidoff and Catherine Hall, *Family Fortunes* (London: Routledge, 2002); *The Routledge History of Women in Europe since 1700,* Deborah Simonton, ed. (New York: Routledge, 2006).

3 Albert Hourani, *Arabic Thought in the Liberal Age, 1798–1939* (Cambridge: Cambridge University Press, 1983), 67–123.

4 Samuel Smiles, *Self-Help: With Illustrations of Conduct and Perseverance,* ed. Peter W. Sinnema (1859; Oxford: Oxford University Press, 2002); C. A. Bayly, *The Birth of the Modern World, 1780–1914* (Malden, MA: Blackwell, 2004), 319.

5 Peter J. Hugill, *World Trade since 1431: Geography, Technology, and Capitalism* (Baltimore: Johns Hopkins University Press, 1993), 174.

6 From Charles Dickens, *Dombey and Son;* as quoted in Myron F. Brightfield, "The Coming of the Railroads to Victorian Britain as Viewed by Novels of the Period (1840–1870)," *Technology and Culture* 3, no. 1 (1962): 45–72, here 52. The

second quote is from "Railroads in the United States," *Hunt's Merchant Magazine,* October 1840, 273–295, here 287.

7 Cavour's review of Pettiti in the *Revue Nouvelle* as cited in Harry Hearder, *Italy in the Age of the Risorgimento* (London: Longman, 1983), 212.

8 A. A. Den Otter, *The Philosophy of Railways: The Transcontinental Railway Idea in British North America* (Toronto: University of Toronto Press, 1997).

9 Cited in *China's Response to the West: A Documentary Survey, 1839–1923,* ed. Ssu-jü Teng and John K. Fairbank (Cambridge, MA: Harvard University Press, 1979), 117–119.

10 Clarence B. Davis, Kenneth E. Wilburn, with Ronald E. Robinson, *Railway Imperialism* (New York: Greenwood Press, 1991). On the cooperation of post–Civil War elites and the creation of a quasi-colonial economy in the South, see C. Vann Woodward, *Origins of the New South, 1877–1913* (Baton Rouge: Louisiana State University Press, 1951); and Robert L. Brandfon, *Cotton Kingdom of the New South: A History of the Yazoo Mississippi Delta from Reconstruction to the Twentieth Century* (Cambridge, MA: Harvard University Press, 1967). Where the older empires—Ottoman and Russian—retained railroad ownership, there was less opportunity for this coalition building, although private magnates emerged via contractual arrangements. The other investment opportunity that served as a sort of melting pot for old and new money was in urban real estate, as cities grew after 1870.

11 Cited by Chabod, *Italian Foreign Policy,* 53.

12 John Lynch, *Caudillos in Spanish America, 1800–1850* (New York: Oxford University Press, 1992); Tulio Halperín Donghi, *Guerra y finanzas en los orígines del Estado Argentina, 1791–1850* (Buenos Aires: Belgrano, 1982); Halperín Donghi, ed., *Projecto y construcción de una nación: Argentina, 1846–1880* (Caracas: Biblioteca Ayacucho, 1980); Fernando López-Alves, *State Formation and Democracy in Latin America, 1810–1900* (Durham, NC: Duke University Press, 2000); Benedict Anderson, *Imagined Communities: Reflections on the Origin and Spread of Nationalism* (London: Verso, 1983).

13 For the Taiping, see Franz Michael and Chang Chung-li, *The Taiping Rebellion: History and Documents,* 3 vols. (Seattle: University of Washington Press, 1966–1971); Jonathan Spence, *God's Chinese Son: The Taiping Heavenly Kingdom of Hong Xiuquan* (New York: W. W. Norton, 1996); Jen Yu-wen (Chien Yu-wen), *The Taiping Revolutionary Movement* (New Haven, CT: Yale University Press, 1973); Vincent Shih, *The Taiping Ideology: Its Sources, Interpretations, and Influences* (Seattle: University of Washington Press, 1967); C. A. Curwen, *Taiping Rebel: The Deposition of Li Hsiu-ch'eng* (New York: Cambridge University Press, 1977).

14 Geoffrey Wawro, *The Austro-Prussian War* (Cambridge: Cambridge University Press, 1996), citation of the Albrecht memo, "Über die Verantwortlichkeit im Kriege," at 291. The Prussians also had much more rapidly reloadable breech-loading rifles (the so-called Needle Guns) vs. Austrian muzzle loaders.

15 George Frederickson, *The Inner Civil War: Northern Intellectuals and the Crisis of the Union* (New York: Harper and Row, 1965), 98–112, on the sanitary commission; for British wartime conditions, see Mark Bostridge, *Florence Nightingale: The Making of an Icon* (New York: Farrar, Straus and Giroux, 2008); also Hugh Small, *Florence Nightingale, Avenging Angel* (New York: St. Martin's, 1998).

16 David Blackbourn, *Marpingen: Apparitions of the Virgin in Nineteenth-Century Germany* (New York: Knopf, 1994); Emmet J. Larkin, *The Making of the Roman Catholic Church in Ireland, 1850–1860* (Chapel Hill: University of North Carolina Press, 1980), among his other works; E. E. Y. Hales, *Pio Nono: A Study in European Politics and Religion in the Nineteenth Century* (Garden City, NY: Doubleday, 1962); Frank Coppa, *Pope Pius IX: Crusader in a Secular Age* (Boston: Twayne, 1979).

17 For a selection of recent analyses of nineteenth-century nationalism, see Anderson, *Imagined Communities;* John Breuilly, *Nationalism and the State,* 2nd ed. (Chicago: University of Chicago Press, 1994); Rogers Brubaker, *Citizenship and Nationhood in France and Germany* (Cambridge, MA: Harvard University Press, 1993); Ernest Gellner, *Nations and Nationalism* (Ithaca, NY: Cornell University Press, 2002); Eric J. Hobsbawm, *Nations and Nationalism since 1780: Programme, Myth, Reality* (New York: Cambridge University Press, 1990); Miroslaw Hroch, *Social Preconditions of National Revolution in Europe: A Comparative Analysis of the Social Composition of Patriotic Groups among the Smaller European Nations* (New York: Columbia University Press, 2000). Works on Asian and African nationalism tend to focus on the twentieth century.

18 I am indebted to Marta Petrusevic for pointing to the role of agricultural improvement societies as proxies for nationalist organization.

19 Alexander Herzen, "From the Other Shore," trans. L. Navrozov, and "To an Old Comrade," both in *Selected Philosophical Works* (Moscow: Foreign Languages, 1956), 343, 577–578.

20 Ernest Satow, *A Diplomat in Japan: An Inner History of the Critical Years in the Evolution of Japan* (Rutland, VT: Charles E. Tuttle, 1983).

21 Carol Gluck, *Japan's Modern Myths: Ideologies in the Meiji Period* (Princeton, NJ: Princeton University Press, 1985).

22 Applied to Japan (as they had long been to European struggles from the seventeenth century), Marxist-derived analyses were represented by E. H. Norman, *Origins of the Modern Japanese State: Selected Writings of E. H. Norman,* ed. John W. Dower (New York: Pantheon, 1975).

23 Karl Marx, *The Eighteenth Brumaire of Louis Bonaparte* (New York: International, 1964); Karl Marx (and Friedrich Engels), *Revolution and Counter-Revolution: Or Germany in 1848,* ed. Eleanor Aveling Marx (New York: Scribner's, 1896).

24 For the major recent account, see James M. McPherson, *Ordeal by Fire: The Civil War and Reconstruction,* 3rd ed. (Boston: McGraw-Hill, 2001).

25 Still valuable, Albert D. Kirwan, *Revolt of the Rednecks: Mississippi Politics, 1865–1925* (Gloucester, MA: P. Smith, 1964).

26 Brian DeLay, *War of a Thousand Deserts: Indian Raids and the U.S.-Mexican War* (New Haven, CT: Yale University Press, 2008); Pekka Hämäläinan, *The Comanche Empire* (New Haven, CT: Yale University Press, 2008). Both books have transformed our vision of the confrontation between Mexico and America.

27 Nelson Reed, *The Caste War of Yucatan* (Stanford, CA: Stanford University Press, 1964).

28 For fine comparative analysis, see López-Alves, *State Formation;* and J. G. Merquior, "Patterns of State-Building in Brazil and Argentina," in *States in History,* ed. John A. Hall (Oxford: Blackwell, 1987), 264–288; also thematic surveys in *Historia General de América Latina,* vol. 6, *La construcción de las naciones latinoamericanas, 1820–1870,* ed. Josefina Z. Vázquez and Manuel Miño Grijalva (Paris: UNESCO, 2003), esp. chaps. 1–6.

29 For Austria-Hungary, see Robert A. Kann, *A History of the Habsburg Empire, 1526–1918* (Berkeley: University of California Press, 1974); Arthur J. May, *The Hapsburg Monarchy, 1867–1914* (1951: New York: W. W. Norton, 1968); C. A. Macartney, *The Habsburg Empire, 1790–1918* (New York: Macmillan, 1969). For key internal developments: Louis Eisenmann, *Le compromis austro-hongrois de 1867* (Paris: G. Bellais, 1904); W. A. Jenks, *The Austrian Electoral Reform of 1907* (New York: Columbia University Press, 1960); and for constitutional issues, Josef Redlich, *Das österreichsche Staats- und Reichsproblem,* 2 vols. (Leipzig: P. Reinhold, 1921).

3. THE HUMAN ZOO

1 The growth of world's fairs or "Expositions Universelles" as registered with the Brussels-based Bureau International des Expositions, chartered in 1928—an NGO representative of the international organizational efforts of the 1920s—is

a revealing development of global history. Cited here are Philadelphia 1876: 1.8 km^2 in area and over 10 million visitors; Paris 1878: 0.27 km^2 and over 13 million visitors; Paris 1889: 0.96 km^2 and 28 million visitors; Chicago ("Columbian Exposition") 1893: 2.4 km^2 and over 27 million visitors. The first major "expo" was the Crystal Palace Exhibit of 1851: 0.092 km^2 within one structure and over 6 million visitors; the largest would be the New York World's Fair of 1939–1940, covering almost 5 km^2 and attracting over 44 million visitors to view supposedly future-oriented exhibits based on "the world of tomorrow." "Tomorrow" turned out to be the Second World War.

2 See Alexander C. T. Geppert, *Fleeting Cities: Imperial Expositions in Fin-de-Siècle Europe* (Houdsmills, Basingstoke: Palgrave-Macmillan, 2010), 121–125.

3 Peter Sloterdijk, *Regeln für den Menschenpark: Ein Antwortschreiben zu Heideggers Brief über den Humanismus* (Frankfurt: Suhrkamp, 1999).

4 Suazanne Marchand, *German Orientalism in the Age of Empire: Religion, Race, and Scholarship* (Washington, DC: German Historical Institute; New York: Cambridge University Press, 2009); Yuri Slezkine, *Arctic Mirrors: Russia and the Small Peoples of the North* (Ithaca, NY: Cornell University Press, 1994); H. Glenn Penny and Matti Bunzl, eds., *Worldly Provincialism: German Anthropology in the Age of Empire* (Ann Arbor: University of Michigan Press, 2003).

5 Rudyard Kipling, "Recessional"; Henry Adams, "The Virgin and the Dynamo," in *Mont-Saint-Michel and Chartres* (1904; Princeton, NJ: Princeton University Press, 1981).

6 Patrice Higonnet has constructed his unsparing history of American interventions around this phrase used by Theodore Roosevelt. See his *Attendant Cruelties* (New York: New Press, 2008). For ecological transformations (and the labor patterns that attended them), see James C. Scott, *Seeing Like a State: How Certain Schemes to Improve the Human Condition Have Failed* (New Haven, CT: Yale University Press, 2008); and for a case study, Clifford Geertz, *Agricultural Involution: The Process of Ecological Change in Indonesia* (Berkeley: University of California Press, 1963).

7 'Der Staat ist ein sittliches Wesen und er hat sittliche Lebensaufgaben." Johann Caspar Bluntschli, *Allgemeines Staatsrecht Geschichtlich Begründet,* 3rd rev. ed. (Munich: J. G. Cotta, 1863), 1:2.

8 Georg Jellinek, *Das Recht des modernen Staates,* vol. 1: *Allgemeine Staatslehre* (Berlin: O. Häring, 1900). "Durch Rechtssätze und Rechtszwang werden daher nationale Selbständigkeit und Macht, wirtschaftliches und geistiges Leben des Volkes auch gefördert, also sociale Resultate durch obrigkeitliche Macht bewirkt.... Briefe befördern, Eisenbahnen betreiben, Schulen gründen, Unter-

richt erteilen, Armenpflege üben, Strassen bauen sind an und für sich private Tätigkeiten, die im socialen, nicht im juristischen Sinne öffentlichen Charakter besitzen. Der Staat kann diese und ähnliche Tätigkeiten, wenn er sie ausübt oder durch Andere ausüben lässt, kraft seiner umfassenden Macht, mit der er Privat- in öffentliches Recht zu verwandeln vermag, zu öffentlichen im Rechtssinne erheben" (572).

9 Rudolph von Gneist, *The History of the English Constitution,* trans. Philip A. Ashworth, 2 vols. (London: William Clowes, 1886). Otto von Gierke, *Das deutsche Genossenschaftsrecht,* 4 vols. (Berlin: Weidman, 1868–1913), selections translated as *Community in Historical Perspective,* ed. Antony Black, trans. Mary Fischer (New York: Cambridge University Press, 1990). For French functionalists, see Léon Duguit, *Le droit social, le droit individuel et la transformation de l'état* (Paris: Felix Alcan, 1908), 37–38 and passim; Arthur Bentley, *The Process of Government: A Study of Social Pressure* (1908; Cambridge, MA: Harvard University Press, 1967). The groups that overthrew communist regimes in the 1990s claimed to be acting for "civil society"—a set of organizations, such as churches, unions, and voluntary associations, that exercised public functions but without relying on the coercive equipment of government in the 1990s— but this concept fell into increased disuse in the following decade as political parties slowly tightened their grip on postcommunist societies and did not relinquish it elsewhere.

10 Cf. Peter Baldwin, "Beyond Weak and Strong: Rethinking the State in Comparative Policy History," *Journal of Policy History* 17, no. 1 (2005): 12–33; for the "hygiene" agenda, emerging since the early nineteenth century, see Pierre Rosanvallon, *L'état on France de 1789 à nos jours* (Paris: Seuil, 1990).

11 Jellinek, *Allgemeine Staatslehre,* 570–572. "Aus den früheren Untersuchungen bereits hat sich ergeben, dass nicht ausschliesslich auf sie beschränkt ist. Durch die Gemeinsamkeit der Herrschaft werden die ihr Unterworfenen Genossen. Die Förderung genossenschaftlicher Zwecke durch gesellschaftliche Mittel ist in stetig steigendem Masse Staatsaufgabe geworden" (570).

12 See James T. Kloppenburg, *Uncertain Victory: Social Democracy and Progressivism in European and American Thought, 1870–1920* (New York: Oxford University Press, 1986); and Daniel T. Rogers, *Atlantic Crossings: Social Politics in a Progressive Age* (Cambridge, MA: Harvard University Press, 1998). The American Economic Association divided between those who looked approvingly at the nascent German welfare state, such as Richard Ely, and those who condemned any infringement of laissez-faire principles. In Britain, social liberalism, which advocated state intervention, was represented preeminently by L. T. Hobhouse.

13 See Carol Gluck, *Japan's Modern Myths: Ideologies in the Meiji Period* (Princeton, NJ: Princeton University Press, 1985).

14 Michel Foucault, *Discipline and Punish: The Birth of the Prison* (New York: Pantheon, 1977), is a parable of state coerciveness and its change from physical punishment to the more universal concept of surveillance. See also Foucault, *The Archaeology of Knowledge,* trans. A. M. Sheridan Smith (New York: Harper and Row, 1972); James C. Scott, *Seeing Like a State.*

15 See James Joll, *The Anarchists* (London: Eyre and Spottiswoode, 1964); Temma Kaplan, *Anarchists of Andalusia, 1868–1903* (Princeton, NJ: Princeton University Press, 1977).

16 Michel Foucault, *Sécurité, territoire, population: Cours au Collège de France, 1977–1978* (Paris: Gallimard Seuil, 2004), esp. 111. See also Foucault's essay on governmentality in *The Foucault Effect,* ed. Graham Burchell, Colin Gordon, and Peter Miller (Chicago: University of Chicago Press, 1991); and cf. Mitchell Deane, *Governmentality: Power and Rule in Modern Society* (London: Sage, 1999). Foucault attributed this growing shift in agenda to the late medieval Catholic Church with its emphasis on pastoral care and administrative organization and argued that the new efforts meant the advent of what he terms bio-politics: concern with bodies as the object of government and statecraft. Historians have also embraced this term, but it risks becoming inflated and overgeneralized.

17 Jacques Donzelot, *L'invention du social: Essai sur le déclin des passions politiques* (Paris: Fayard, 1984).

18 For Britain, see Mary Poovey, *History of the Modern Fact: Problems of Knowledge in the Sciences of Wealth and Society* (Chicago: University of Chicago Press, 1998).

19 Matthew Edney, *Mapping an Empire: The Geographical Construction of British India* (Chicago: University of Chicago Press, 1997); Raymond B. Craib, *Cartographic Mexico: A History of State Fixations and Fugitive Landscapes* (Durham, NC: Duke University Press, 2004), 126–192.

20 Sabine Dabringhaus, *Territorialer Nationalismus in China: Historisch-geographisches Denken, 1900–1948* (Cologne: Böhlau, 2006).

21 Foucault, *Discipline and Punish.*

22 James C. Scott, *The Art of Not Being Governed: An Anarchist History of Upland Southeast Asia* (New Haven, CT: Yale University Press, 2009).

23 John Torpey, *The Invention of the Passport: Surveillance, Citizenship, and the State* (Cambridge: Cambridge University Press, 2000).

24 See John Wesley Powell, *Report on the Lands of the Arid Region of the United States* (Cambridge, MA: Harvard University Press, 1962).

25 Francis Amasa Walker, "The Eleventh Census of the United States," *Quarterly Journal of Economics* 2 (1848): 135–161, cited in Matthew O. Hannah, *Governmentality and the Mastery of Territory in Nineteenth-Century America* (New York: Cambridge University Press, 2000), 122. This material borrows from Hannah, who emphasizes Walker's efforts in his maps of climate, states, etc., to establish a sort of American exceptionalism.

26 Hannah, *Governmentality,* 139–140.

27 I borrow Vanessa Ogle's arguments about the so-called internationalism of the late nineteenth century; see Ogle, "Clocks, Calendars, and Conversion Charts: Reorganizing Time during the First Wave of Globalization, 1883–1930" (PhD diss., Harvard University, 2011).

28 Roberto Michels, *Political Parties: A Sociological Study of the Oligarchical Tendencies of Modern Democracy,* trans. Eden Paul and Cedar Paul (New York: Crowell-Collier, 1962); Moisei Ostrogorski, *Democracy and the Organisation of Political Parties* (New York: Macmillan, 1902), focusing on Britain, with an interesting preface by the observer of American politics Ambassador James Bryce; and Ostrogorski, *Democracy and the Party System in the United States: A Study in Extra-Constitutional Government* (New York: Macmillan, 1910).

29 On rightist political currents in late nineteenth- and early twentieth-century Europe, see, among a vast literature, Richard Drake, *Byzantium for Rome: The Politics of Nostalgia in Umbertian Italy, 1878–1900* (Chapel Hill: University of North Carolina Press, 1980); John W. Boyer, *Political Radicalism in Late Imperial Vienna: Origins of the Christian Social Movement, 1848–1897* (Chicago: University of Chicago Press, 1981); Eugene J. Weber, *Action Française: Royalism and Reaction in Twentieth-Century France* (Stanford, CA: Stanford University Press, 1962); Zeev Sternhell, *La Droite révolutionnaire: Les origines françaises du fascisme* (Paris: Fayard, 2000).

30 Cited by Wolfgang J. Mommsen, *Max Weber and German Politics, 1890–1920,* trans. Michael S. Steinberg (Chicago: University of Chicago Press, 1984), 69.

31 Carl Schmitt, *The Nomos of the Earth in the Jus Publicum Europaeum,* trans. G. L Ulmen (New York: Telos Press, 2003). For the Berlin conference and the process of partitioning Africa, see H. L. Wesseling, *Divide and Rule: The Partition of Africa, 1880–1914,* trans. Arnold J. Pomerans (Westport CT: Praeger, 1996). On the Congo, see Adam Hochschild, *King Leopold's Ghost: A Story of Greed, Terror and Heroism in Colonial Africa* (New York: Houghton Mifflin, 1998).

32 For the Marxist texts in recent versions, see Rosa Luxemburg, *The Accumulation of Capital,* trans. Agnes Schwarzschild (London: Routledge, 2003); Rudolf Hilferding, *Finance Capital: A Study of the Latest Phase of Capitalist Development,* ed. Tom Bottomore (London: Routledge and Kegan Paul, 1961); V. I. Lenin, *Imperialism: The Highest Stage of Capitalism,* ed. Norman Lewis and James Malone (London: Junius, 1996).

33 Hans Ulrich Wehler, *Bismarck und der Imperialismus,* 2nd ed. (1965; Frankfurt: Suhrkamp Verlag, 1984).

34 The Indian journal *Subaltern Studies,* founded by Ranajit Guha in 1982, served as the vehicle for this movement. See David Ludden, ed., *Reading Subaltern Studies: Critical History, Contested Meaning and the Globalization of South Asia* (London: Anthem, 2002); for the impact of colonialism on metropole as well as colonial institutions, see Frederick Cooper and Ann Laura Stoler, *Tensions of Empire: Colonial Cultures in a Bourgeois World* (Berkeley: University of California Press, 1997); and for a less confrontational interpretation stressing the now-fashionable idea of hybridity, see Homi Bhabha, *The Location of Culture* (London: Routledge, 1994).

35 Frederic C. Cooper, *Colonialism in Question: Theory, Knowledge, History* (Berkeley: University of California Press, 2003).

36 Mahmood Mamdani, *Citizen and Subject: Contemporary Africa and the Legacy of Late Colonialism* (Princeton, NJ: Princeton University Press, 1996). For a concise description of the post-1918 colonial states that the French and British created out of the Ottoman provinces in the Middle East, see Roger Owen, *State, Power, and Politics in the Making of the Modern Middle East* (London: Routledge, 1992), 8–31. For a general description, see Jüergen Osterhammel, *Colonialism: A Theoretical Overview* (Princeton, NJ: Markus Wiener, 1997). For the British colonial administration's experience, see John W. Cell, "Colonial Rule," in *The Oxford History of the British Empire,* vol. 4: *The Twentieth Century,* ed. Judith M. Brown and Wm. Roger Louis (New York: Oxford University Press, 1998–1999), 232–254.

37 See C. A. Bayly, *Indian Society and the Making of the British Empire,* vol. 2, pt. 1 of *The New Cambridge History of India* (Cambridge: Cambridge University Press, 1988), for the crises and transitions before the uprising of 1857. For a survey of the post-1857 organization of the Indian states (including their diverse origins), see Barbara M. Ramusack, *The Indian Princes and Their States,* vol. 3, pt. 6, of *The New Cambridge History of India* (Cambridge: Cambridge University Press, 2004), with a fine bibliography.

38 John R. McLane, *Indian Nationalism and the Early Congress* (Princeton, NJ: Princeton University Press, 1977), 22–26.

39 Michael O'Dwyer, *India as I Knew It, 1885–1925* (London: Constable and Co., 1925), 406; cf. Florence Deprest, *Géographes en Algérie (1880–1950): Savoirs universitaires en situation coloniale* (Paris: Bélin, 2009), for the tensions between colonialist hard-liners and those sympathetic to the Berber or Arab natives and their precapitalist economy.

40 See Alice Bullard, *Exile to Paradise: Savagery and Civilization in Paris and the South Pacific, 1790–1900* (Stanford, CA: Stanford University Press, 2000).

41 Stanislaw Lem, "Alfred Zellermann: 'Gruppenführer Louis XVI,'" in *A Perfect Vacuum,* trans. Michael Kandel (Evanston, IL: Northwestern University Press, 1999). The stories are cast in the form of book summaries that supposedly unite "elements that would appear to be totally irreconcilable . . . a thing that is at once the truth and a lie" (58). For a nonfictional and contested account of a state where ritual is claimed to be the whole purpose of rule, see Clifford Geertz, *Negara: The Theater State in Nineteenth-Century Bali* (Princeton, NJ: Princeton University Press, 1980). But state ritual certainly serves to codify stratification and domination.

42 Calculated from the figures provided (£360,000 costs, £75,000,000 revenues) in McLane, *Indian Nationalism,* 43.

43 See Margery Perham, *Lugard,* 2 vols. (London: Collins, 1960–1961); and Edmund Burke III, *Prelude to Protectorate in Morocco: Precolonial Protest and Resistance, 1860–1912* (Chicago: University of Chicago Press, 1976).

44 John William Burgess, *Political Science and Comparative Constitutional Law* (1890; Boston: Ginn and Co., 1900), 45–46.

45 George Steinmetz, *The Devil's Handwriting: Precoloniality and the German Colonial State in Qingdao, Samoa, and Southwest Africa* (Chicago: University of Chicago Press, 2007), 406–410; at the same time he recognized a value to Chinese civilization and saw himself as a type of super Mandarin.

46 Hevla, *English Lessons,* 223, 228. The looting of artifacts aroused criticism in the Western press. It had been outlawed by the Hague Conventions a couple of years earlier, and when the lapse had to be addressed, racial differences were cited as explanation.

47 See Yoshihisa Tak Matsusaka, *The Making of Japanese Manchuria, 1904–1932* (Cambridge, MA: Harvard University Press, 2001); also the introduction to Ronald Suleski, *The Modernization of Manchuria: An Annotated Bibliography* (Hong Kong: Chinese University Press, 1994). I owe bibliography to the Harvard

dissertation research by Victor Seow on the coal-mining industry of Manchuria. See also Ramon Myers and Mark R. Peattie, eds., *The Japanese Colonial Empire* (Princeton, NJ: Princeton University Press, 1984).

4. STATES OF EXCEPTION, EXCEPTIONAL STATES

1 Carl Schmitt, *Political Theology: Four Chapters on the Concept of Sovereignty* (Chicago: University of Chicago Press, 1985), 5. The German version, like the English, retains some ambiguity: did sovereignty imply the right to decide when an exceptional state existed and/or the right to decide when and to decree the measures needed? Did sovereignty mean more than just the de facto power to impose a state of emergency as in a coup d'état or was it sanctified with no more than force? From the context, he evidently believed that provision for determining and resolving the state of exception was implicitly a metaconstitutional measure. See also, for elaboration, Giorgio Agamben, *State of Exception* (Chicago: University of Chicago Press, 2005).

2 Again Foucault is the reference point for many contemporary historians, of Asia as well as Europe and the Americas. Whereas his earlier writing (e.g., *Discipline and Punish: The Birth of the Prison* [New York: Pantheon, 1977]) argued that the elaboration of a soft-power but carceral state represented only a modernization of concern with power, the late lectures separated the agenda of governmentality from sovereignty. See Eric Paras, *Foucault 2.0: Beyond Power and Knowledge* (New York: Other Press, 2006). Paras's valuable book originated as a Harvard doctoral dissertation, of which I was a second reader, and although I did not recall his work when I decided on the title of this work, his formulation of a second Foucault may well have stuck in my mind.

3 W. G. Beasley, *Japanese Imperialism, 1894–1945* (Oxford: Oxford University Press, 1987), 41–68.

4 A vast literature exists on this: see the relevant volumes of the monumental series by the Carnegie Endowment for International Peace, *Social and Economic History of the World War,* ed. James T. Shotwell (New Haven, CT: Yale University Press, 1928–); Gerald Feldman, *Army, Industry and Labor in Germany, 1914–1918* (Princeton, NJ: Princeton University Press, 1964); Keith Middlemas, *Politics in Industrial Society: The Experience of the British System since 1911* (London: A. Deutsch, 1979); Charles S. Maier, *Recasting Bourgeois Europe: Stabilization in France, Germany, and Italy in the Decade after World War I* (Princeton, NJ: Princeton University Press, 1975).

5 Niall Ferguson, *The War of the World: History's Age of Hatred* (London: Allen Lane, 2006). It is a view shared by scholars who generally take a political stance

quite different from Ferguson's. See Robert Vitalis, "The Noble American Science of Imperial Relations and Its Laws of Race Development," *Comparative Studies in Society and History* 52, no. 4 (2010): 909–938, esp. 911: "In the science of imperial relations, the world's biological boundaries mattered much more to theory building than did territorial boundaries." For the debate between "primordialists" and "constructivists," on the nature of ethnicity, see the recent discussion in Rogers Brubaker et al., *Nationalist Politics and Everyday Ethnicity in a Transylvanian Town* (Princeton, NJ: Princeton University Press, 2006); for a compromise stance I find congenial, see Anthony D. Smith, *The Antiquity of Nations* (Cambridge: Polity Press, 2004).

6 See Monica Wilson and Leonard Thompson, eds., *The Oxford History of South Africa,* 2 vols. (Oxford: Oxford University Press, 1971), 2:313–364, statistics on 338. For a comparison of South African and US racial practices, see John W. Cell, *The Highest Stage of White Supremacy: The Origins of Segregation in South Africa and the American South* (Cambridge: Cambridge University Press, 1982).

7 For the ambiguities of semicolonial status (as applied to China), see Tong Lam, "Policing the Imperial Nation: Sovereignty, International Law, and the Civilizing Mission in Late Qing China," *Comparative Studies in Society and History* 52, no. 4 (2010): 881–908.

8 Jack London, *The Iron Heel* (New York: Macmillan, 1907); Georges Sorel, *Réflexions sur la violence,* 4th ed. (1908; Paris: Marcel Rivière, 1919), which includes the preface saluting Lenin; "Agathon," pseudonym for Alfred deTarde and Henri Massis, *Les jeunes gens d'aujourd'hui: Le gout de l'action, la foi patriotique; Une renaissance catholique, le réalisme politique* (Paris: Plon-Nourrit, 1913); Robert Wohl, *The Generation of 1914* (Cambridge, MA: Harvard University Press, 1979).

9 Likhit Dhiravegin, *The Meiji Restoration, 1868–1912, and the Chakkri Reformation, 1865–1910: A Comparative Perspective* (Bangkok: Faculty of Political Science, Thammasat University, 1984); David K. Wyatt, *The Politics of Reform in Thailand: Education in the Reign of King Chulalongkorn* (New Haven, CT: Yale University Press, 1969); Walter E. J. Tips, *Gustave Rolin-Jaequemyns and the Making of Modern Siam: The Diaries and Letters of King Chulalongkorn's General Adviser* (Bangkok: Cheney, White Lotus, 1996); Bahru Zewde, *A History of Modern Ethiopia, 1855–1891,* rev. ed. (Columbus: Ohio University Press, 2001); Harold G. Marcus, *A History of Ethiopia* (Berkeley: University of California Press, 1994), 77–115; Marcus, *The Life and Times of Menelik II: Ethiopia, 1844–1913* (Oxford: Clarendon Press, 1975).

10 What they were *not* was a protest against economic stagnation. The years from 1896 to 1914 brought robust technological innovation and economic growth, certainly unevenly distributed but still vigorous and perhaps higher than any earlier period, and any era afterward until the 1950s and 1960s. Economics, however, did not assuage political discontent any more than the cross-border flows of capital, workers, and goods prevented war.

11 Cited from Nikki Keddie, "Iran under the Later Qajars, 1848–1922," in *The Cambridge History of Iran,* vol. 7: *From Nadir Shah to the Islamic Republic,* ed. Peter Avery, Gavin Hambly, and Charles Melville (Cambridge: Cambridge University Press, 1991), 174–212, quotation at 196; see also Keddie, *Religion and Rebellion in Iran: The Tobacco Protest of 1891–1892* (London: Frank Cass, 1966).

12 Mangol Bayat, *Iran's First Revolution: Shi'ism and the Constitutional Revolution of 1905–1909* (New York: Oxford University Press, 1991); Nikki Keddie, *Roots of Revolution: An Interpretive History of Modern Iran* (New Haven, CT: Yale University Press, 1981); Firoozeh Kashani-Sabet, *Frontier Fictions: Shaping the Iranian Nation, 1804–1946* (Princeton, NJ: Princeton University Press, 1999); also Gavin R. G. Hambly, "The Pahlavi Autocracy: Riza Shah, 1921–1941," and P. Kazemzadeh, "Iranian Relations with Russia and the Soviet Union, to 1921," both in *The Cambridge History of Iran,* 213–225, 314–349.

13 Benjamin C. Fortna, "The Reign of Abdülhamid II," and M. Sükrü Hanioğlu, "The Second Constitutional Period, 1908–1918," both in *The Cambridge History of Turkey,* vol. 4, *Turkey in the Modern World,* ed. Reşat Kasaba (Cambridge: Cambridge University Press, 2008), 38–61, 62–101; also M. Sükrü Hanioğlu, *Preparation for a Revolution: The Young Turks, 1902–1908* (New York: Oxford University Press, 2001); Feroz Ahmad, *The Young Turks: The Committee of Union and Progress in Turkish Politics, 1908–1914* (Oxford: Clarendon Press, 1969); A. L. Macfie, *The End of the Ottoman Empire, 1908–1923* (New York: Addison Wesley Longman, 1998).

14 Hasan Kayali, "The Struggle for Independence," in *The Cambridge History of Turkey,* 4:112–146; Erik Jan Zürcher, *The Unionist Factor: The Role of the Committee of Union and Progress in the Turkish National Movement, 1905–1926* (Leiden: Brill, 1984); Andrew Mango, *Atatürk: The Biography of the Founder of Modern Turkey* (Woodstock NY: Overlook Press, 1999).

15 John Womack Jr., "The Mexican Revolution, 1910–1920," in *The Cambridge History of Latin America,* vol. 5: *c. 1870 to 1930,* ed. Leslie Bethell (Cambridge: Cambridge University Press, 1986), 79–152, quotation at 81; for the end of the Porfiriato, the presidential years of Porfirio Díaz, see also Friedrich Katz, "Mexico: Restored Republic and Porfiriato, 1867–1910," in Bethell, *The Cam-*

bridge History of Latin America, esp. 62–78. On the role of foreign investment, see John Mason Hart, *Empire and Revolution: The Americans in Mexico since the Civil War* (Berkeley: University of California Press, 2002).

16 I draw on Friedrich Katz's monumental account, *The Life and Times of Pancho Villa* (Stanford, CA: Stanford University Press, 1998), esp. 354–487.

17 Jean Meyer, "Mexico: Revolution and Reconstruction in the 1920s," in Bethell, *The Cambridge History of Latin America,* 155–194.

18 Min Tu-Ki, *National Polity and Local Power: The Transformation of Late Imperial China* (Cambridge, MA: Harvard University Press and Harvard Yenching Institute, 1989), 89–179.

19 For a survey of Chinese development throughout the period covered in this chapter, see Jonathan D. Spence, *The Search for Modern China* (New York: W. W. Norton, 1990). Cf. Tong Lam, "Policing the Imperial Nation," esp. 907 for Lee Tinghou's lessons drawn from contemporary Japanese experience. On the reform movement of 1890–1898 and its aborting by the empress dowager's faction at the court, see Hao Chang, "Intellectual Change and the Reform Movement," in *The Cambridge History of China,* vol. 11, pt. 2, *Late Ch'ing, 1800–1911,* ed. John K. Fairbank and Kwang-ching Liu (Cambridge: Cambridge University Press, 1980), 274–338. See, in the same volume: on the Chinese military defeat by France in 1884 and by Japan in 1894, Kwang-ching Liu and Richard J. Smith, "The Military Challenge: the Northwest and the Coast," esp. 251–273; on the Boxers, Immanuel C. Y. Hsu, "Late Ch'ing Foreign Relations, 1866–1905," esp. 109–130; Michael Gasster, "The Republican Revolutionary Movement," 463–534.

20 On the hapless fate of the parliamentary experiments, see Andrew J. Nathan, "A Constitutional Republic: The Peking Government, 1916–28," and on warlordism, see James E. Sheridan, "The Warlord Era: Politics and Militarism under the Peking Government, 1916–28," both in *The Cambridge History of China,* vol. 12, pt. 1, *Republican China, 1912–1949,* ed. John K. Fairbank (Cambridge: Cambridge University Press, 1983), 256–283, 284–321. On Guomindang and Communist development and falling-out in the south, see, in the same volume: Jerome Ch'en, "The Chinese Communist Movement to 1927," 505–526, and C. Martin Wilbur, "The Nationalist Revolution: From Canton to Nanking, 1923–28," 527–721. See also William C. Kirby, *Germany and Republican China* (Stanford, CA: Stanford University Press, 1984).

21 On the interwar tensions faced by the colonial powers and the difficulty of reform, see Frederick C. Cooper, *Decolonization and African Society: The Labor Question in French and British Africa* (Cambridge: Cambridge University Press,

1996). For British difficulties in relinquishing control in Asia and the Middle East, see *The Oxford History of the British Empire*, vol. 4: *The Twentieth Century*, ed. Judith M. Brown and Wm. Roger Louis (New York: Oxford University Press, 1998–1999), 398–489.

22 V. I. Lenin, *What Is to Be Done? Burning Questions of Our Movement* (Moscow: Foreign Languages Publishing House, 1950).

23 Czesław Miłosz, *The Captive Mind*, trans. Jane Zielonka (New York: Vintage, 1955). Many similar critiques emerged by the 1940s and 1950s; among the fictional accounts, see Arthur Koestler's *Darkness at Noon*, trans. Dorothy Hardie (London: Jonathan Cape, 1940), and George Orwell's *Nineteen Eighty-Four: A Novel* (London: Secker and Warburg, 1949).

24 Georg Lukács, *History and Class Consciousness*, trans. Rodney Livingstone (Cambridge, MA: MIT Press, 1971), 319–320, 326–327.

25 On the purges, see Anne Applebaum, *Gulag: A History* (New York: Doubleday, 2003), esp. 584–585 for the effort to establish a tally of the victims; also Robert Conquest, *The Great Terror: A Reassessment* (New York: Oxford University Press, 2008). Of the works that sought to challenge the Stalin-centered narrative, see J. Arch Getty, *Origins of the Great Purges: The Soviet Communist Party Reconsidered, 1933–1938* (Cambridge: Cambridge University Press, 1985). For statistical analyses, see Paul R. Gregory, *Terror by Quota: State Security from Lenin to Stalin: An Archival Study* (New Haven, CT: Yale University Press, 2009). For insights into how ordinary Russians coped with this period, see Sheila Fitzpatrick, *Everyday Stalinism: Ordinary Life in Extraordinary Times: Soviet Russia in the 1930s* (New York: Oxford University Press, 1999). For the postwar purges in Communist Eastern Europe, see George H. Hodos, *Show Trials: Stalinist Purges in Eastern Europe, 1948–1954* (New York: Praeger, 1987).

26 On the sprawling organization of terror in Germany, see Helmut Krausnick et al., *Anatomie des SS-Staates* (Munich: Institut für Zeitgeschichte, 1968), translated as *Anatomy of the SS State* (London: Collins 1968). Timothy Snyder, *Bloodlands: Europe between Hitler and Stalin* (New York: Basic Books, 2010), for the toll in the vulnerable area of Poland and Ukraine; for the most recent detailed survey of the murder of the Jews by region, see David Cesarani, ed., *The Final Solution: Origins and Implementation* (London: Routledge, 1994).

27 Sorel, *Réflexions sur la violence*; and Sorel, *Les Illusions du Progrès* (Paris: Marcel Rivière, 1911). For Sorel's influence, see Steven Hirsch and Lucien van der Walt, eds., *Anarchism and Syndicalism in the Colonial and Postcolonial World, 1870–1940: The Praxis of National Liberation, Internationalism, and Social Revolution* (Leiden: Brill, 2010).

28 For the projects, see Steven Kotkin, *Magnetic Mountain: Stalinism as a Civilization* (Berkeley; University of California Press, 1995). The vast transformative projects not only characterized the totalitarian regimes but also were part of the vision of the 1930s—including the TVA and the New Deal. See Wolfgang Schivelbusch, *Three New Deals: Reflections on Roosevelt's America, Mussolini's Italy and Hitler's Germany, 1933–1939,* trans. Jefferson Chase (New York: Metropolitan Books, 2006).

29 Erez Manela, *The Wilsonian Moment: Self-Determination and the International Origins of Anticolonial Nationalism* (New York: Oxford University Press, 2007); Arno J. Mayer, *Wilson vs. Lenin: Political Origins of the New Diplomacy, 1917–1918* (Cleveland: World Publishers, 1964); Maier, *Recasting Bourgeois Europe.*

30 Rocco, "La Trasformazione dello Stato," in *Scritti e discorsi politici di Alfredo Rocco,* 3 vols. (Milano: A. Giuffrè, 1938), 3:775–778; Mussolini, "Fascismo," in *Enciclopedia italiana* (Roma: Istituto della Enciclopedia Italiana [Treccani], 1932), 14:848, 850; both cited in Sabino Cassese, *Lo Stato Fascista* (Bologna: Il Mulino, 2010), s.v. *Cassese,* 47, 37.

31 Notes on fascism and its institutions: For a narrative, see Adrian Lyttelton, *The Seizure of Power: Fascism in Italy, 1919–1929,* rev ed. (London: Routledge, 2004); and the multivolume biography of Mussolini by Renzo De Felice, *Mussolini il Fascista: L'organizzazione dello stato fascista, 1925–1929* (Turin: Einaudi, 1968); *Mussolini Il Duce: Lo stato totalitario, 1936–1940* (Turin: Einaudi, 1981); on institutions, see Alberto Aquarone, *L'organizzazione dello stato totalitario* (Turin: Einaudi, 1965); on parallel organizations, G. Melis, *Due modelli di amministrazione fra liberalismo e facissmo: Burocrazie tradizionali e nuovi apparati* (Roma: Ministero per I Beni culturali e ambientali, 1988); for comparative fascist movements, Michael Mann, *Fascists* (Cambridge: Cambridge University Press, 2004), a broad and sensible analysis.

32 Federico Finchelstein, *Los Origenes ideológicos de la dictadura* (Buenos Aires: Editorial Sudamericana, 2008); also Finchelstein, *Ideology, Violence and the Sacred in Argentina and Italy, 1919–1945* (Durham, NC: Duke University Press, 2010).

33 Of the numerous sources on the Nazi regime, see Richard Evans, *The Third Reich in Power, 1933–1939* (New York: Penguin, 2005); and Evans, *The Third Reich at War, 1939–1945* (London: Allen Lane, 2008); Ian Kershaw, *Hitler, 1889–1936: Hubris* (New York: W. W. Norton, 1999); Kershaw, *Hitler, 1936–1945: Nemesis* (London: Penguin, 2000); Karl Dietrich Bracher; *Die deutsche Diktatur: Entstehung, Struktur, Folgen des Nationalsozialismus,* 6th ed. (Frankfurt am Main: Ulstein, 1979).

332 ~~~ Notes to Pages 267–285

34 See Karen Painter, *Symphonic Ambitions* (Cambridge, MA: Harvard University Press, 2007); also Erik Levi, *Music in the Third Reich* (Basingstoke: Macmillan, 1994). On jazz, see Michael H. Kater, *Different Drummers: Jazz in the Culture of Nazi Germany* (New York: Oxford University Press, 1992).

35 Carl Schmitt, *The Crisis of Parliamentary Democracy,* ed. Ellen Kennedy (1923; Cambridge, MA: MIT Press, 1988); Schmitt, *The Concept of the Political,* trans. George Schwab (Chicago: University of Chicago Press, 1996), with a useful forward by Tracy Strong.

36 Carl Schmitt, *The Nomos of the Earth in the Jus Publicum Europaeum,* trans. G. L. Ulmen (New York: Telos Press, 2003).

37 István Bibó, *Misère des petits états d'Europe de l'est,* trans. György Kassai (Paris: Albin Michel, 1993).

38 For the narrative of expansion, see W. G. Beasley, *Japanese Imperialism, 1894–1945* (Oxford: Clarendon, 1987); and, among the many English-language contributions, Mark R. Peattie, *Ishiwara Kanji and Japan's Confrontation with the West* (Princeton, NJ: Princeton University Press, 1975); Hugh Borton, *Japan since 1931: Its Political and Social Development* (New York: Institute of Pacific Relations, 1940). For the debate on whether the regime was or was not fascist, see Marcus Willensky, "Japanese Fascism Revisited," *Stanford Journal of East Asian Affairs* 5, no. 1 (Winter 2005): 52–77. For ideological currents, see Maruyama Masao, *Thought and Behaviour in Modern in Japanese Politics* (London: Oxford University Press, 1963); on responsibilities, Herbert P. Bix, *Hirohito and the Making of Modern Japan* (New York: HarperCollins, 2000).

39 André Gide, *Retour de l'U.R.S.S.* (Paris: Gallimard, 1936); George Orwell, *Homage to Catalonia* (London: Secker and Warburg, 1938). The Auden line is from his poem "September 1, 1939."

40 On collectivization, see Moshe Lewin, *Russian Peasants and Soviet Power: A Study in Collectivization,* trans. Irene Nove (London: Allen and Unwin, 1968); Stephen F. Cohen, *Bukharin and the Bolshevik Revolution: A Political Biography, 1888–1938* (New York: Vintage, 1975); Alexander Erlich, *The Soviet Industrialization Debate, 1924–1928* (Cambridge, MA: Harvard University Press, 1960).

41 Renzo De Felice, ed., *Il Fascismo: Le interpretazioni dei contemporanei e degli historici* (Rome: Laterza, 1998).

42 Herbert Marcuse, *Reason and Revolution: Hegel and the Rise of Social Theory* (London: Oxford University Press, 1941); Franz Neumann, *Behemoth: The Structure and Practice of National Socialism, 1933–1944* (New York: Oxford University Press, 1944).

43 Snyder, *Bloodlands;* Andrea Graziosi, *Lettere da Kharkov: La carestia in Ucraina e nel Caucaso del Nord nei rapporti dei diplomatici italiani, 1923–33* (Torino: Einaudi, 1991). Also, Graziosi, *The Great Soviet Peasant War: Bolsheviks and Peasants, 1917–1933* (Cambridge, MA: Harvard University Press and Ukrainian Research Center, 1996).

44 Ian Kershaw has emphasized the Nazi concept of "working toward the Führer." See Kershaw, *Hitler, 1936–1945: Nemesis,* 249–250.

45 David Rousset, *L'Univers concentrationnaire* (Paris: Éditions Du Pavois, 1946); Ernst Fraenkel, *The Dual State: A Contribution to the Theory of Dictatorship,* trans. E. A. Shils in collaboration with Edith Lowenstein and Klaus Knorr (New York: Oxford University Press, 1941). Fraenkel attributed "the prerogative state" (versus the constitutional state) to the emergency decrees issued at the outset of the regime, and he cited Schmitt: "The state continues to exist while the legal order is inoperative" (25).

46 Arendt, *The Origins of Totalitarianism* (New York: Harcourt, Brace, 1951); see also the more mechanistic account by Carl J. Friedrich and Zbigniew K. Brzezinski, *Totalitarian Dictatorship and Autocracy* (New York: Praeger, 1965); for a history of the concept, see Abbot Gleason, *Totalitarianism: The Inner History of the Cold War* (New York: Oxford University Press, 1995). There are many efforts to differentiate the different regimes and experiences. See the essays collected in Michael Geyer and Sheila Fitzpatrick, eds., *Beyond Totalitarianism: Stalinism and Nazism Compared* (Cambridge: Cambridge University Press, 2009), and the search for important qualifications of the model in the contributions to Paul Corner, ed., *Popular Opinion in Totalitarian Regimes: Fascism, Nazism, Communism* (Oxford: Oxford University Press, 2009). For a political-science approach, see Juan J. Linz, *Totalitarian and Authoritarian Regimes* (Boulder, CO: Lynne Rienner, 2000).

47 Among the helpful insights into such genocidal mentalities, see Jacques Semelin, *Purify and Destroy: The Political Uses of Massacre and Genocide,* ed. Cynthia Schoch (New York: Columbia University Press, 2007). For an approach that tends to dissolve genocidal violence into a broader process of stressful social change, see Christian Gerlach, *Extremely Violent Societies: Mass Violence in the Twentieth-Century World* (Cambridge: Cambridge University Press, 2010).

48 Peter Baldwin, *The Politics of Social Solidarity: Class Bases of the European Welfare State, 1875–1975* (Cambridge: Cambridge University Press, 1990); Susan Pedersen, *Family, Dependence, and the Origins of the Welfare State: Britain and France, 1914–1945* (Cambridge: Cambridge University Press, 1993); Gøsta Esping-Andersen, *The Three Worlds of Welfare Capitalism* (Princeton, NJ:

Princeton University Press, 1990). The most interesting general coverage of Europe after 1945 is Tony Judt, *Postwar: A History of Europe since 1945* (New York: Penguin, 2005).

49 See Daniel Chirot, *Modern Tyrants: The Power and Prevalence of Evil in Our Age* (New York: Free Press, 1994).

POSTSCRIPT

1 Anne-Marie Slaughter, *A New World Order* (Princeton: Princeton University Press, 2004), 268–269. For a comprehensive discussion, see Jon Pierre and B. Guy Peters, *Governance, Politics and the State* (London: Macmillan, 2000).

Selected Bibliography

Adelman, Jeremy. *Sovereignty and Revolution in the Iberian Atlantic.* Princeton, NJ: Princeton University Press, 2006.

Ahmad, Feroz. *The Young Turks: The Committee of Union and Progress in Turkish Politics, 1908–1914.* Oxford: Clarendon Press, 1969.

Anderson, Benedict. *Imagined Communities: Reflections on the Origin and Spread of Nationalism.* London: Verso, 1983.

Anderson, Fred, and Andrew Cayton. *The Dominion of War: Empire and Liberty in North America, 1500–2000.* New York: Viking, 2005.

Applebaum, Anne. *Gulag: A History.* New York: Doubleday, 2003.

Aquarone, Alberto. *L'organizzazione dello stato totalitario.* Turin: Einaudi, 1965.

Arendt, Hannah. *The Origins of Totalitarianism.* New York: Harcourt, Brace, 1951.

Baldwin, Peter. "Beyond Weak and Strong: Rethinking the State in Comparative Policy History." *Journal of Policy History* 17, no. 1 (2005): 12–33.

———. *The Politics of Social Solidarity: Class Bases of the European Welfare State, 1875–1975.* Cambridge: Cambridge University Press, 1990.

Banner, Stuart. "Why *Terra Nullius*? Anthropology and Property Law in Early Australia." *Law and History Review* 23, no. 1 (2005): 95–132.

Barkey, Karen. *An Empire of Difference: The Ottomans in Comparative Perspective.* Cambridge: Cambridge University Press, 2008.

Bayat, Mangol. *Iran's First Revolution: Shi'ism and the Constitutional Revolution of 1905–1909.* New York: Oxford University Press, 1991.

Bayly, C. A. *The Birth of the Modern World, 1780–1914: Global Connections and Comparisons.* Malden, MA: Blackwell, 2004.

———. *Indian Society and the Making of the British Empire.* Vol. 2, part 1, of *The New Cambridge History of India,* edited by Gordon Johnson. Cambridge: Cambridge University Press, 1988.

Bazant, Jan. *Alienation of Church Lands in Mexico: Social and Economic Aspects of the Liberal Revolution, 1856–1875.* Edited and translated by Michel P. Costeloe. Cambridge: Cambridge University Press, 1971.

Beasley, W. G. *Japanese Imperialism, 1894–1945.* Oxford: Clarendon Press, 1987.

Bentley, Arthur F. *The Process of Government: A Study of Social Pressure.* Edited by Peter H. Odegard. Cambridge, MA: Belknap Press of Harvard University Press, 1967.

Bibó, István. *Misère des petits états d'Europe de l'est.* Translated by György Kassai. Paris: Albin Michel, 1993.

Bix, Herbert P. *Hirohito and the Making of Modern Japan.* New York: HarperCollins, 2000.

Blum, Jerome. *The End of the Old Order in Rural Europe.* Princeton, NJ: Princeton University Press, 1978.

Bluntschli, Johann Caspar. *Allgemeines Staatsrecht.* 3rd ed. Munich: J. G. Cotta, 1863.

Bose, Sugata. *Peasant Labour and Colonial Capital: Rural Bengal since 1770.* Vol. 3, part 2, of *The Cambridge History of India,* edited by Gordon Johnson. Cambridge: Cambridge University Press, 1993.

Boyer, John W. *Political Radicalism in Late Imperial Vienna: Origins of the Christian Social Movement, 1848–1897.* Chicago: University of Chicago Press, 1981.

Bracher, Karl Dietrich. *Die deutsche Diktatur: Entstehung, Struktur, Folgen des Nationalsozialismus.* 6th ed. Frankfurt: Ulstein, 1979.

Brandfon, Robert L. *Cotton Kingdom of the New South: A History of the Yazoo Mississippi Delta from Reconstruction to the Twentieth Century.* Cambridge, MA: Harvard University Press, 1967.

Brubaker, Rogers. *Citizenship and Nationhood in France and Germany.* Cambridge, MA: Harvard University Press, 1992.

Buchheim, Hans, et al. *Anatomie des SS-Staates.* Munich: Institut für Zeitgeschichte, 1968.

Bullard, Alice. *Exile to Paradise: Savagery and Civilization in Paris and the South Pacific, 1790–1900.* Stanford, CA: Stanford University Press, 2000.

Burchell, Graham, Colin Gordon, and Peter Miller, eds. *The Foucault Effect: Studies in Governmentality.* Chicago: University of Chicago Press, 1991.

Burke, Edmund, III. *Prelude to Protectorate in Morocco: Precolonial Protest and Resistance, 1860–1912.* Chicago: University of Chicago Press, 1976.

The Cambridge History of China, vols. 10 and 11: *Late Ch'ing, 1800–1911,* edited by John K. Fairbank and Kwang-ching Liu. Cambridge: Cambridge University Press, 1980.

The Cambridge History of China, vol. 12: *Republican China, 1912–1949,* part 1, edited by John K. Fairbank. Cambridge: Cambridge University Press, 1983.

The Cambridge History of Egypt, vol. 2: *Modern Egypt from 1517 to the End of the Twentieth Century,* edited by M. W. Daly. Cambridge: Cambridge University Press, 1998.

The Cambridge History of Iran, vol. 7: *From Nadir Shah to the Islamic Republic,* edited by Peter Avery, Gavin Hambly, and Charles Melville. Cambridge: Cambridge University Press, 1991.

The Cambridge History of Latin America, vols. 4 and 5: *c. 1870 to 1930,* edited by Leslie Bethell. Cambridge: Cambridge University Press, 1986.

The Cambridge History of Turkey, vol. 3: *The Later Ottoman Empire, 1603–1839,* edited by Suraiya N. Faroqhi. Cambridge: Cambridge University Press, 2008.

The Cambridge History of Turkey, vol. 4: *Turkey in the Modern World,* edited by Reşat Kasaba. Cambridge: Cambridge University Press, 2009.

Cassese, Sabino. *Lo stato fascista.* Bologna: Mulino, 2010.

Cell, John W. *The Highest Stage of White Supremacy: The Origins of Segregation in South Africa and the American South.* Cambridge: Cambridge University Press, 1982.

Cesarani, David, ed. *The Final Solution: Origins and Implementation.* London: Routledge, 1994.

Chabod, Federico. *Italian Foreign Policy: The Statecraft of the Founders.* Translated by William McCuaig. Princeton, NJ: Princeton University Press, 1996.

Cohen, Stephen F. *Bukharin and the Bolshevik Revolution: A Political Biography, 1888–1938.* New York: Vintage, 1975.

Commins, David Dean. *Islamic Reform: Politics and Social Change in Late Ottoman Syria.* New York: Oxford University Press, 1990.

Cooper, Frederick. *Colonialism in Question: Theory, Knowledge, History.* Berkeley: University of California Press, 2003.

———. *Decolonization and African Society: The Labor Question in French and British Africa.* Cambridge: Cambridge University Press, 1996.

Cooper, Frederick, and Ann Laura Stoler, eds. *Tensions of Empire: Colonial Cultures in a Bourgeois World.* Berkeley: University of California Press, 1997.

Corner, Paul, ed. *Popular Opinion in Totalitarian Regimes: Fascism, Nazism, Communism.* Oxford: Oxford University Press, 2009.

Craib, Raymond B. *Cartographic Mexico: A History of State Fixations and Fugitive Landscapes.* Durham, NC: Duke University Press, 2004.

Crosby, Alfred W., Jr. *The Columbian Exchange: Biological and Cultural Consequences of 1492.* Westport, CT: Greenwood, 1972.

Dabringhaus, Sabine. *Territorialer Nationalismus in China: Historisch-geographisches Denken, 1900–1948.* Cologne: Böhlau, 2006.

Davis, Clarence B., and Kenneth E. Wilburn Jr., with Ronald E. Robinson, eds. *Railway Imperialism.* New York: Greenwood, 1991.

Dean, Mitchell. *Governmentality: Power and Rule in Modern Society.* London: Sage, 1999.

Dean, Warren. *With Broadax and Firebrand: The Destruction of the Brazilian Atlantic Forest.* Berkeley: University of California Press, 1995.

Deane, Phyllis, and W. A. Cole. *British Economic Growth, 1688–1959: Trends and Structure.* 2nd ed. London: Cambridge University Press, 1967.

De Felice, Renzo, ed. *Il fascismo: Le interpretazioni dei contemporanei e degli historici.* Rev. ed. Rome: Laterza, 1998.

———. *Mussolini il duce: Lo stato totalitario, 1936–1940.* Turin: Einaudi, 1981.

———. *Mussolini il fascista: L'organizzazione dello stato fascista, 1925–1929.* Turin: Einaudi, 1968.

DeLay, Brian. *War of a Thousand Deserts: Indian Raids and the U.S.-Mexican War.* New Haven, CT: Yale University Press, 2008.

Den Otter, A. A. *The Philosophy of Railways: The Transcontinental Railway Idea in British North America.* Toronto: University of Toronto Press, 1997.

Deprest, Florence. *Géographes en Algérie, 1880–1950: Savoirs universitaires en situation coloniale.* Paris: Belin, 2009.

De Vries, Jan. *The Industrious Revolution: Consumer Behavior and the Household Economy, 1650 to the Present.* Cambridge: Cambridge University Press, 2008.

Donzelot, Jacques. *L'invention du social: Essai sur le déclin des passions politiques.* Paris: Fayard, 1984.

Drake, Richard. *Byzantium for Rome: The Politics of Nostalgia in Umbertian Italy, 1878–1900.* Chapel Hill: University of North Carolina Press, 1980.

Duguit, Léon. *Le droit social, le droit individuel et la transformation de l'état.* Paris: Félix Alcan, 1908.

Edney, Matthew H. *Mapping an Empire: The Geographical Construction of British India, 1765–1843.* Chicago: University of Chicago Press, 1997.

Elliott, John H. *Empires of the Atlantic World: Britain and Spain in America, 1492–1830.* New Haven, CT: Yale University Press, 2006.

Elvin, Mark. *The Retreat of the Elephants: An Environmental History of China.* New Haven, CT: Yale University Press, 2004.

Evans, Richard J. *The Third Reich at War, 1939–1945.* London: Allen Lane, 2008.

———. *The Third Reich in Power, 1933–1939.* New York: Penguin, 2005.

Feldman, Gerald. *Army, Industry and Labor in Germany, 1914–1918.* Princeton, NJ: Princeton University Press, 1966.

Ferguson, Niall. *The War of the World: History's Age of Hatred.* London: Allen Lane, 2006.

Finchelstein, Federico. *Transatlantic Fascism: Ideology, Violence, and the Sacred in Argentina and Italy, 1919–1945.* Durham, NC: Duke University Press, 2010.

Foucault, Michel. *Discipline and Punish: The Birth of the Prison.* Translated by Alan Sheridan. New York: Pantheon, 1977.

———. *Sécurité, Territoire, Population: Cours au Collège de France, 1977–1978.* Paris: Gallimard, 2004.

Fraenkel, Ernst. *The Dual State: A Contribution to the Theory of Dictatorship.* Translated by E. A. Shils in collaboration with Edith Lowenstein and Klaus Knorr. New York: Oxford University Press, 1941.

Friedrich, Carl J., and Zbigniew K. Brzezinski. *Totalitarian Dictatorship and Autocracy.* 2nd rev. ed. New York: Praeger, 1965.

Gall, Lothar. *Bismarck: Der weisse Revolutionär.* Frankfurt: Propyläen, 1980.

Geertz, Clifford. *Agricultural Involution: The Process of Ecological Change in Indonesia.* Berkeley: Association of Asian Studies/University of California Press, 1963.

———. *Negara: The Theater State in Nineteenth-Century Bali.* Princeton, NJ: Princeton University Press, 1980.

Gellner, Ernest. *Nations and Nationalism.* 2nd ed. Ithaca, NY: Cornell University Press, 2008.

Geppert, Alexander C. T. *Fleeting Cities: Imperial Expositions in Fin-de-Siècle Europe.* New York: Palgrave-Macmillan, 2010.

Gerth, H. H., and C. Wright Mills, eds. *From Max Weber: Essays in Sociology.* Translated by H. H. Gerth and C. Wright Mills. New York: Oxford University Press, 1958.

Geyer, Michael, and Sheila Fitzpatrick, eds. *Beyond Totalitarianism: Stalinism and Nazism Compared.* Cambridge: Cambridge University Press, 2009.

Gleason, Abbot. *Totalitarianism: The Inner History of the Cold War.* New York: Oxford University Press, 1995.

Gluck, Carol. *Japan's Modern Myths: Ideologies in the Late Meiji Period.* Princeton, NJ: Princeton University Press, 1985.

Gneist, Rudolph. *The History of the English Constitution.* Translated by Philip A. Ashworth. 2 vols. London: W. Clowes, 1886.

Gray, Jack. *Rebellions and Revolutions: China from the 1800s to the 1980s.* New York: Oxford University Press, 1990.

Graziosi, Andrea. *The Great Soviet Peasant War: Bolsheviks and Peasants, 1917–1933.* Cambridge, MA: Ukrainian Research Center, Harvard University/Harvard University Press, 1996.

Hagen, William W. *Ordinary Prussians: Brandenburg Junkers and Villagers, 1500–1840.* Cambridge: Cambridge University Press, 2002.

Hall, John A., ed. *States in History.* New York: Basil Blackwell, 1987.

Halperín Donghi, Tulio. *Guerra y finanzas en los orígines del estado argentina, 1791–1850.* Buenos Aires: Belgrano, 1982.

Hämäläinan, Pekka. *The Comanche Empire.* New Haven, CT: Yale University Press, 2008.

Hanioğlu, M. Şükrü *Preparation for a Revolution: The Young Turks, 1902–1908.* New York: Oxford University Press, 2001.

Hannah, Matthew G. *Governmentality and the Mastery of Territory in Nineteenth-Century America.* New York: Cambridge University Press, 2000.

Hart, John Mason. *Empire and Revolution: The Americans in Mexico since the Civil War.* Berkeley: University of California Press, 2002.

Hearder, Harry. *Italy in the Age of the Risorgimento, 1790–1870.* London: Longman, 1983.

Hevia, James L. *English Lessons: The Pedagogy of Imperialism in Nineteenth-Century China.* Durham, NC: Duke University Press, 2003.

Hobsbawm, Eric. *The Age of Extremes: The Short Twentieth Century, 1914–1991.* London: Michael Joseph, 1994.

———. *Nations and Nationalism since 1780: Programme, Myth, Reality.* Cambridge: Cambridge University Press, 1990.

Hochschild, Adam. *King Leopold's Ghost: A Story of Greed, Terror and Heroism in Colonial Africa.* Boston: Houghton Mifflin, 1998.

Hugill, Peter J. *World Trade since 1431: Geography, Technology, and Capitalism.* Baltimore: Johns Hopkins University Press, 1993.

Inalcik, Halil. *The Ottoman Empire: Conquest, Organization and Economy.* London: Variorum, 1978.

Jackson, Robert. *Sovereignty: Evolution of an Idea.* Cambridge: Polity, 2007.

Jellinek, Georg. *Das Recht des modernen Staates.* Vol. 1, *Allgemeine Staatslehre.* Berlin: O. Häring, 1900.

Jen Yu-wen. *The Taiping Revolutionary Movement.* Edited by Adrienne Suddard. New Haven, CT: Yale University Press, 1973.

Joll, James. *The Anarchists.* London: Eyre and Spottiswoode, 1964.

Jonas, Raymond. *The Battle of Adwa: African Victory in the Age of Empire.* Cambridge, MA: Harvard University Press, 2011.

Kang, David C. *East Asia before the West: Five Centuries of Trade and Tribute.* New York: Columbia University Press, 2010.

Kaplan, Temma. *Anarchists of Andalusia, 1868–1903.* Princeton, NJ: Princeton University Press, 1977.

Kasaba, Reşat. *A Moveable Empire: Ottoman Nomads, Migrants, and Refugees.* Seattle: University of Washington Press, 2009.

Kashani-Sabet, Firoozeh. *Frontier Fictions: Shaping the Iranian Nation, 1804–1946.* Princeton, NJ: Princeton University Press, 1999.

Katz, Friedrich. *The Life and Times of Pancho Villa*. Stanford, CA: Stanford University Press, 1998.

———, ed. *Riot, Rebellion, and Revolution: Rural Social Conflict in Mexico*. Princeton, NJ: Princeton University Press, 1988.

Keddie, Nikki R., with Yann Richard. *Roots of Revolution: An Interpretive History of Modern Iran*. New Haven, CT: Yale University Press, 1981.

Kershaw, Ian. *Hitler, 1889–1936: Hubris*. New York: W. W. Norton, 1999.

———. *Hitler, 1936–1945: Nemesis*. New York: W. W. Norton, 2000.

Kirby, William C. *Germany and Republican China*. Stanford, CA: Stanford University Press, 1984.

Kirwan, Albert D. *Revolt of the Rednecks: Mississippi Politics, 1865–1925*. Gloucester, MA: P. Smith, 1964.

Kloppenberg, James T. *Uncertain Victory: Social Democracy and Progressivism in European and American Thought, 1870–1920*. New York: Oxford University Press, 1986.

Knowlton, Robert J. *Church Property and the Mexican Reform, 1856–1910*. DeKalb: Northern Illinois University Press, 1976.

Koselleck, Reinhard. "Crisis," translated by Michaela W. Richter. *Journal of the History of Ideas* 67, no. 2 (2006): 357–400.

Kotkin, Stephen. *Magnetic Mountain: Stalinism as a Civilization*. Berkeley: University of California Press, 1995.

Kourí, Emilio. *A Pueblo Divided: Business, Property, and Community in Papantla, Mexico*. Stanford, CA: Stanford University Press, 2004.

Krasner, Stephen D. *Sovereignty: Organized Hypocrisy*. Princeton, NJ: Princeton University Press, 1999.

Kuhn, Philip A. *Origins of the Modern Chinese State*. Stanford, CA: Stanford University Press, 2002.

———. *Rebellion and Its Enemies in Late Imperial China*. Cambridge, MA: Harvard University Press, 1970.

Larkin, Emmet. *The Making of the Roman Catholic Church in Ireland, 1850–1860*. Chapel Hill: University of North Carolina Press, 1980.

Lenin, V. I. *Imperialism: The Highest Stage of Capitalism*. London: Junius, 1996.

———. *What Is to Be Done? Burning Questions of Our Movement*. Moscow: Foreign Languages, 1950.

Lewin, Moshe. *Russian Peasants and Soviet Power: A Study in Collectivization*. Translated by Irene Nove with John Biggart. London: Allen and Unwin, 1968.

Linz, Juan J. *Totalitarian and Authoritarian Regimes*. Boulder, CO: Lynne Rienner, 2000.

López-Alves, Fernando. *State Formation and Democracy in Latin America, 1810–1900.* Durham, NC: Duke University Press, 2000.

Lukács, Georg. *History and Class Consciousness.* Translated by Rodney Livingstone. Cambridge, MA: MIT Press, 1971.

Lynch, John. *Argentine Dictator: Juan Manuel de Rosas, 1829–1852.* Oxford: Clarendon Press, 1981.

Lyttelton, Adrian. *The Seizure of Power: Fascism in Italy, 1919–1929.* Rev. ed. London: Routledge, 2004.

Macartney, C. A. *The Habsburg Empire, 1790–1918.* New York: Macmillan, 1969.

Macfie, A. L. *The End of the Ottoman Empire, 1908–1923.* New York: Longman, 1998.

Maier, Charles S. "Consigning the Twentieth Century to History: Alternative Narratives for the Modern Era." *American Historical Review* 105, no. 3 (2000): 807–831.

———. " 'Fictitious Bonds . . . of Wealth and Law': On the Theory and Practice of Interest Representation." In *Organizing Interests in Western Europe: Pluralism, Corporatism, and the Transformation of Politics,* edited by Suzanne Berger. Cambridge: Cambridge University Press, 1981.

———. "Nation and State." In *The Palgrave Dictionary of Transnational History,* edited by Akira Iriye and Pierre-Yves Saunier. Basingstoke, UK: Palgrave Macmillan, 2009.

———. *Recasting Bourgeois Europe: Stabilization in France, Germany, and Italy in the Decade after World War I.* Princeton, NJ: Princeton University Press, 1975.

Mamdani, Mahmoud. *Citizen and Subject: Contemporary Africa and the Legacy of Late Colonialism.* Princeton, NJ: Princeton University Press, 1996.

Manela, Erez. *The Wilsonian Moment: Self-Determination and the International Origins of Anticolonial Nationalism.* New York: Oxford University Press, 2007.

Mann, Michael. *Fascists.* Cambridge: Cambridge University Press, 2004.

Marcus, Harold G. *A History of Ethiopia.* Berkeley: University of California Press, 1994.

———. *The Life and Times of Menelik II: Ethiopia, 1844–1913.* Oxford: Clarendon Press, 1975.

Marichal, Carlos. "Las finanzas y la construcción de las nuevas naciones latinoamericanas." In *Historia general de América Latina,* vol. 6, edited by Josefina Z. Vázquez and Manuel Miño Grijalva. Paris: UNESCO, 2003.

Martin, James R. "The Theory of Storms: Jacob Burckhardt and the Concept of 'Historical Crisis.' " *Journal of European Studies* 40, no. 4 (2010): 307–327.

Marx, Karl. *The Eighteenth Brumaire of Louis Bonaparte.* New York: International, 1964.

————. *Revolution and Counter-revolution, or, Germany in 1848.* Edited by Eleanor Marx Aveling. New York: C. Scribner's Sons, 1896.

Matsusaka, Yoshihisa Tak. *The Making of Japanese Manchuria, 1904–1932.* Cambridge, MA: Harvard University Asia Center/Harvard University Press, 2001.

May, Arthur J. *The Hapsburg Monarchy, 1867–1914.* New York: W. W. Norton, 1968.

Mayer, Arno J. *Wilson vs. Lenin: Political Origins of the New Diplomacy, 1917–1918.* Cleveland: World, 1964.

McLane, John R. *Indian Nationalism and the Early Congress.* Princeton, NJ: Princeton University Press, 1977.

McPherson, James M. *Ordeal by Fire: The Civil War and Reconstruction.* 3rd ed. Boston: McGraw-Hill, 2001.

Medrano, Ethelia Ruiz. *Mexico's Indigenous Communities: Their Lands and Histories, 1500–2010.* Translated by Russ Davidson. Boulder: University Press of Colorado, 2010.

Michael, Franz, with Chung-li Chang. *The Taiping Rebellion: History and Documents.* 3 vols. Seattle: University of Washington Press, 1966–1971.

Michels, Robert. *Political Parties: A Sociological Study of the Oligarchical Tendencies of Modern Democracy.* Translated by Eden Paul and Cedar Paul. New York: Collier, 1962.

Middlemas, Keith. *Politics in Industrial Society: The Experience of the British System since 1911.* London: A. Deutsch, 1979.

Miłosz, Czesław. *The Captive Mind.* Translated by Jane Zielonko. New York: Vintage, 1955.

Min, Tu-Ki. *National Polity and Local Power: The Transformation of Late Imperial China.* Edited by Philip A. Kuhn and Timothy Brook. Cambridge, MA: Harvard Yenching Institute/Harvard University Press, 1989.

Mintz, Sidney W. *Sweetness and Power: The Place of Sugar in Modern History.* New York: Viking, 1985.

Mironov, Boris N. *The Social History of Imperial Russia, 1700–1917.* 2 vols. Boulder, CO: Westview Press, 2000.

Mommsen, Wolfgang J. *Max Weber and German Politics, 1890–1920.* Translated by Michael S. Steinberg. Chicago: University of Chicago Press, 1984.

Myers, Ramon H., and Mark R. Peattie, eds. *The Japanese Colonial Empire, 1895–1945.* Princeton, NJ: Princeton University Press, 1984.

Neumann, Franz. *Behemoth: The Structure and Practice of National Socialism, 1933–1944.* Rev ed. New York: Oxford University Press, 1944.

Norman, E. H. *Origins of the Modern Japanese State: Selected Writings of E. H. Norman.* Edited by John W. Dower. New York: Pantheon, 1975.

Osterhammel, Jürgen. *Colonialism: A Theoretical Overview.* Translated by Shelley L. Frisch. Princeton, NJ: M. Wiener, 1997.

———. *Die Verwandlung der Welt: Eine Geschichte des 19. Jahrhunderts.* Munich: C. H. Beck, 2009.

Ostrogorski, Moisei. *Democracy and the Organization of Political Parties.* Translated by Frederick Clarke. New York: Macmillan, 1902.

———. *Democracy and the Party System in the United States: A Study in Extra-Constitutional Government.* New York: Macmillan, 1910.

Owen, Roger. *State, Power, and Politics in the Making of the Modern Middle East.* London: Routledge, 1992.

The Oxford History of the British Empire, vol. 4: *The Twentieth Century,* edited by Judith M. Brown and Wm. Roger Louis. New York: Oxford University Press, 1999.

The Oxford History of South Africa. 2 vols. Edited by Monica Wilson and Leonard Thompson. Oxford: Oxford University Press, 1969–1971.

Perdue, Peter C. *China Marches West: The Qing Conquest of Central Eurasia.* Cambridge, MA: Harvard University Press, 2005.

Perham, Margery. *Lugard.* 2 vols. London: Collins, 1960–1961.

Perkins, Dwight H., with Yeh-chien Wang, Kuo-ying Wang Hsiao, and Fung-ming Su. *Agricultural Development in China, 1368–1968.* Chicago: Aldine, 1969.

Pflanze, Otto. *Bismarck and the Development of Germany.* 3 vols. 2nd ed. Princeton, NJ: Princeton University Press, 1990.

Philbrick, Nathaniel. *The Last Stand: Custer, Sitting Bull, and the Battle of the Little Bighorn.* New York: Viking, 2010.

Pocock, J. G. A. *The Machiavellian Moment: Florentine Political Thought and the Atlantic Republican Tradition.* Princeton, NJ: Princeton University Press, 1975.

Polanyi, Karl. *The Great Transformation.* Boston: Beacon Press, 1957.

Pomeranz, Kenneth. *The Great Divergence: China, Europe, and the Making of the Modern World Economy.* Princeton, NJ: Princeton University Press, 2000.

Quataert, Donald. *The Ottoman Empire, 1700–1922.* New York: Cambridge University Press, 2000.

Ramusack, Barbara M. *The Indian Princes and Their States.* Vol. 3, part 6, of *The New Cambridge History of India,* edited by Gordon Johnson. Cambridge: Cambridge University Press, 2004.

Redlich, Josef. *Das österreichsche Staats- und Reichsproblem: Geschichtliche Darstellung der inneren Politik der habsburgischen Monarchie von 1848 bis zum Untergang des Reiches.* 2 vols. Leipzig: P. Reinhold, 1920–1921.

Reed, Nelson. *The Caste War of Yucatan.* Stanford, CA: Stanford University Press, 1964.

Reid, Brian Holden. *The Civil War and the Wars of the Nineteenth Century.* New York: HarperCollins/Smithsonian Books, 2006.

Reid, James J. *Crisis of the Ottoman Empire: Prelude to Collapse, 1839–1878.* Stuttgart: F. Steiner, 2000.

Reinhard, Wolfgang. *Geschichte der Staatsgewalt: Eine vergleichende Verfassungsgeschichte Europas von den Anfängen bis zur Gegenwart.* Munich: C. H. Beck, 1999.

Richter, Daniel K. *Facing East from Indian Country: A Native History of Early America.* Cambridge, MA: Harvard University Press, 2001.

Roberts, Andrew. *A History of Zambia.* New York: Africana, 1976.

Robinson, Geroid Tanquary. *Rural Russia under the Old Régime: A History of the Landlord-Peasant World and a Prologue to the Peasant Revolution of 1917.* New York: Macmillan, 1967.

Rodgers, Daniel T. *Atlantic Crossings: Social Politics in a Progressive Age.* Cambridge, MA: Harvard University Press, 1998.

Rosanvallon, Pierre. *L'état en France de 1789 à nos jours.* Paris: Seuil, 1990.

———. *Le moment Guizot.* Paris: Gallimard, 1985.

Rowe, William T. *China's Last Empire: The Great Qing.* Cambridge, MA: Harvard University Press, 2009.

Sarmiento, Domingo. *Facundo, or, Civilization and Barbarism.* Translated by Mary Mann. New York: Penguin, 1998.

Schivelbusch, Wolfgang. *Three New Deals: Reflections on Roosevelt's America, Mussolini's Italy and Hitler's Germany, 1933–1939.* Translated by Jefferson Chase. New York: Metropolitan, 2006.

Schmitt, Carl. *Der Begriff des Politischen.* Berlin: Duncker und Humblot, 1932.

———. *The Crisis of Parliamentary Democracy.* Translated by Ellen Kennedy. Cambridge, MA: MIT Press, 1985.

———. *The Nomos of the Earth in the Jus Publicum Europaeum.* Translated by G. L. Ulmen. New York: Telos, 2003.

———. *Political Theology: Four Chapters on the Concept of Sovereignty.* Translated by George Schwab. Chicago: University of Chicago Press, 2005.

Scott, James C. *The Art of Not Being Governed: An Anarchist History of Upland Southeast Asia.* New Haven, CT: Yale University Press, 2009.

———. *Seeing Like a State: How Certain Schemes to Improve the Human Condition Have Failed.* New Haven, CT: Yale University Press, 2008.

———. *Weapons of the Weak: Everyday Forms of Peasant Resistance.* New Haven, CT: Yale University Press, 1985.

Skinner, Quentin. *The Foundations of Modern Political Thought.* 2 vols. Cambridge: Cambridge University Press, 1978.

Smith, Anthony D. *The Antiquity of Nations*. Cambridge: Polity, 2004.

Smith, Denis Mack. *Cavour and Garibaldi, 1860: A Study in Political Conflict*. Cambridge: Cambridge University Press, 1954.

Snyder, Timothy. *Bloodland: Europe between Hitler and Stalin*. New York: Basic Books, 2010.

Sorel, Georges. *Réflexions sur la violence*. 4th ed. Paris: M. Rivière, 1919.

Spence, Jonathan D. *God's Chinese Son: The Taiping Heavenly Kingdom of Hong Xiuquan*. New York: W. W. Norton, 1996.

———. *The Search for Modern China*. Rev ed. New York: W. W. Norton, 1999.

Steinmetz, George. *The Devil's Handwriting: Precoloniality and the German Colonial State in Qingdao, Samoa, and Southwest Africa*. Chicago: University of Chicago Press, 2007.

Sternhell, Zeev. *La droite révolutionnaire: Les origines françaises du fascisme*. Rev. ed. Paris: Fayard, 2000.

Szabo, Franz A. J. *Kaunitz and Enlightened Absolutism, 1753–1780*. Cambridge: Cambridge University Press, 1994.

Teng, Ssu-yü, and John K. Fairbank, eds. *China's Response to the West: A Documentary Survey, 1839–1923*. Cambridge, MA: Harvard University Press, 1979.

Thompson, E. P. *The Making of the English Working Class*. New York: Vintage, 1963.

———. "The Moral Economy of the English Crowd in the Eighteenth Century." *Past and Present*, no. 50 (1971): 76–136.

Tips, Walter E. J. *Gustave Rolin-Jaequemyns and the Making of Modern Siam: The Diaries and Letters of King Chulalongkorn's General Adviser*. Bangkok: White Lotus, 1996.

Tucker, Richard P., and J. F. Richards, eds. *Global Deforestation and the Nineteenth-Century World Economy*. Durham, NC: Duke University Press, 1983.

Vázquez, Josefina Z., and Manuel Miño Grijalva, eds. *La construcción de las naciones latinoamericanas, 1820–1870*. Vol. 6 of *Historia general de América Latina*. Paris: UNESCO, 2003.

Vlastos, Stephen. *Peasant Protests and Uprisings in Tokugawa Japan*. Berkeley: University of California Press, 1986.

Watts, Sheldon. *Epidemics and History: Disease, Power, and Imperialism*. New Haven, CT: Yale University Press, 1997.

Wawro, Geoffrey. *The Austro-Prussian War: Austria's War with Prussia and Italy in 1866*. Cambridge: Cambridge University Press, 1996.

Weber, Eugen. *Action Française: Royalism and Reaction in Twentieth-Century France*. Stanford, CA: Stanford University Press, 1962.

Weber, Max. *Gesamtausgabe.* Part 1, vol. 17: *Wissenschaft als Beruf: Politik als Beruf.* Edited by Wolfgang J. Mommsen, Wolfgang Schluchter, and Birgitt Morgenbrod. Tübingen: Mohr, 1992.

Wehler, Hans-Ulrich. *Bismarck und der Imperialismus.* Rev. ed. Frankfurt: Suhrkamp, 1984.

Wesseling, H. L. *Divide and Rule: The Partition of Africa, 1880–1914.* Translated by Arnold J. Pomerans. Westport, CT: Praeger, 1996.

Wohl, Robert. *The Generation of 1914.* Cambridge, MA: Harvard University Press, 1979.

Woodward, C. Vann. *Origins of the New South, 1877–1913.* Baton Rouge: Louisiana State University Press, 1951.

Wyatt, David K. *The Politics of Reform in Thailand: Education in the Reign of King Chulalongkorn.* New Haven, CT: Yale University Press, 1969.

Zewde, Bahru. *A History of Modern Ethiopia, 1855–1891.* Rev. ed. Athens: Ohio University Press, 2001.

Acknowledgments

I want to acknowledge the Woodrow Wilson International Center for Scholars in Washington, D.C., which named me Distinguished Fellow and provided a stimulating milieu for writing the brunt of this book in the spring of 2011. I am grateful in particular to my former student Vanessa Ogle, now teaching at the University of Pennsylvania, who commented on chapter drafts; to my American editors, Akira Iriye and Emily Rosenberg; and to my colleagues Niall Ferguson and Sven Beckert, who read the work and offered much-appreciated encouragement. Steven Press, currently an advanced doctoral researcher in the History Department at Harvard University, graciously gave a final scrutiny to the manuscript of the paperback edition. Any remaining errors, though, are my responsibility alone.

When it was published as a segment of the volume *A World Connecting, Leviathan 2.0* was dedicated "to the fellow faculty and student advisees of the past three decades in the Harvard History Department, who have collectively encouraged the most encompassing study of the past." My wife, Pauline, was thanked for having "put up with [my] mental and physical absences after she completed her own splendid book, *Ratification*." During the summer of 2013, while this separate book version of *Leviathan 2.0* was in preparation, Pauline was stricken with devastating rapidity by cancer and died two months after diagnosis. She and I did history together for over half a century. This book was not the larger effort currently under way that I was planning to dedicate to her, but this work, too, like everything else achieved, emerged from a shared life of teaching and writing (and of course much else). Insufficient tribute as it may be, it is offered to the memory of our common work and family.

Index